T0061547

ADVANCE PRAISE FOR

IVY LODGE

"Using translation of languages as a metaphor to search for the meaning of family relationships, Linda Murphy Marshall takes the readers on a journey of recollection and compassion to understand her parents. Ultimately, *Ivy Lodge* is a story of self-discovery through the language of love, written in elegant prose. It is an extraordinary book."

—Allison Hong Merrill,
author of *Ninety-Nine Fire Hoops: A Memoir*

"With carefully crafted narrative, Linda Murphy Marshall has written the next great memoir about her painful and still-mysterious childhood. After both parents' deaths, she returns to the family home, *Ivy Lodge*—a grand façade that shrouds the emptiness inside. She moves from room to room, examining distressing memories that stem from her emotionally detached parents. A multi-linguist, Murphy-Marshall applies her considerable language skills to translate the dialogue that still echoes, ultimately accepting that some languages may be too intricate to understand. I highly recommend this first-time author and look forward to her next release!"

—Donna Koros Stramella, author of *Coffee Killed My Mother*

"A comfortably white middle class American family living in the Midwest: what could go wrong? No poverty or alcoholism, no racial discrimination or physical abuse: how could someone raised in such favorable circumstances emerge so wounded? Linda Murphy Marshall's memoir takes us deep into the dysfunction of one such family. In intriguing detail, she examines how seemingly ideal conditions can result in a lifelong attempt to 'translate' parents' actions into meaning. Many will relate to the lives it describes, prevalent and arguably influential in shaping our country's social fabric as they are."

—Chivvis Moore, Author of *First Tie Your Camel, Then Trust in God: An American Feminist in the Arab World*

IVY
LODGE

IVY
LODGE

A Memoir of
Translation & Discovery

Linda Murphy Marshall

SHE WRITES PRESS

Published 2022
Printed in the United States of America
Print ISBN: 978-1-64742-367-4
E-ISBN: 978-1-64742-368-1
Library of Congress Control Number: 2022900233

For information, address:
She Writes Press
1569 Solano Ave #546
Berkeley, CA 94707

She Writes Press is a division of SparkPoint Studio, LLC.

Book design by Stacey Aaronson

All company and/or product names may be trade names, logos, trademarks, and/or registered trademarks and are the property of their respective owners.

This book is a memoir. It reflects the author's present recollections of experiences over time. Some names and characteristics have been changed, some events have been compressed, and some dialogue has been recreated.

"... writing is translation,
and the opus to be translated is yourself."
~ E.B. WHITE

"A room is the summation of all that has happened in it."
~ AMOR TOWLES, *A Gentleman in Moscow*

Ivy Lodge

TABLE OF CONTENTS

prologue

◦❦◦

*M*y memories of that day remain sketchy. A foggy lens held at a great distance with unsteady hands. A scrim of years obscures the first time I saw Ivy Lodge the winter of 1959–1960. Like a movie you watched so long ago that you only remember liking it or not, not details of the plot.

Accompanied that day by my parents, my two older brothers, and my little sister, we had a mission to fulfill. Our father wanted to buy Ivy Lodge, wanted us to see it—wanted our mother to see it—although I doubt our opinions of the property impacted his final decision.

In this memory I'm nine years old, in fourth grade, short for my age—all six of us were. Janet was four, not yet in school. She looked like a mini-me, a smaller version with the same dark eyes, chin-length dark hair, Dutch-girl bangs. Steve stood several inches taller than me, in seventh grade, with dark features similar to Janet's and mine, features our uncle referred to as "Black Irish." My friends routinely had crushes on Steve because of his movie star looks, his charismatic personality. Sam, the eldest, in ninth grade, took after our mother with his lighter brown hair, blue eyes, more reserved personality. Steve, Janet, and I resembled our swarthy father.

Our parents met in college, marrying in 1942 at the height

of World War II. More than ten years separated their eldest and youngest children, Sam and Janet, but moving into Ivy Lodge would create a chasm that made that age difference pale in comparison. The move would ultimately lay waste to our family of six, almost as though the home had been dropped on top of our little three-dimensional, six-sided cube, our personal Rubik's puzzle—our family—shattering it in the process.

We didn't go inside Ivy Lodge that day, so I never took off my coat, but if I had, my outfit wouldn't have featured black. According to my mother, "fast" women wore black, women who had questionable morals, who tried to seduce men, whatever that meant. My mother forbade me to wear black until years later, high school. Even then I owned a single black jumper with nickel-sized gold buttons and a faux insignia. The buttons ran down the middle of my jumper. I balanced the black of the jumper with a white Peter Pan blouse underneath; the outfit made me look more nun-like than wanton woman. My mother needn't have worried; I knew far less than my friends about boys. I didn't learn about the "birds and the bees" until well into the eighth grade.

Even though only a few blocks separated Ivy Lodge from our home on Gill Avenue, I'd never driven past Ivy Lodge with my parents. It wasn't on the way to or from anywhere in my limited world: not on the way to my grade school or the junior high or high school, not on the way to the shops in downtown Kirkwood, nor to downtown St. Louis. Nor en route to my grandparents' home or any of my aunts' or uncles' homes. Besides, at only nine years old, I hadn't ventured too far from Gill Avenue.

Seeing the words "Ivy Lodge" etched into the corner pillars that first day, I may have wondered about living in a house that had such a fancy name, not to mention two sets of pillars. I'd been to Wilderness Lodge and Trout Lodge, both just outside St.

Louis, but they were large resorts, open to the public. Why would someone's private home be called a lodge? Weren't lodges where men hunted, where deer antlers, bear heads, and game fish had been mounted on paneled walls? It made no sense, especially in Kirkwood, Missouri.

From my vantage point that day, I would have looked at the seemingly enormous home, much larger than the one on Gill that we would move out of, just three blocks away, and been puzzled. Maybe I deemed it too big for the six of us, thought it looked more like a hotel than a home, at least from the outside.

Long before I became a translator, an aficionado of words, my favorite word was "cozy." Nothing about Ivy Lodge evoked that image for me. Cozy meant hugs and smiles, crowding onto a couch with a bowl of popcorn along with people who loved you, snuggled with you. With my active imagination, I might have thought this large, dark house would swallow us alive, that it had nothing to do with being cozy. I'd have wondered how the six of us would manage to find each other once we moved inside such a cavernous-looking place.

I split away from everyone, wandering around through the life-sized stone planters and giant trees, thinking it felt more like a graveyard or a cemetery than someone's home. I saw no swing set, no climbing trees with lower branches I could reach. No evidence kids had ever lived here. All I saw were statues, sky-high trees that loomed over me, fancy carved pillars, as well as a fountain with two basins, and two empty sky-blue pots on either side of the front door.

My memories of the day we actually moved into Ivy Lodge are more vivid. Since nothing had been unpacked or set up, my paternal grandmother brought over a big casserole dish of spaghetti for us. It tasted all right, but I didn't like how the noodles felt, stuck in my throat before they slid down to my stomach, like still-alive worms that had been dug up in our new back-yard. They didn't taste right; nothing felt right in this dark house.

The Essex family originally built Ivy Lodge in in the 1860s. Captain Lorraine Jones bought the home in 1881 for his wife and seven children. In 1939 they had the enormous home razed and rebuilt it using the same stones and material from the original home in the same location, but with a somewhat smaller footprint.

My parents bought the Tudor-style home from the Jones family in 1960. Mr. Jones, a fifty-year-old bachelor, had lived there for years with his mother. That year, 1960, marked one hundred years since the original home had been built. Jones's descendants still lived across the street from Ivy Lodge as well as catty-corner in homes built on the grounds of the former large estate.

Ivy Lodge had been the manor home of the estate, but developers eventually carved up acre lots and sold them to home-owners following the home's smaller reconstitution in the 1940s. Some homes still retained the original feel of that estate, though. A home across from Ivy Lodge—on the Bodley side of Ivy Lodge's corner lot—had once been a barn on the estate. It still resembled a barn. Another home a few houses away had been the site of the stable, with a small "IVY LODGE" stone marker located to the side of its driveway.

Although I didn't know much of the story back then, I sometimes overheard my father talking to my mother after we moved in about what a "deal" Ivy Lodge had been. Why? To convince her because perhaps she didn't like the house? Because he needed to brag about the deal he'd made? I didn't know. But I overheard him tell her that the seller—Mr. Jones—had been angry, "insulted," according to my father, because of the low offer my father had made, one Mr. Jones had finally accepted.

Kirkwood had been experiencing the effects of "white flight" following the 1954 Supreme Court decision in Brown v. Board of Education in which the Supreme Court ruled racial segregation in schools unconstitutional. Lucrative real estate deals could be made in the wake of that controversial decision. I learned later that "white flight," with its resultant diminishing real estate prices, had been behind my father's decision to buy Ivy Lodge, a good investment. My grade school and eventual junior high school (seventh through ninth grades) had already been integrated but became the first schools in the Kirkwood school district to receive a large influx of additional African American students from the nearby all-black neighborhood in Kirkwood, so homes in our area became "bargains" in the eyes of some people.

The funereal atmosphere I sensed back in 1960 soon permeated all corners of Ivy Lodge, including those of us living inside the home, like shadows overtaking the light. Missing was whatever lightheartedness we'd shared in our former house on Gill Avenue, any closeness, spontaneity, casualness, any genuine sense of family. We'd been plucked out of a more homespun world, thrown into a new one where we played certain roles. The gloomy atmosphere of Ivy Lodge saturated all of us, a gradual yet unrelenting metamorphosis.

In a sense, we all became prisoners of Ivy Lodge: prisoners of the opulent façade it portrayed, prisoners of the dark atmosphere both inside and out, prisoners of our parents' plans for our lives in that home. Even after forty years, with the addition of a mountain's worth of belongings, it still retains the somber spirit I felt that first day. Maybe chemistry played a role. Ivy Lodge plus the six of us created cracks in our foundation that no one could fix.

one

IVY LODGE

Kirkwood, Missouri
February 2000

*T*he weather fits my mood: a dreary, overcast, wintry day in a suburb of St. Louis. I'm outside my parents' home in the aftermath of their deaths, waiting for my three siblings to arrive so we can go through it, room by room, object by object, memory by memory; decide what to keep, what to discard. Stepping out of my rental car, part of me feels like a trespasser now, while another part feels like I never left.

I look up at the vacant windows of my former childhood bedroom on the second story. I have no memories of my father tucking me in at night, here or at the home on Gill Avenue where we lived before, or even a time when he initiated a hug. The norm consisted of me hurling myself at him octopus-style or, as I grew older, taking the first step to embrace him in greeting or farewell. Nor did he take my hand to cross a busy street. Any type of touching was rare.

Our family moved into Ivy Lodge in February exactly forty years ago, February to February, winter to winter. In 1960, much of our furniture would have been delivered through the back door. In the not-so-distant future, it would all come out again. For everything there is a season, I guess.

It seems like decades since my father lay in a small clinic in Barcelona, stricken with strokes during our family's Mediterranean cruise, but it has only been a year. After we got him back to St. Louis, he made progress, then had setbacks, then made more progress, then more setbacks, until he fell into a coma, dying in June of 1998. My mother's death followed a year and a half later. During the periods both parents became ill, I came back from the East Coast as much as I could and had been at Ivy Lodge less than a month ago for my mother's funeral. Aside from my brother transporting valuables to his home for safekeeping, nothing inside has changed much since I last stayed here, the innards—furniture, dishes, knickknacks, clothes, art— like orphans waiting to see if they'll be adopted. But a sense of loss bubbles up beyond my parents' deaths, a foreign substance seeping in, unbidden.

Ivy Lodge sits on an acre corner lot of a tree-lined street, a regal-looking Tudor home with oversized limestones and diamond casement windows. Several spans of private sidewalks intersect the lawn. In only a few short months it will belong to someone else, another family beginning its own memory-making. The walls will begin to absorb the scenes of new lives. As I look up at the limestones, the arched Gothic entrance, the gabled windows, the oversized trees, the small stone porch off my brothers' former room, the larger L-shaped porch at the back of the house, the small pillars marking the entrance of both the side and front driveways, powerful memories surface. My parents can no longer interpret my life for me; that's my job now.

My brothers and sister have no desire to buy the home from the estate. My parents didn't believe in throwing things out, adding to the size of our job. Forty years is a long time to live in the same place, or to keep returning to the same place as I have done: home base.

In addition to the physical aspects of the work, I'm here to recreate my own personal story, my own narrative. For years—a lifetime, really—when I thought about my life, I saw it through the lens of other people, usually my parents, sometimes my siblings. If they told me I was this, that, or the other type of person, I usually took their words at face value, even when the descriptions sounded negative, even when I fought their pronouncements. But translation is all about making decisions, hundreds, even thousands of decisions. Maybe a new way exists to look at myself, at my life. At long last, I'll take those same words and events to come up with different meanings, different interpretations, ones I've reached on my own, stripping away others' interpretations of who I am.

WALKABOUT

Heading across the back of the house to the front yard, I want to keep moving until my siblings arrive. I'm reminded how impressive my former home looks. It's beautiful when viewed from this vantage point, even in February—from the outside as well as from a distance. This might have been my parents' goal when they commissioned a well-known illustrator, Walter DuBois Richards, to create a lithograph of it. A time before people had artists paint their homes, mansions or not. A time when such paintings or sketches were featured in art museums or in the mansions themselves, when they hung in gilded frames above oversized fireplaces. Paintings done for the well-to-do featured large estates owned by oil magnates or bank presidents or CEOs or movie stars or British royalty, not ambitious families in solidly middle-class Kirkwood, Missouri. But maybe in my parents' eyes, the lithograph illustrated how successful they'd been. Maybe part of the appeal of living in such a grand home lay in showing people they had money, that they mattered. After all, perception is reality. You can dress up a house or a person or words to give off a different impression than what lies beneath that surface glimpse.

Many of my parents' friends—fellow alumni from Washington University in the late 1930s and early 1940s—lived in upscale St. Louis suburbs with zip codes reflecting opulence. Ladue and Frontenac are such places where wealthy people live. It's like wearing a Tiffany bracelet. All you have to see is the blue on the box to know what lies inside. Similarly, you know what's inside a Ladue home without looking. An imposing home on a fair amount of land with a sweeping driveway and sky-high trees meant inside you'd find plush carpets, Waterford crystal, sterling silver tea services, kitchens with the latest modern conveniences, dark-paneled studies, solid wood heirloom furniture, spacious bedrooms.

"Ah. You say you live in Ladue? Nice." Nothing else needed to be said. Ladue is fairly homogeneous in that regard. Not so with Kirkwood, with its pockets of affluence averaged out by more modest—even poor—sections. It's an ambiguous area. Follow-up questions have to be asked. "Where, exactly, in Kirkwood did you say you live?"

Following my parents' deaths, I dug a copy of the lithograph out of my dresser drawer to reexamine. Our parents gave my siblings and me several copies. Sometimes clichés are too fitting to avoid, especially since they capture the essence of a situation. In this case, a picture is worth a thousand words. If these walls of my childhood home could communicate, what stories they would tell, each room in the house with memories, mementos of our lives together, forty years of family history. The closed-in walls of the small breakfast nook would tell of time spent eating our meals together, my father's voice dominating the five other voices. Even the cramped walls of the second-story bathroom my parents, sister, and I all shared contain secrets, not to mention the walls of my parents' bedroom, where they spoke in hushed tones, shutting the door so we couldn't hear.

The years we lived in Ivy Lodge formed part of a glorious façade, the lithograph coming to life. We made up the façade, the four children raised here, two boys, two girls, perfect even in our symmetry. By the time the four of us had grown up, left home behind, we had earned eight college degrees among us, and each had a successful career. We all looked good on paper, just like the house featured in the lithograph. But, like the paper on which the artist created the lithograph, the house in which we lived represented a thin veneer of respectability, a surface hiding darker realities just below the surface: cavernous unfinished areas juxtaposed with silver- and crystal-studded rooms; credentialed, successful family members hiding secrets.

I catch myself wondering if my siblings and their spouses went out to lunch together before convening at our parents' home. I know this isn't a productive way to spend my time, but since I've moved out of the area, I often have the feeling I'm missing something. A piece of news, a lunch date, a family celebration, a niece or nephew's play/graduation/dinner, a confidentiality, even a phone call.

I feel like an outlier, or at least some kind of "out." I'm out of touch, out of step, out of bounds. In fairness, all four of us probably always felt like outliers in our own way. We each tried to devise our own way of surviving. For Janet, it meant being loyal to our mother, from an early age promising never to leave the area, to stay nearby. For Steve, it meant excelling all through school, beginning in elementary school when he won a national speech competition, traveling to Washington, DC, as part of his prize. He also skillfully navigated our father's moods. For Sam, it translated into being the rebel, the trailblazer.

Even now, though, I'm the only female member of my family who works full-time, left the area, got a divorce: a trifecta of defects, at least in my mind. Odd [wo]man out. Self-proclaimed black sheep. Even though I lived in Kirkwood until I was thirty-five, whenever I come back, a sibling will imply that it's no longer my town, my home. My mother sometimes told people after I left the area, "She made her bed . . ." her voice trailing off to let people finish the sentence for themselves. Not being an active part of the family is the price I pay, my neediness poking through any façade I hoped to have created. In fairness, though, I realize what I want is to be part of both worlds. I want my siblings to warmly welcome me whenever I'm back in Kirkwood, but I'm equally drawn to the East Coast where I have a fulfilling career as a translator. I'm a multi-linguist working in over a dozen languages: Spanish, Portuguese, French, German, Russian, along with a handful of African languages: Xhosa, Sotho, Shona, Amharic, Zulu, and Swahili. I lead a completely different life than people close to me probably expected. Maybe my siblings' message—as well as my parents' before their deaths—signified that my choices have consequences. I can't have it both ways.

Looking at the lithograph the week before returning to Kirkwood, I notice more details about the house than I ever had growing up. A few of these details lie in the gabled windows on the second story. Using a magnifying glass, I could appreciate the way the artist depicted the narrow, stained glass windows on either side of the front door, windows with elaborate metal lattice work framing the oversized domed front entrance, not to mention a large bay window that extends off the dining room. French doors lead from the formal dining room to the large, L-shaped porch, features not visible in the lithograph. A small, elevated stone porch is visible off one of the two first-floor bedrooms, all adding to the stately appearance of the large home. Even interior details held no appeal for me growing up, such as the hand-hammered brass doorknobs in various rooms, delicate crystal doorknobs in others, the ornate crystal chandelier in the dining room, the knotty pine paneling in the finished portion of the basement, the eight-tone doorbell.

The L-shaped porch is where my sister and I made command performances during our parents' cocktail hour. We'd each try on outfits our mother had purchased for us on shopping trips to the Helen Wolff boutique in Clayton, or at Saks Fifth Avenue, Famous Barr, or Stix Baer Fuller. One at a time we'd model our outfits, twirling in place to show our father, careful to thank him for our beautiful clothes. We were performers in a show.

Our father nodded politely, briefly looking up from his newspaper or stopping his conversation with our mother to make a positive comment. Janet would sometimes return after the end of the fashion show to eat the coveted maraschino cherries at the bottom of our parents' old-fashioned cocktails.

Living in Ivy Lodge always made me feel different than my classmates; the house seemed like a living, breathing person. Yet the lithograph contradicted what lay inside. My friends saw me as rich, but this was a false front, like one of those towns you see on movie sets, a Potemkin village. I didn't know how to counter the false image, especially since friends seldom entered my home. My parents only entertained occasionally, but when they did, guests remained in the front of the house, certainly not venturing upstairs. I have no memory of Steve or Sam having friends overnight and, since Janet and I shared a room until I reached my teenage years, also sharing a bathroom with our parents, neither of us had overnight guests for years.

I continue to wander outside my parents' home to wait for my siblings. A hodgepodge of memories of my years living here flood my mind: playing hotbox in the yard, practicing cartwheels for cheerleading tryouts, playing tag with the large Catholic family across the street on summer evenings, half a dozen boys pouring into our yard at dusk to see if we wanted to play.

A less pleasant memory rises up, unbidden. Visiting my parents once in the 1990s, long after I'd moved out, I sat on the L-shaped screened-in porch at the back of the house with my father. I decided to broach the subject of the clutter in their home.

My father looked handsome, had been especially good-looking in his youth, swarthy, with dark brown eyes that sparkled when he laughed, but could just as easily blaze a hole in you when he became angry. His dark hair, even in his sixties, prompted friends to joke that he must be dying it with a cheap drugstore product known as Grecian Formula. Additionally, although he stood at only about five feet seven inches or so, he had such an imposing, larger-than-life personality you soon forgot his lack of height when you were with him.

Waiting for a pause in the conversation that day on my parents' porch, I asked my father if he thought he and my mother might want to put a dent in tossing out or donating a portion of their things, at least the things they didn't seem to use anymore, particularly those in their giant basement or in the massive unfinished section of the second story, the so-called "attic." Both areas—"attic" and basement—had become dumping grounds for everything model train-related (in the case of the basement) or not deemed worthy of being in the public areas of the home (in the case of the attic). Tripping over my string of softening words, I said, "Do you think you might want to maybe think about going through your things to downsize a little? You have so much in the attic alone. I think it's becoming a fire hazard. Don't you think?"

Shaking his head, he leaned forward in the wrought iron porch chair, taking his time to place his cocktail on the wooden table at his side. "We're not doing that. I'll tell you why," he snapped. "This will be *your* problem to sort out when we're gone, not ours." Thinking about it now, I wonder if he thought any clutter or excesses constituted payback for having borne the financial and physical burden of four children for more than four decades, children who no doubt exhibited varying degrees of gratitude.

I said nothing more, changed the subject, my pulse racing. But at the time I thought what a mess it would be—sorting through everything in a large home with many oversized rooms filled to the brim with random things—at least to me.

The translator in me—always at work, even in English— wants to understand the intent of his words. This is where the meaning must lie, right? With the filters turned off, the translator's mind is unfettered by others' words, actions, or opinions, or even by their mere presence.

Now, catching a glimpse of the porch where this conversation took place, I anticipate a mausoleum of memories, long-abandoned paraphernalia from various hobbies, a mountain of who-knows-what. The house has a lot to say to me, through what has been left behind. I'll need to translate it all, though, create meaning from the mountain of objects and their attached memories.

I have always been a translator, seeking meaning from fragments of language, sounds, experiences. Whether it's words spoken, whispered, or shouted at me, the actions of those around me, or even the objects the people I love have surrounded themselves with, I believe they all contain a kernel of truth, if only I can decipher it, find the meaning.

Tell me who I am, I'd asked my parents in so many ways. Easier.

Ivy Lodge reminds me of those houses a great aunt lived in —without the lace doilies or the scent of dying roses or stale Chanel N°5 perfume. As I walk around the perimeter, I sense decay: in the way the rooms were laid out, in what's missing, in what was added. It has always been an old person's home, even when we first moved in. But it's an old person's home with model trains—lots of trains—as though a ten-year-old had hidden in the body of an octogenarian.

As I walk, I am transported back to the trees: elm, silver maple (with its helicopter seedpods), oak, a peach tree, an apple tree, an Ohio buckeye, an Osage orange, several black walnut trees, a dogwood, a mulberry tree back in the corner of our property, a sycamore, several snowball bushes, honeysuckle vines, pine trees, others I've forgotten. It's like noticing them for the first time, all except for the elms, of course—victims of Dutch elm disease. I never appreciated them in my chronic homesickness for our previous home on Gill Avenue. Just walking the extensive grounds of Ivy Lodge, my mind takes me where my heart leads, to that earlier home, where I haven't set foot in forty years.

GILL AVENUE:
BEFORE THE GLITTER

*O*ur home on Gill Avenue, only three blocks south of Ivy Lodge, might as well have been in another town. It had a traditional layout, with a dining room on the north side as you faced it, a living room on the south, a large den off the living room. Up the stairs, which bisected the front of the home, my sister and I shared one room, my brothers shared another, my parents, the third. It felt cozy but not cramped. The kitchen was at the back, and we ate at a small Formica kitchen table or in the dining room. My older brothers sat at the kitchen table, sometimes shoving unwanted mashed potatoes in their blue jeans' pockets, the potatoes showing up later in the laundry: dried and crusty. I thought my brothers acted bravely, the potato misdeed sure to be discovered later.

The Gill home's family room had room for a TV, a sizable red faux-leather couch we could sprawl on, comfortable chairs, other furniture. My brothers built forts with lightweight red and white cardboard "bricks" the size of shoe boxes, or they constructed miniature buildings with chunky wooden blocks or with their Lincoln Logs. They wore their moss-green jungle helmets as they crawled around on their hands and knees with their toy metal periscopes, pretending to be guerrilla soldiers.

The room had space for my doll house. I listened to my red plastic record collection on my portable record player. "Hush Little Baby, Don't You Cry" stood out as my favorite. I'd sing along to the words, all these verses about things "Papa" planned to buy for his daughter. Or I played board games like Candy Land on the floor, or solitaire, or put on puppet shows for my little sister with my Spanish señorita marionette or my gray kitten puppet with the marble eyes. Even though I shared a room with Janet, this family room made it possible to spread out, to avoid feeling trapped in a single space, to spend time with my older brothers, watching *The Honeymooners*, or *Ozzie and Harriet* or *Bonanza*. Once a year we gathered around the TV to watch the annual showing of *The Wizard of Oz* together.

Weekends on Gill Avenue sometimes included family outings to a local drive-in, either the single-screen 66 Park-In Theatre in nearby Crestwood, or Ronnie's, also close. The four of us would put our pajamas on and pile into the station wagon, enjoying snacks our mom brought in a tiny beige cosmetic case: red licorice whips, Necco tabs, Cracker Jacks. The staticky speaker hung off the front window of our car where our dad sat. We had blankets and pillows to curl up in when Janet and I inevitably fell asleep. Once we moved to Ivy Lodge, though, those magical evenings ended. Maybe we had outgrown them by then.

At Ivy Lodge, the tiny breakfast nook served as a much smaller stand-in for a family room. The living room didn't have a TV for years, nor did my brothers' bedrooms. A more formal atmosphere prevailed. My mother didn't encourage us to lounge around in the living room, the only communal space available. One look around told you not to spread out games, play with dolls, or put your feet up on the couch. The only exceptions were at Christmas, since the tree went in the living room, or when practicing an hour each day on the Steinway grand piano.

My friends had posters of teen idols on their bedroom walls —the Beatles, the Rolling Stones, Twiggy, the Mamas and the Papas—bulletin boards crammed with swimming badges, party invitations, dried prom corsages, graduation tassels, notes dangling precariously at odd angles.

The bedrooms in Ivy Lodge had a generic look: fancy, impersonal, like showrooms of a model house before it's occupied, with nothing allowed on the walls. No one told me not to personalize the room I shared with Janet when I moved in at age nine. But I knew not to deface the plaster walls in my bedroom, not to mar the "look" of the house.

At thirteen I moved downstairs from the room I shared with my sister to take over my brother Steve's room on the first floor; he moved to Sam's room down the hall when Sam left for college. My mother had a decorator redo my new room: lime green, Kelly green, yellow florals, with white wallpaper covered in delicate green-and-yellow blossoms meandering on vines. It looked a little Japanese to me. Although I liked it, its inspiration had come from an outsider's perspective. I hadn't been involved in the selection of the color scheme or the items selected for the room: the wing chair with its little ottoman, the bedspreads with different shades of green vines spreading across the fabric to match the wallpaper.

Sam's room—eventually it would be Steve's—at the end of the hall in Ivy Lodge had grown-up looking, black-and-white flocked wallpaper with raised paisley designs. No old license plates or posters of hot rods ever touched the walls. Sam had a plastic horse collection, but it stood on one of the wide bedroom windowsills.

PIANO DREAMS

I began taking piano lessons at age seven at a studio in the home of a Gill neighbor. My teacher had recently graduated from Juilliard and worked for Mr. Holscher, who owned the studio and lived in the attached home with his wife. Years before, the boxy-shaped building had been a depot for the streetcar, when it still ran through Kirkwood.

Every Thursday afternoon, I walked with my sheet music out my back door on Gill, up a few steps onto the sidewalk on Fillmore, and past the home of the Hartmanns, good friends. Paul Hartmann, a lifelong bachelor, lived with his elderly mother, who made sock monkeys the way other women knitted. I sometimes stopped by their home after my lesson to see the progress of her latest monkey.

After we moved to Ivy Lodge, though, I no longer walked to the Holschers' studio; my piano teacher came to our home for my lessons. This meant my mother heard every wrong note, every word I spoke with Mr. Hannon. I pictured her listening, damp dishrag in hand, one of her purchases from regular visits by the door-to-door Fuller Brush salesman. Mr. Hannon rang the eight-tone doorbell of the formal front door of Ivy Lodge where my mother greeted him, but their exchanges were brief, cordial. Above all, they were formal, followed by my mother summoning me to the living room. The soft curls in her brunette hair were the handiwork of weekly visits to Mr. William at Crestwood Plaza. She lightly brushed her bangs out of her eyes, always glamorous, even in the middle of the day with the piano teacher, when no one could witness her beauty except us.

Whenever we spoke, my mother's eyes met mine, but only for the briefest moment since she avoided eye contact. I longed to meet her eyes, provided she wasn't angry with me. I wanted to see affection, a connection. But her icy blue eyes looked down at the floor or to either side of me after resting on me a microsecond. Then she would grimace with distaste, as though she sensed an unpleasantness about me. I never knew the origin of her distaste, but she'd assume this expression around me.

From an early age, probably kindergarten, I devised a type of game in response to feeling disconnected from my parents. Sitting on the back stoop of Pitman Elementary School with my best friend, I'd sometimes play a secret game in which I pretended someone—a teacher I admired, a favorite aunt, grandparent, neighbor, babysitter—was watching me, admiring me as I played ball, interacted with friends, played the piano, or raised my hand in class armed with the right answer. Maybe I used the game to compensate, to get the attention I thought I wasn't receiving at home. Maybe I believed I wasn't worthy of being looked at, counted, as my home was a world in which I felt invisible.

My need for attention eventually revealed itself in less benign ways. I talked incessantly throughout grade school, middle school, high school, and was frequently disciplined for disrupting class. In this way I announced to everyone, "See how funny I am? How nice? Don't forget me! I'm here!" Somebody—anybody—had to notice me, consider me special. Whatever it took. In fourth grade, my teacher marked me down for "attentiveness," in fifth, for "self-discipline." Talking too much eventually gave way to my goal of being categorized as "sweet," the word used to describe me the most in high school yearbooks. With this "sweet" label, I thought I'd succeeded in being noticed, liked, maybe even a little popular.

Back when I had my piano lessons at the Holschers' studio on Gill Avenue, Mr. Hannon sometimes helped me with long division. I disliked math, struggled with it in school, but Mr.

Hannon remained patient, pulling the yellow number two pencil from behind his ear to show me how to solve problems. He never made me feel stupid or slow or instructed me to try harder. Nor did he ever reprimand me, tell me he wasn't my schoolteacher, that we didn't have time for math, or that it wasn't his job. After we moved to Ivy Lodge, I no longer asked for his help. My parents wouldn't have liked it, would have considered it a bad idea, wasteful of the money they spent on lessons. "We're not paying him to do your homework," they might have said.

Ten years later, when I was seventeen, Mr. Hannon encouraged me to apply to Juilliard, but my parents balked, even though I had won local competitions, had played on a St. Louis classical radio station. I knew without anyone explicitly stating it that my job involved finding a suitable husband at college. My parents may have thought a pool of appropriate candidates wouldn't exist at Juilliard, or maybe—a simpler explanation—they didn't think I had the talent. I never knew.

Playing the piano became my first foreign language. Before I had the words in English to articulate my feelings, I played them on the piano, the eighty-eight keys a surrogate for strong, inexpressible emotions. It's no coincidence that the majority of the pieces I played tended to be dramatic, flashy selections—Chopin scherzos and polonaises, Beethoven sonatas—ones that gave my pent-up emotions free rein.

Long before I discovered I had an interest in and a gift for languages, I excelled at the piano. What's more, it represented the only way—in my child's mind—to garner attention from either parent, make them stop their activities, listen to me, notice me.

A lackluster student till I left for college, if I had applied to Juilliard and been accepted, it would have been a chance to excel, to be above average for once, but it wasn't to be. No liberal arts colleges wanted to admit a student with a grade point average teetering between C and C+.

Not applying to Juilliard produced a watershed moment in my life. From then on, piano playing took a back seat to other activities I soon deemed more important: hanging onto the fringes of the popular crowd at high school, working on my tan in the summer, devising strategies to date popular boys, trying to look pretty, making it onto my male classmates' unofficial lists of the Top Ten Pretty Girls, being rail thin. No use killing myself at the piano if I wasn't particularly talented, I must have reasoned, giving up on what had been a pipe dream at best.

DOG DAYS

After we moved to Ivy Lodge, a new neighbor frightened me one night with his behavior. His actions precipitated nightmares, resulted in childhood prayers. He lived behind us and staggered over one summer night—I must have been ten or eleven—to complain about our German shepherd trespassing on his property. My maternal grandparents, in town from New York, sat on the back porch for cocktail hour. I had joined them when he staggered up to the porch. Even from a distance I smelled alcohol on his breath, wondered why he slurred his words.

"You need to keep your goddamned dog out of my yard or I'm going to get out my shotgun, put a bullet in your dog, then toss its stinking carcass back in your yard. D'ya hear me? I'm sick of it chasing the squirrels in my yard. I'll put a stop to it if you don't." The neighbor pointed his finger at my father in a menacing way.

I sat frozen in my chair, frightened at his words. An image

seared my mind of my cherished dog Heidi being riddled with bullets.

My father calmly walked over to the screen door, pointed his finger at the neighbor and used his sternest voice. "You. Keep. Away. From. My. Dog. Understand? If you go near her, you'll be sorry." He paused. Deepening his voice, he added, "Now get the hell off my property; we have company." Although he appeared calm, I knew that was for the benefit of my grandparents. I also knew it would take little for that deceptive calm to turn explosive. I'd seen it happen too many times.

I'm not sure who frightened me more, the drunken neighbor or my potentially explosive father defending our family dog, but from then on, I included a phrase in my nightly prayers to "please keep Heidi away from Mr. Allen." I recited the prayer for years, even though we never saw or heard from him again. I wonder now if my prayers weren't also designed to keep my father's anger at bay, if part of me perhaps suspected I could just as easily have been at the wrong end of his temper that day. I'd seen this side of my father, the sudden outbursts, but my mother had usually been quick to get him to dial back his anger. Not that night, though.

My father admitted to my husband and me decades later that he actually saw a line of red whenever his rage erupted; his feelings were that intense. You never knew what would provoke his wrath and couldn't prepare for it. Perhaps to downplay his outbursts, he would sometimes remark: "We Murphys aren't crazy; we're just *mean*," stressing the word *mean*, as though that was a better label than *crazy*.

MOTHER'S HELPER

My parents occasionally entertained at Ivy Lodge and hired our "ironing lady," Marzie, for the evening. She also stayed with us when they traveled, once my father's real estate business began growing and he could afford to go on trips with my mother. At my parents' parties, Marzie prepared and passed out fancy hors d'oeuvres on silver trays, wearing a short white apron over a black uniform, her hair piled on top of her head with a white maid's cap. None of the guests ventured upstairs during these parties, remaining in the front of the house: the foyer, the living room, and the dining room, occasionally leaving coats in the bedroom closest to the kitchen.

One job assigned to me involved sweeping the front walk up from the driveway, along with the wide flagstone terrace outside the front door. A series of broad, shallow steps led from the long sidewalk up to the entryway, the flagstones creating an extensive mosaic of flat stones, graduated pillars flanking both sides. Back and forth, back and forth, I swept, scattering pine needles that rained down from the sky-high pine trees far above the house, the small twigs and leaves that fell onto the pavement. But my mother rarely approved of the job I did, instructing me to do it again, so I would continue to sweep, removing invisible leaves, twigs, pine needles.

"I did sweep it," I'd mutter under my breath, stomping my foot in frustration when she glanced out the front door to inspect my work, already dressed for her party in a slinky, maroon velvet, knee-length dress, shaking her head in disapproval, her recently styled hair making her look glamorous, the scent of her Chanel N°5 wafting in my direction. She looked like a movie star. "I've been out here forever. Can't you see that? It looks fine,"

I argued in vain when she failed to respond, thus living up to my "Last-Word-Linda" reputation. It wasn't that I'd been asked to do more than my fair share of family chores, but I knew I'd have to do this again—and other tasks as well—to meet her unattainable standards.

Nothing ever seemed good enough, never done to her—or my father's—liking, but I'd try to anticipate what they wanted. They must have had X-ray vision, seeing imperfections I couldn't see, I thought, like those special lights they put on hotel bedspreads in documentaries to reveal all the unmentionable bacteria not visible otherwise. Recent evidence of this had occurred at a Thanksgiving family get-together in 1997. Making small talk with various relatives, one family friend had approached my mother and me, remarking how fortunate it had been that I'd been with my parents in Barcelona during my father's health crisis after our cruise the summer of 1997, that I spoke Spanish and could interpret for both my parents. Pausing just a beat, my mother forced a small smile at the woman. Then, still smiling, she looked over at me while responding to the relative's remarks, her voice sounding disingenuous. "Yes . . . so *very* lucky." She continued, "Yet you didn't know the word for *catheter* in Spanish, did you, Linda?" In that moment, I knew I hadn't measured up, again, despite the thousands of words I had spoken and translated those long days and nights. That was the pattern: I either fell just short of meeting their expectations or wasn't even close.

My mother rarely resorted to losing her temper or shouting at any of us in the style of my father; in fact, her voice sounded virtually free of emotions, as though calmly instructing a wayward employee how to behave. She chose the best words to ensure no backlash, but her message arrived loud and clear. "Your friend Patty has *such* a cute figure, don't you think?" Or "Did you hear

your friend Mary got a *perfect* score on the SATs? She's so smart!"
Or "Your brother works *so* hard; I'm so worried about him!"

Even though she never swore, the words she used privately
with me frequently varied from the ones she used in public with
others. Harsher, angrier words, surprising for such a refined person. Her private lexicon was another language for me to master.
She referred to certain people as "phonies," or accused them of
"acting cute." She referred to food I ate and shouldn't have been
eating as "slop," and outfits I wore that she didn't like she called
"getups." She'd warn me to "get off your high horse" or "keep
your shirt on!" or "get a hold of yourself!" My behavior—or others'—fell into the "disgusting" category. "How revolting!" she'd
exclaim when I dared to confide in her, sharing a less-than-flat-
tering fact about myself.

Once I'd begun studying languages, thinking about her behavior reminded me of the different sociolinguistic registers
people use. Registers are the particular type of language people
use in different settings, for different purposes, ranging from
formal on down to intimate. With most people, my mother acted
extremely formal, standoffish, using words that reflected that
stance, in her almost regal attitude. But with me, it went beyond
intimate, beyond the kind of communication style you share
with a spouse or a sibling or a parent. It felt as though she had
morphed into a completely different person, as though she'd
assumed a different persona, identity.

When I didn't understand the double or triple meanings of
what she told me, she'd accuse me of being "thick." *Where did
ground truth lie?* I always wondered. *What constituted the underlying meaning of people's words, words written or spoken in Spanish
or Swahili or German?* Perhaps deciphering these other lexicons
might better equip me to understand the words of those closest
to me, those who had raised me.

But no one ever saw. No one ever heard. She made sure of that. Yet if I dared to raise my voice to her, to muster the courage to speak up, to cobble together a sort of flimsy defense on my behalf, suddenly her loyal entourage would appear out of nowhere to put me in my place: my sister, my father, my brothers, my sisters-in-law, her small army of loyal supporters. After her death, when I read about gaslighting, I wondered if that's what she'd done. I just happened to be the one singled out in an elaborate psychological game. She enlisted the support of other family members, perhaps telling them lies about me, secret lies, making it impossible for me to defend myself.

Once, a family member stopped speaking to me for two years. An aunt I had a close relationship with asked her why. The family member confided in her that my mother had claimed I'd made an unflattering comment about this family member. Instead of asking me about it, she'd taken it at face value, cut me out of her life until my aunt had defended me. "That doesn't sound like Linda," she'd said, prompting her to finally reach out, to ask me point-blank about the incident. Then she apologized for believing my mother. Who knows how common this was with my mother, how many people she poisoned against me? I'll never know.

In the presence of my cousins, she acted friendly, but behind their backs she'd rip them apart, describing one as "horribly fat, disgusting." Another one "wasn't smart at all," despite an Ivy League pedigree. Three others weren't that intelligent, either, in her estimation, even though they'd graduated from elite West Coast colleges. Another one, who'd chosen an unconventional profession, was "mediocre at it," she told me when the cousin's name came up. My cousins never suspected, as far as I know. It became a competition, though. She couldn't tolerate others—not even family members—doing better than her own children, putting her in a less favorable light when she measured her worth against her children's accomplishments, intelligence, looks.

My mother acted in a much more subtle way than my father, her messages cloaked in hidden messages, secret codes, languages I'd never studied yet had to try to decipher. Consequently, I learned to doubt myself, doubt my first instincts, doubt what her words actually meant, rather than question her motivation. I always assumed everyone's words had double or triple meanings; I overanalyzed everyone's speech, not just hers.

My parents first met at Washington University where they were both students, my father almost two years older than my mother. Their paths crossed when he was president of the student body. He "sentenced" her in kangaroo court to carrying her books around in a shopping cart for a week, for not wearing her freshman beanie on campus. They married shortly after my mother graduated from college, after my father had earned his law degree. Following a stint in the FBI during World War II, my father practiced law before joining the Missouri legislature in 1950, where he served for eight years, commuting from Kirkwood to Jefferson City. In 1958 he went into private practice, eventually expending his time and energy in commercial real estate, a field he loved. My mother was a stay-at-home wife and mother, as dictated by the times. After we had all left the house, she did part-time work as a coin appraiser, intricate, demanding work. She also pursued numerous hobbies: digging for arrowheads, panning for gold, Egyptology, collecting rare coins.

MIXED MESSAGES

The spillover from those years of stifling my opinions to avoid pushback, of sometimes daring to speak up, risking fiery consequences, is that, from a young age, I alternated between the two extremes, causing confusion for people who knew me. Sometimes I acted assertive, bordering on aggressive, when I cared passionately about an issue, boldly speaking my mind against all odds; while other times I'd hang back, appear meek, desperate to please people. I still send mixed messages. *Please, please like me*, I signal, while other times demanding to be heard when I feel injustices have been committed, or when an incident reminds me too much of a similar one from childhood, when someone unknowingly channels one parent or the other.

In elementary school I secretly wondered what it would be like to be Pat Boone's daughter. He looked so kind in magazine photographs, his eyes warm. I'd listen to "Moody River," "April Love," "Love Letters in the Sand," on my record player, imagining him singing to me at seven, eight, nine years old. Perry Como singing "Catch a Falling Star," "It's Impossible," "Till the End of Time" had a similar effect. What would he be like as a father? Would he listen to me, smile at me, laugh at my lame jokes? I once saw a publicity photo of Perry Como in a magazine. It pictured him stretched out on the floor, reading to his children. I'd rarely seen my father act so informally, down on the floor playing with us or reading to us. A childhood fantasy, though I thought it disloyal to have such thoughts, so I never shared them, not even with close friends. Another song I loved to hear and sing along to was the 1958 Laurie London version of "He's Got the Whole World in His Hands." It comforted me to think that someone watched over me, knew I existed, had hands so big that I fit into them. I'd cup my small hands as the music played, trying to envision the entire world in what must be giant hands, lovingly careful not to drop a single person.

three

⚜

FOUNTAIN OF YOUTH

The showpiece of Ivy Lodge's front yard is an ornate stone fountain. It's large enough to be used as a small wading pool with sizable twin basins, one at ground level—a separate pond with a spillover for water tumbling down from the basin above. A second receptacle stands at eye level, balancing on a tall pedestal that looks like it sprang out of the base. This upper basin holds a finely sculpted cherub, a curly-haired angel with water shooting out of a large shell on her lap. It reminds me of Italian sculptures and fountains you see in grand homes in Rome —now museums—part of a show for tourists to enjoy.

The fountain looks nothing like it did back in 1960, of course. Forty years in fickle Midwestern weather have beaten up the former gleaming white paint, chipped and peeling over much of the statue, as though the sculptor couldn't decide what color it should be: the color of its heyday, the white of Greek seaside homes, the gray of a dying fire ember, or the black of decay, neglect. Dead leaves are matted against both basins, as though stenciling their shapes onto the forgotten statuary.

Noticing it for the first time in years, its neglected twin

basins filled with winter's dead leaves, twigs, pine needles with brackish water left over from a recent rain, I feel like I've fallen back in time to a summer evening a number of months after moving here in 1960. Lonely and bored, I scavenged a Ping-Pong ball from our "rathskeller," the term sometimes used for a finished basement. Then I ran outside to try my hand at balancing the ball on the fountain's spouting water. My father had taken over the Ping-Pong table as a staging area for a few of his model trains shortly after we moved in; I knew a ball or two wouldn't be missed. No one played Ping-Pong anymore. Watching the white ball bobbing in the bubbling water, I had been mesmerized by its precariousness, the balancing act involved in remaining on top while water spurted up from the shell in the cherub's lap. I stared at it as if in a trance, rooting for the white orb to stay afloat. I felt like that ball, trying to stay upright against the forces of churning, unpredictable waters. A zigzag kind of life, but all I knew, although I had glimpses of friends' parents, whose relationships appeared to be more equal, more like partnerships. Since my mother always sang my father's praises, even when he treated her less than ideally, I took her at her word, despite evidence to the contrary right before my eyes. She made comments about their perfect marriage when I must have suspected a different truth deep inside, a different reality.

Many years later, I'm still like that Ping-Pong ball, although I live halfway across the country, married, with my own family. I'm still stuck, trying to please the people I care about while trying to maintain my own identity. Life comes at me in bursts, the slightest current threatening to knock me down, destroy my equilibrium.

Tiring of my solitary fountain game that same summer evening in 1960, I retrieved the Ping-Pong ball and walked a few feet to a buckeye tree bordering our neighbors' property to look for stray buckeyes on the ground. They supposedly brought good luck. Finding several, I used a corner of my T-shirt to polish the small, brown, wooden globes to a sheen and took them inside, misshapen treasures to display on the windowsill of the bedroom I shared with my sister. I collected objects thought to bring good luck: buckeyes, four-leaf clovers, store-bought rabbits' feet, pennies on the street. I avoided stepping on sidewalk cracks or telling anyone what I wished for as I blew out my birthday candles. Otherwise, my wish wouldn't come true.

I liked to bring these bits of the outside world inside: colorful fall leaves, maple "squirts," as we called them. The twin seedpods from the maple squirts doubled as helicopters when you tossed them just right, or you could squirt their juice at unsuspecting friends. In addition, my collection included delicate lavender-colored violets I found in the yard in the early spring. I then presented them to my mother in small bouquets, violets her favorite flower. But my little bouquets wilted within hours of my mother putting them in a special little ceramic vase—a violet painted on its side—as though they, too, couldn't thrive in their new environment.

My collection included pebbles with interesting shapes, fragrant honeysuckle flowers, their hard-earned nectar tasting sweet in my mouth; yellow dandelions, feathers, the occasional four-leaf clover, necklaces I braided from clover flowers by threading the stem of one flower into the base of another, the buckeyes, shells from our family's annual trips to Jones Beach on Long Island—whatever I found of interest. As I wander aimlessly around Ivy Lodge's grounds now, I'm on the lookout for such treasures to help me hold onto what will be my last stroll around the grounds.

four

❦

ANIMAL INSTINCTS

s a child, I sometimes came across abandoned baby rabbits or birds on the grounds of Ivy Lodge, the orphaned rabbits perhaps victims of my father mowing the lawn on his blue tractor. But I never succeeded in keeping them alive.

Once, a baby bird fell from a nest built in the antique light fixture over our front door. It was young enough that it still had its eyes closed, its delicate pink flesh without a single tuft of a feather. It looked like a miniature version of the raw turkeys my mother bought at the grocery store each Thanksgiving. Answering the door for visitors, I had noticed the fallen bird behind them, sprawled out on the pavement, barely moving. I ran to the basement to locate one of my father's empty cigar boxes. Using an old dust rag and a handful of grass, I scooped him up from the newly cut lawn; I knew not to directly touch him, or his parents would abandon him. I used another cloth and a spoon to carefully transfer him to his new nest. Then, rinsing a medicine dropper from ear drops for my chronic infections, I mixed a concoction of sugar and water.

Information was less accessible then: no internet to instantly instruct me on what to do with the tiny creature, no one I could readily call, and the library had closed by then. At some level, I must have known this bird wouldn't survive, that I was giving it my own version of hospice. Maybe I also knew not to get my hopes up, knew they'd be crushed when my new little friend inevitably died. In retrospect, maybe it had to do with having control over my environment, making a difference, being of use. Otherwise, I felt superfluous, adding nothing to my self-sufficient family members, needed by no one, even making things worse at times. But these orphaned creatures needed me, I reasoned.

When the animals I rescued invariably died, along with the hamsters and parakeets I owned, I had a special place for them. Located in a small square of land just outside Ivy Lodge's elevated stone porch, beneath my eldest brother's first-story bedroom on the south side of the house, a dozen or so cigar boxes are buried. Each one contains the tiny body of a former friend.

I held a small service below the stone porch for each animal after digging a shallow grave, marking each plot with a pile of tiny stones, long before I'd heard of cairns. I cobbled together a cross made from stray twigs secured with long pieces of grass or string from my mother's kitchen junk drawer. Then I offered up a small prayer for the bird, squirrel, hamster, or mouse that had died, leaning on my shovel as I paid my respects.

Perhaps attracted to my subterranean crypt, a bat once gave birth to half a dozen offspring on the small porch's sunless stone walls, the babies hanging upside down like black fingers from a glove. Intrigued by the bats, I watched their progress, but from a safe distance. Bats played roles in the frightening movies I'd seen; I feared they'd get tangled up in my hair or bite my neck like vampires if I got too close. On top of that, experts still believed that bats carried rabies. The thought of having shots in my stomach appalled me.

With the exception of the time the bats claimed the wall of the stone porch to have their babies, I'd stand at the edge of the little plot of land surveying my animal cemetery. I only stepped on the ground itself when I had to bury a new little friend, not wanting to be disrespectful to the ones already buried in my little graveyard. I felt like their guardian, responsible for them even after their deaths.

My parents knew about my pet burial ground, watched me drag the heavy metal shovel from our stand-alone garage at the edge of the property. The garage looked like a miniature of our home, a small stone building where my father kept his tools, tractor, and train paraphernalia—never our cars—but my cemetery was a tiny, sunless, out of the way parcel of land that no one in my family paid any attention to. After all, it wasn't part of the manicured lawn. Nothing grew there because of the ever-present shadows. Nor did it interfere with the outdoor route of my father's model railroad. No statues or fountains decorated the tiny parcel, making it easier for my animals to rest in peace. In a sense, it was the only part of the property I didn't have to share with anyone.

I head to the tiny plot, my little pets long gone, dead leaves shrouding the small patch of sacred land, the cairns, the crosses now ancient history. I wonder if the cigar boxes—coffins—are still below ground, or if other animals have dug them up. Standing next to the tiny graveyard, I find comfort in the knowledge that a few years ago, I finally succeeded in my efforts to keep wounded or abandoned creatures alive when two baby squirrels were thrown onto the roof of my Maryland home during a storm. After my husband retrieved them, I placed them on soft rags in a shoebox and took them to a local Maryland organization—All Creatures Great and Small—where an animal-loving woman cared for them, eventually releasing them into a nearby park.

five

STONE SOLDIERS

*O*n the north side of the house, opposite the driveway pillars, shoulder-high stone planters still dot the lawn, permanent fixtures that predate our arrival decades ago. In the early morning or evening, or on foggy days, the planters look like shadowy, ominous sentries from another time, frozen in place while patrolling the grounds, wearing curly, green plant-helmets, and stiff, whitish-gray uniforms.

I sometimes used these planters to gauge my growth, standing next to them, wanting to feel like I had mastery of height over part of my somber yard. The statuesque figures reminded me of tall headstones in a cemetery, minus the inscriptions, their essence linked to having been on the property for decades. Other times they reminded me of tall statues I'd seen at nearby Oak Hill cemetery where numerous Murphy relatives are buried. Ivy Lodge itself sometimes felt like a cemetery to me, all of us buried inside.

I look at my watch again, wondering where my siblings are, if they realize how much work we have ahead of us. But another dark incident at Ivy Lodge interrupts my reverie. Three years after we moved here, on November 22, 1963, the dark feelings I had about the house came to the surface. I sat in my eighth-grade speech class with Mr. Beckman, working on my presentation about the benefits of having fluoride in the municipal water supply, when the principal came on the intercom to make the somber announcement that President Kennedy had been shot.

Like my classmates, like everyone else in the world, I felt shocked, saddened. Overnight, the world had changed, become an even darker place, a place I could no longer rely on. I'd thought of the Kennedy presidency as "Camelot" before it became a catchphrase, watching the Kennedys on TV, falling in love with JFK, Jackie, Caroline, little John-John, as everyone referred to him. Inconceivably, JFK had died; even more horrifying, someone had killed him. An anchor in my life—one I didn't realize I relied on—had been destroyed.

Returning home from school, still numb, I convinced my parents to let me spend the night at a friend's house, having no idea who that friend would be. Caught up in their own sadness, they agreed. I then had to find a friend, any friend, someone whose family wouldn't object to having an outsider spend the night on such a tragic day, a day most families came together, not apart.

Without being able to articulate it or understand why, I knew I had to get away: from Ivy Lodge, from my parents, from my siblings. I knew at some level that nothing I needed could be found within those walls. No one could do anything but make me feel worse, and I knew I couldn't afford to feel worse. Their words—or lack of words—would only sink my spirits further.

After being rebuffed by a number of close friends whose parents wanted privacy, a turning inward, an intimate path to healing, not socializing, I found someone—Sharon Ashton, more of an acquaintance—whose parents said I could spend the night. I'd never spent the night with her before. Although she acted friendly enough, I knew my insistence puzzled her. If the

Ashton family had turned me down, I'd have continued calling every person in my eighth-grade class until I found someone. Anyone. I had to.

When I returned home late the next morning, my original fears were reinforced as I faced my parents' usual attitude in crises. Traumas that should have been viewed as affecting us all seemed to be theirs alone. In their eyes, the president's assassination was their tragedy, their pain; what did it have to do with me, a child?

"Well, I certainly hope you enjoyed your time with Sharon," my mother remarked tersely when I walked in the back door. "President Kennedy's death upset most of us, but we didn't have time to escape from the news with frivolous overnights."

In their eyes I couldn't possibly feel things as deeply as they did. They talked to each other about what had happened, but never with my siblings or me.

Thirty-five years later, when my father died, my mother would display this same attitude, oblivious to the fact that, though she had suffered a grievous loss, losing her husband of fifty-six years, my siblings and I had lost our father. In her eyes, the pain she felt, the sympathy displayed toward her by others belonged to her alone; the four of us weren't entitled to our own feelings of sadness. I'd wanted to honor my father by delivering a eulogy. My teenage daughter had agreed to read it on my behalf since I knew I wouldn't be able to get through it without crying. But my mother vetoed that idea. "We're not having any eulogies," she said. "None of that. We'll have the visitation the afternoon before, with the service the following day; no one is going to stand up or say a word." A friend attending the service called it the most impersonal, anonymous funeral she'd ever attended, said that it could have been for any John Doe, not my father.

six

REMEMBERING THE ALAMO

*T*he site of my former fort was located on the north side of our yard, just outside the L-shaped porch, next to the life-sized planters. It had four natural walls, all made of brambly bushes that pricked me when I rushed into this muffled, protected area, painful reminders of what it cost to escape, even for just a few minutes. I imagine a series of flower-laden trellises hung overhead when Ivy Lodge still formed part of a grand estate.

A trellis served as a partial open-air roof with thick, long-dead vines twining through narrow rotting boards. A small opening in the bushes, not entirely visible from the outside, on the far side of the yard, allowed me to slip through to the dark interior if I stood sideways.

Honeysuckle vines wove themselves through the brambles, their fragrant flowers jutting through them in places like slim threads of perfumed light. They served as an aromatic reward for having made it into the dark space, a counterweight to the gloom.

The ground inside the fort lay matted with grass, dirt, and

pine needles. A few horizontal green blades of grass had survived the lack of sunlight, and a handful of large, fragrant pine cones dotted the ground. These small missiles of wood had escaped from the mammoth pine trees high above our home carrying secret, indecipherable messages to me, in another language.

I don't know why I dubbed the fort the Alamo. Maybe because of the semblance of privacy it afforded me, the brown bushes laden with berries and tiny wildflowers peeking out from the shrubbery, providing a false sense of safety, always my first goal. It's where I disappeared from the eyes of the world. Whenever I stood inside the fort, it felt like a hideaway, a sanctuary.

Many years later, I still feel the need to carve out my own space wherever I am, whenever I can, to create a sanctuary where I'm not disturbed, where people can visit but not stay too long. Friends routinely mistake that part of me that longs to be liked for someone outgoing, easygoing, but I need a place where I can escape, be alone, somewhere I don't have to act upbeat, friendly, solicitous, accommodating.

I should have predicted the fate of the fort. Eventually my father's model trains would take precedence over nature's canopy of silence and invisibility. He tore down most of the Alamo to make way for the first of several outdoor loops for his ever-expanding model train collection, the diminutive, O-gauge train cars roaring their way through all of our lives while the larger, child-size, coal-powered locomotive engines spewed soot and noise in their wake.

The trains reflected the famed ivy of Ivy Lodge, gradually encroaching on space. Unlike the ivy, though, the trains traveled both inside and outside the house. Remnants of the Alamo remained visible since my father retained its oval outline when building the tracks for his train.

Years after I'd left Ivy Lodge, I read with interest that the actress Candice Bergen had once remarked that, as a child, she saw herself as being in competition with her ventriloquist father's famous wooden puppet, Charlie McCarthy. Trains were my father's Charlie McCarthy; I couldn't compete with them for his time, his interest, or his attention.

Even back when we lived on Gill, I would lie in bed at night, listening to the faint melancholy sound of the train whistle rising up from the basement where my father worked on his trains, a smaller set then, the sound a sad reminder of where his priorities lay. Decades after his death, whenever I hear a nearby train whistle, I am catapulted back to my father's trains. It reminds me of the cryptic Portuguese word, *saudade*, which—loosely translated—means a deep longing. That's what the sound of the train whistle elicited, still elicits.

seven

THE SIBLINGS ARRIVE

*F*rom the rear of the house, I hear the rapid-fire metallic sound of several car doors slamming, announcing the arrival of my three siblings with their spouses. I head their way to greet them, everyone offering a half-wave and smile. We've never been much for hugging.

Walking down the back sidewalk, we converge at the small circular flower garden my mother planted in the early 1960s. It's just outside the back door, with petunias, pansies, and marigolds that have seen better days. She planted the garden around a small stone birdbath, but the garden mysteriously sank several inches each year until she discovered she had unknowingly planted it on top of a cistern, an old well, built years earlier and filled in before we moved into the house, maybe after plumbing and running water had been installed.

I wonder why the owners filled in the well, whether anything had ever disappeared into the cistern or still lay buried beneath. I avoid stepping directly onto the garden's soil, still obsessed with horror movies featuring quicksand that I'd seen as a child. Back then I feared if I stepped into the garden I'd be sucked down into the cistern below, its brick lining still visible when the garden's soil sank each spring. Once, when my parents had the nearby driveway resurfaced, workmen found a large, turn-of-the-century, brown glass bottle with "PUREX" printed on the side in oversized letters, completely intact. Who knows what else lies beneath the large property? It reinforces my feeling—fear, perhaps—that much more to this home exists than meets the eye, spirits of its former inhabitants lingering both above and below ground, still present at Ivy Lodge, watching us, maybe even disapproving of us.

This fearfulness, or perhaps just mystery, was reinforced by what I found inside the house early on, remnants of other lives. I came across objects, treasures when we first moved in. I occupied my solitary time wandering around the large house, trying to acquaint myself with everything. A heavy (nearly half a pound), hand-carved iron key measuring almost six inches long by two inches wide and half an inch thick, abandoned on the stone ledge of an unfinished room hidden in the interior of the basement, a chilly, cave-like room built from the same limestone walls as the exterior. We called the room the "fruit cellar," although I later learned its proper name is "root cellar." The room's only source of light came from a single bulb dangling from the ceiling on a long chain.

The large key looked like the handiwork of a blacksmith, several dozen hammer marks on both sides, inscribed with the number "29" below the word "Barbarossa," the name of a notorious fifteenth-century pirate. If its dimensions were any indication, the key would open a giant's home. My young mind never stopped wondering who had used it, where, and how it ended up in the bowels of this old Midwestern home, far from the ocean, far from pirates.

Wandering through the house in those early days, I came

across a small, unfinished piece of beaded embroidery—one inch wide by three and a half inches long—in a second-story bedroom. It featured two whimsical men with top hats, crafted by alternating the colors of the tiny ceramic beads. Given the simple squared-off pattern, it looks like the work of a child who had lost interest in the project before completion or had to abort her handiwork for some reason. Loose, unknotted threads extend off the top of the piece—perhaps intended to be a bookmark—as though it had been left behind when its owner departed in a hurry.

Looking at the tiny beaded work in 1960, I had wondered at the story behind it. This didn't seem to be a home where children ran, played hide-and-seek, not in recent decades anyway. This had the feel of a home where somber adults had lived and died quietly amid darkly upholstered couches, oversized vases, dimly lit rooms. Through the eyes of the child of nine or ten that I'd been when I discovered it, I could only speculate that, like other parts of Ivy Lodge, its past still wielded mysterious influences on the present, still made itself known, competing with my family, representing the present day.

Seeing my siblings, I feel a wave of nostalgia roll over me. Why, though? Nostalgia is longing for what existed in the past. With the exception of isolated instances of togetherness, there isn't much to be nostalgic for. Even during the cruises our parents invited us on, we all went our separate ways during the day for the most part, convening for cocktail hour or dinner at night. Nonetheless, watching my siblings walk toward the house, joking about this or that, I am reminded of the few times we did click, decades ago, on and off when still children, and again when all of us were in our twenties or early thirties, not yet parents. The time we went bowling, the time we played the poker-like game Tripoley, the times we went out to dinner together with our spouses or to someone's home, even the time several of us went camping together. Is that the nostalgia I feel? It's like being given a thimbleful of delicious ice cream, forever remembering how wonderful it tasted, longing to try it again, even though it had barely registered on my palate.

Mostly I feel like I've been locked outside another house—the house of sibling togetherness, I'll call it— my nose pressed to its glass walls. Once, twice, three times or more I've been invited inside, but then banished outside again to catch only furtive glimpses as my siblings go their separate ways, out of my range of vision. The few times I'd been invited into the life of my siblings and their spouses happened long ago, years before I moved to Maryland, before my father's commercial real estate deals took off, thrust into our lives like a stick of dynamite, blowing up any sense of family we had.

Walking behind them as we head up the two steps to the back porch, through the kitchen door, I wonder if our lack of closeness isn't due in part to my parents' approach to child-rearing. My father never got involved enough with his children to foster togetherness or family activities, too busy with his legal career, physically absent during much of the eight years he spent in the legislature, occupied and preoccupied with his hobbies, model railroading the main one. He didn't concern himself with our getting along, as long as we behaved appropriately, stayed out of trouble, didn't besmirch his name. We could have been strangers in the house as long as we behaved.

The sight of my siblings carries me back to a conversation I had with my father ten years ago. In his late seventies, perhaps thinking he'd created bridges between his adult children, he made an impromptu comment to me one day when just the two of us were sitting in my parents' living room. His tone almost gleeful as we waited for my mother to come downstairs to join us for dinner, my father broke through the always awkward silence we shared when no one else was around. On this occasion he appeared calm, almost rehearsed in his delivery.

"Lin, you kids may not realize it now, but you will always be linked, even after your mother and I are long gone. I've tied up my real estate portfolio into such a tangled knot you'll never be able to unravel it; you'll be forced to deal with each other the rest of your lives." He paused, looking over at me, ensuring that his words had sunk in.

I thought it an odd remark to make at the time. Thinking about it now as we get ready to tackle Ivy Lodge's warehouse of objects, it strikes me as an unconventional, not to mention disastrous, way to be certain your children will continue to have a relationship after your death, linking us through money, buildings, documents. If he'd wanted us to have a healthy relationship, why hadn't that been the goal growing up, when we still had time, instead of creating this Gordian knot? Why had he and my mother alternately ignored us and compared us to each other, pitted us against one another, encouraged us to compete for their finite attention? This method—to what end?—only meant we would forever be shackled to each other, no one having the key. But that's the language my father understood: money, commercial real estate, legal documents, deals . . . and trains, of course.

Ultimately, his remarks would be prescient, because nearly twenty years after our father's death, well into 2018, my siblings and I would still be trying to unravel the legal knots, still trying to disentangle ourselves from the "deals," the property. The linkage would strangle the scant affection out of our relationships. My eldest brother, Sam, would nearly die of heart disease in 2006, sixty-two at the time, his ill health possibly exacerbated by the stress of the family financial nightmare, at least according to people close to him. Janet would die in 2011 at only fifty-six due to undiagnosed heart disease and diabetes, and maybe also because of the stress—emotional, physical, financial—of watching the family disintegrate before her eyes. Although we didn't know it at the time, this day in 2000, together for a specific, compulsory reason, would mark the last time—except for a memorial dedication at our parents' church a year later—we'd all be together. From then on, our dealings would exclusively be in business matters, but we would never carry equal weight in those financial matters.

eight

❦

KITCHEN:
THE HEART OF THE HOME

*T*he kitchen is where I begin excavating mementos and memories, and their meaning. This is where I spent many hours of my childhood. I'm sitting in the middle of the floor, surrounded by utensils, dishes, pots, pans, in addition to various chipped ceramic and papier-mâché bowls made by me or one of my siblings in grade school. A sizable pile of loose, unused birthday candles, crumpled scraps of paper with cryptic messages, broken pencils, screws, nails, pens, paper clips, torn recipe cards, match boxes, and unidentifiable odds and ends have all been emptied from crammed drawers, surrounding me like a giant mountain of multi-shaped confetti, a trash bag at my side. I've already caught my sister-in-law ready to throw out a family treasure: an ancient five-inch tall, two-cup, dented and stained aluminum percolator coffee maker, its thimble-sized glass dome cracked, standing at an angle, smoky with residual coffee.

"Don't throw that out!" I thunder at her. My grandfather Chivvis salvaged this tiny coffee pot back in the 1950s when the handle fell off. He replaced it with an old wooden clothes-iron handle; I have to save it.

Giving me a withering look to show her disdain for such a worthless piece of junk, my sister-in-law hands me the coffee pot, its jury-rigged clothes-iron handle extending the full length of the pot. I cram it into my tote bag. I feel more strongly about this beat-up, miniature coffee pot than I do about the boatload of valuable sterling silver coffee and tea service pieces, silver flatware, and ornate serving dishes displayed in the formal dining room till Steve took them to his house for safekeeping. This coffee pot is special, irreplaceable. A treasure my maternal grandfather Chivvis lovingly transformed using his hands and his ingenuity. It represents the philosophy of a kind man, one who had his own way of doing things, even if they looked odd, different, even if they clashed with his wife's more refined practices.

He brought the beat-up coffee pot to my grandmother's formal dining room table at breakfast one day, placing it on a sterling silver trivet, next to all the sterling silverware, the silver serving dishes my grandmother had placed on the table. "What do you think of my handiwork, your highness?" he asked me, no doubt noting my shocked expression. In my opinion it rivaled all my grandmother's silver.

Of my four grandparents, my grandfather Chivvis displayed the most warmth to me, was the most accessible and paid the most attention to me growing up. Even though he lived across the country in Bronxville, New York, dying when I was only twelve, he served as a counterpoint to my other grandparents who acted more distant (my paternal grandparents) or, in the case of my maternal grandmother, quick to point out my shortcomings: my too-long bangs; the way I stacked dishes to carry them into the kitchen after a meal, my weight, my sometimes-ravenous appetite, my lackluster grades, to name a few. Even more painful was her accusation once that I'd neglected my pet parakeet, not fed him. She told me I'd been responsible for his premature death, a charge that forever haunted me. In addition, she disliked my habit of watching TV in the dark, saying it was hard on my eyes, and when she caught me nursing my single daily Diet Coke, she never failed to mention it, even in the last months of her life when I had flown across the country to help my mother take care of her. But the most painful charge against me occurred when she habitually compared me to my older cousin Anne, a brilliant student who had attended Radcliffe before it became part of Harvard. It was "Anne this" and "Anne that" whenever my grandmother visited. I knew I could never measure up to such brilliance, although I loved spending time with Anne, who never once lorded her intelligence over me.

My paternal grandparents lived less than half a mile away from our home on Gill as well as from Ivy Lodge. Their good-sized home had a full screened-in porch in front, an enclosed porch at the back, a beautiful garden my grandfather cared for. The kitchen was the size of a closet, converted by my grandfather so the original kitchen could serve as a dining room for the family of seven. A single bathroom on the second floor served five children (four boys and a girl) as well as both my grandparents when my father and his siblings were children.

I saw no sign of toys in my paternal grandparents' home, for the eventual eleven in-town grandchildren. My grandmother had a set of ornate, colorful, handmade cloth dolls, intricately sewn. They mysteriously disappeared when she died in 1965. Before our grandmother's death, Janet and I loved to look at them, touching their elaborate costumes and hair, but we never played with them. I sometimes asked if she could bring out the box in which they were kept, each one carefully wrapped in white tissue paper.

Even though this dark, pipe-smelling home lacked toys, my paternal grandmother played pin-the-tail-on-the-donkey with Janet and me once, a departure from her quiet, almost reclusive ways. She pinned the donkey target outside on the door of their front porch, watching as Janet and I took turns, blindly trying to hit the mark. Another time, she taught me a game in which she drew an abstract doodle on a page of blank paper. I then had to transform it into a concrete sketch of a bird or a house or a flower. A small, out of tune, upright piano stood against a wall in their living room but, similar to my mother, I rarely heard my grandmother play it. She lived in the shadow of my grandfather Murphy. Like my father, he was the patriarch.

Conversely, the home of my maternal grandparents outside New York City had an entire playroom over the garage. Once a year we would make the trip by car from Kirkwood to Bronxville to visit our grandparents, aunt, uncle, and four cousins. My brothers would sleep in the playroom, which had twin beds on simple metal frames and, best of all, was filled with toys and games: pick-up-sticks, Changeable Charlie with eleven blocks you mixed and matched to create a different face, and a beautiful baby doll with blond ringlets and eyes that closed. There were also intricately made miniature wind-up cars you could send skittering across the wood floor in races, as well as Carrom, the Indian board game popularized after World War I: a large wooden board with small, netted areas in each corner, and wooden disks to play. The playroom also featured bookshelves filled with children's books from the early twentieth century, like *Penrod and Sam* by Booth Tarkington, along with many beautifully illustrated books my mother, Aunt Jane, and Uncle Bill had owned as children.

My maternal grandfather of improvised-coffee-pot fame called me "Princess" or "Your Highness" (Janet, younger by five years, had the title of "Duchess"). He sent me dozens of post-cards from his trips with my grandmother, all addressed to "Princess Linda." He even wrote me letters when I could barely read, telling me about his travels, asking me how I was. He made me feel special. Loved.

When we visited my grandparents in New York each summer, he sat on the living room floor of their beautiful home to play Tiddlywinks with me, using the squares of their Oriental carpet as a makeshift playing board. My mother's side of the family is steeped in British ancestry; I like to think they brought the 1888 game over with them when they immigrated to the US in the late 1800s.

My grandfather was a tall, lanky man, so it must have been a challenge to fold his long frame in order to play with me on their rug. Tall enough to play basketball in college, he towered over my under-five-foot grandmother. His smile lit up his face, a perpetual twinkle in his eyes. He always appeared to be happy, happy with me, able to defuse my grandmother's more patrician nature by showering me with his charm. He fondly referred to his wife as "Little Anne" and adored her. My mother called him Daddy, while addressing my more formal grandmother as Mother.

When we played Tiddlywinks, he lined up the colorful nickel-sized plastic discs, launching them across the Oriental carpet into the tiny dishes, using the larger, quarter-sized discs. I loved it all: the game, but mostly spending time with him. To watch him, you'd think he'd never had more fun, that nothing else could bring him greater pleasure. "You almost got it in the cup, Your Highness!" he'd exclaim during a match, clapping his hands for my benefit, his face beaming, pleased with my amateurish efforts.

One of my grandfather's wonderful eccentricities consisted

of changing the meaning of words on a whim; for instance, "lugubrious" became a word to describe delicious, gooey desserts, losing its "sad" or "dismal" meaning, a beloved malaprop. I understood from this, from other examples, too, that you could play around with language, with words and their meaning, create a private language of sorts. I loved that idea and began mispronouncing select words, "coincidence," for instance. I changed the stress, putting it on the third syllable instead of the second. "What a co-in-CI-dence!" I'd proclaim to anyone listening, trying my new word on for size.

I adored my grandfather Chivvis, maybe because he singled me out, or because he truly knew me. I loved him because he wasn't afraid to come down to my level, to be almost childlike, to shorten the distance between us, to talk to me. I now understand, years after his death, that he made me believe I could be myself with him. That who I was, at least in his eyes, was fine, more than fine. Perfect.

Taking care to put the miniature coffee pot in my large tote bag, I continue to sort through the kitchen clutter: dishes, utensils, pots, pans, odds and ends and whatnots. Looking around, I am reminded of all the time I've spent in this smallish, drab kitchen at the back of the house, a counterbalance to the grandeur found in the front rooms. Its walls have faded, never-updated wallpaper depicting old-fashioned coffee grinders and bottled spices, darkened from years of smoky cooking emissions. White tiles more appropriate to a bathroom act as a backsplash. A buckled, brown-stained linoleum floor looks like the inexpensive flooring you'd put in an unfinished basement, with dull brown kitchen cabinets framing the room. No space for a table, for chairs.

Everything is a different shade of beige, either by choice or through years of grimy build-up. The exception is a white

Formica countertop dotted with tiny gold flecks of metal. Pea-green curtains hang over the sink where a small window lets in scant light, partially blocked by my mother's plants on the windowsill.

For years, one of her plants was a rangy cactus Sam gave her when he was in grade school. It looked like a green snake rising out of a too-small ceramic pot, small barbs poking out of its body. Like a snake, it eventually coiled all over the tiled window ledge, then up and around the knob that opened the small window. When it outgrew the pot, falling over from its own weight, she staked it to a thin wooden post, tying various sections to parts of the window frame to keep it from toppling over.

Standing next to the sink, the window ledge is about chest level. My thoughts of those plants mingle with memories of one of my mother's habits, talking to these same plants, just as Prince Charles claimed he did. Already a follower of the British royal family, in 1953 my mother referred to the scandal when Queen Elizabeth's sister Margaret announced she would marry Captain Peter Townsend. Even though I was only three or four at the time, I could see how interested my mother was in the royal family's life, an interest shared by many American women.

The queen was six years younger than my mother, who closely followed Elizabeth's coronation in 1953, fascinated by this woman assuming power at such a young age. Maybe she contrasted her life with that of Elizabeth, the most powerful woman in the British Empire, an "empire on which the sun never set." My mother had little power over anything in the small orbit of her own life, even in her own home. Truthfully, she probably had less power than her peers, given my father's sometimes demanding nature.

In 1957 and 1959, when Queen Elizabeth visited the US for the first and second times, my mother followed her stops—

Washington, DC, in 1957, Chicago in 1959—cutting articles out of the *Globe Democrat* and *Post-Dispatch*, watching coverage on TV. Perhaps because my mother's grandmother immigrated to the US from England, or because Americans followed members of the British aristocracy like teen idols. As a young child, though, I wondered what connection we had to these crown-wearing, tea-sipping women in England; why else would my mother talk about them so much?

It came as no surprise, then, after Prince Charles admitted to talking to plants in the 1970s, that the idea took off in the US. My mother followed close behind, occasionally talking to the plants in our home: those on the kitchen window, larger ones in the bay windowsill in the dining room, ones on the floor next to the bay window, too large for the windowsill.

One morning I walked into the dining room as she greeted the plants. "Good morning! Nice to see you all," she whispered lovingly, or words to that effect, using a quiet but singsong voice I rarely heard, bending over her green, twiggy charges. Dressed for the day, she wore a print shirtwaist dress with stockings, her permed hair styled into soft curls.

"Who are you talking to?" I asked, walking into the room, my skepticism obvious, unaccustomed to hearing such effusiveness from my mother.

"What can it hurt," she replied defensively, startled at seeing me, pulling herself up to her full height of five feet two inches as she straightened her dress. "If it's good enough for Prince Charles, it's good enough for me. Besides, who knows? It may affect them. You never know."

I had trouble reconciling this person who talked to plants, bending over them, gingerly wiping their leaves of dust with a damp cloth as though tending a nursery full of newborn babies, with the woman who, most days, revealed few emotions. Once again, my mother was complex, a mystery, the meaning of her words elusive, foreign.

I wonder if any of us—family or friends—ever really knew her, what hopes and dreams she'd buried before she became a mother, before she married our father. I imagine how different her life would have been if she'd been born fifty years later, say, in 1969 instead of 1919, if she'd waited longer after graduating from college to get married. Maybe she would have had a career, or never married, or never had children, or moved out of St. Louis. Who knows? But years after we'd moved out, she sharpened her already impressive numismatic skills. A number of people hired her to do coin appraisals, intricate work requiring skill, patience, a keen eye. I've never seen her happier than those days when she used her considerable expertise, becoming part of the workforce, at least part-time. What's more, she had colleagues with similar interests; her circle had broadened beyond church friends and the wives of our father's friends and associates. These were professional associations she cultivated.

Regardless of conversations with the plants, Sam's cactus died after almost twenty years of care, leaving a blank space on the kitchen windowsill. But other Ivy Lodge plants survived. Following my mother's death, before the house went on the market, my sister dug up many of our mother's outdoor flowerbeds, distributing cuttings from these, as well as from her indoor plants to all four of us: marigolds, begonias, petunias, gladiolas, pansies, along with nonflowering varieties. Mine are displayed on a tall cabinet in a sunny room in my Maryland home. Although I ignore them except for weekly watering, I know I'd be sad if they died. They represent a living piece of my mother, their tiny pink flowers surviving despite my lack of a green thumb. I have plants my own children gave me when they were in grade school. I'm obsessive about them: a small succulent from my son, a spider plant from my daughter. I overwater them, take them to a local nursery for doctoring when they look sickly or have spindly branches, hoping to undo the damage I've unwittingly done by trying too hard.

I can still see my mother, the curls of her short, permed, brown hair bobbing a little as she had her intimate conversations, her small frame bent over her green charges as though waiting for sounds to emanate from them, hovering over her plants in Ivy Lodge's dining room, attentive, gentle, affectionate sounding, whispering sweet nothings as she gazed lovingly at each one, touching their leaves with her outstretched hands.

I walk the few steps to the dining room to ensure the plants are still alive. This is where I realize that I might have actually been a little jealous of those plants. She didn't admonish them for their unattractive appearance, for their brown leaves or spots, or reprimand them for being lazy. She didn't compare one plant to another one. She didn't humiliate them into doing better, being better, looking better. No. She showed them warmth and affection, like a concerned parent who unconditionally loved all her green children. What a crazy thought, although at the time I would never have made such a preposterous connection. Jealous of some plants? Me? Ridiculous. But most of them thrived in her care; they've outlived her, still in the dining room bay window.

Back in the kitchen, the appliances date back at least twenty years, except for an upscale Viking stove my father bought my mother after my siblings and I had moved out. But one Thanksgiving, the turkey proved to be too heavy for my tiny mother. As she lifted it out of the oven, it slid out of her hands, onto the floor. Twenty pounds of dead bird, skidding across the kitchen floor in a trail of hot grease. Witnessing the debacle, I ran to find my husband before my father got wind of the accident. My husband captured "Tom," wrestling him back into the pan. Witnesses were sworn to secrecy amid muffled laughter. If my father had seen what happened, he would not have been happy. Looking at my mother's face, I knew this, observed as she nervously watched Bill save the day, making us promise to never tell. Even at dinner, she put her finger to her lips when he wasn't looking to ensure we would keep the secret.

The slippery turkey incident reminds me of a similar near-crisis that happened when I was home from college. My mother asked for help removing the air conditioner in my bedroom window. We forgot it was bulky, heavier outside the window than inside. When we opened the window, it tumbled into the bushes below.

In a rare flash of solidarity, laughing as we dashed outside to inspect the damage, we managed to wrestle the unit out of the bushes, placing it on the grass, as though this had been our plan all along, just minutes before my father got home from work. My mother was afraid he would witness the mistake.

A small, narrow pantry closet in the corner of the kitchen—lit with a single bulb attached to a long metal chain—is the main place to store unrefrigerated food. My mother kept all the cookies and crackers in this closet, in addition to her cans of Sego—meal replacement drinks—along with her tasteless Metrecal cookies. The cookies were eventually taken off the market following claims they had caused several deaths.

The diet drinks and cookies represent competing yet interconnected pulls, to be slender on the one hand, and to indulge in sweet, comforting foods on the other. My mother was steadfast in her pursuit of slimness. I, on the other hand, succumbed to the repetitive cycle of starving, then overindulging, and finally trying to hide the evidence.

Everyday dishes and glasses in the kitchen consist primarily of inexpensive plasticware, but also of plain, beige ceramic dishes. A number of older glasses and bowls are stacked in cabinets. They came from gas station giveaways or grocery stores where you could buy cottage cheese or jelly and be left with a ready-to-use container when the food had been eaten. She kept the good china in the dining room, using it only for special occasions, usually when we had guests.

As I run my fingers over the countertop, I visualize my mother endlessly scrubbing, removing invisible dirt, sometimes slamming the cabinet doors, angry at unseen, unarticulated enemies.

She left empty cookie boxes on display on the counter, humiliating evidence of my having devoured the contents when no one was around. I'd sneak into the kitchen late at night or when no one was home to grab a sweet-tasting cookie from the pantry. Before I knew it, I'd finished off the entire box. The sweets tasted like love to me, but I felt remorseful, fat afterward. Yet I never stopped trying, thinking maybe this time the cookie or cake or pie I ate would do the trick, fill the void inside me. After devouring the sweets, though, the dilemma lay in choosing between disposing of the box or buying myself time by putting the empty box back into the pantry. No matter. Either way, she always found out, a complete inventory of the contents of the kitchen etched in her mind, displaying the empty box on the countertop for all to see, leaving it as evidence for days. I felt like Hester Prynne with my own scarlet letter.

Several times, I launched my meager defense, asking her why she'd put the empty boxes out on the countertop since they were empty. Why hadn't she pitched them? In reply, eyebrows arched, a slight smile on her face as though she had been waiting for just that moment, she answered, "Yes. My thoughts exactly. After *you* ate the whole box, why didn't *you* throw it out?" I hadn't thrown it out because I knew she would find the box in the trash; leaving it in the pantry bought me time. Either way, though, I'd been caught.

I mustered the courage in high school once to confess to her that sometimes late at night, my defenses down, I would raid the kitchen, targeting sweets, racked with guilt the next morning at the memory of my overindulgence. "I don't know what comes over me, Mom; I lose control, head for anything sweet," I explained. I found it difficult to confess my behavior to a woman for whom indulging meant nibbling on one cookie for fifteen minutes. Looking at me the way you'd look at a stranger invading your space to complain about the weather, she quickly left the room.

I avoided the subject till the fateful afternoon I told both parents I'd been seeing a therapist for my food issues. Even though I'd graduated from college, gotten married, I thought it would help them understand my bizarre teenage behavior, maybe even make us closer to learn of my struggles. But my mother walked out of the room again, saying she had to get ready for a party. My fantasy solution would have been for her to pause on her way out, to stop, maybe give me a hug—no words needed, just a hug as she left. I think that would have worked far better than words. By this time, we had all slung so many words at each other—many disingenuous, others hurtful, superfluous—that a hug would have accomplished much more. Fantasy on my part. After leaving the room, she made no mention of pamphlets I left in her mailbox to explain my obsession with food, my last-ditch effort to explain my bewildering behavior, years before people discussed eating disorders. Needless to say, my behavior was slow to change, my midnight forays into the kitchen continuing well into my college years and beyond.

By never overeating, never being overweight, hiding her true emotions from my father, my mother sent a message that she had risen above everyone, perhaps had evolved to a greater degree, didn't need anything from anyone, including food, including my father, my siblings, and me. Maybe, also, it had become the one thing in her life over which she had control: what she ate, how much she weighed. She used that phrase with me when I became emotional. "Rise above it!" she'd lecture me, elongating the word *rise*. But I couldn't rise above my demons. Looking back on it, I'm actually grateful I developed this work-around strategy of overindulging on sweets, though for years I hated myself for my weakness. Who knows what would have happened without my stash of sweets, my quick fix? Maybe I would have turned to alcohol or drugs.

Looking at the newly stripped-down kitchen, I'm satisfied that little of sentimental or monetary value remains. My siblings apparently agree because they've disappeared into other parts of the large home. I'll keep the warped, yellow papier-mâché bowl from grade school, a few squiggles of green and red paint added to jazz it up, my vain attempt to be artistic. A shallow ceramic dish with an uneven lip, a sad little flower painted in the middle. I set aside a dozen or so small wooden angel candle holders for my sister and me to keep, their paint chipped off in numerous places from the heat of the flames. My mother put candles in the little wooden angels for our childhood birthdays.

Family cakes were never store-bought, always homemade angel food cakes with our choice of either a homemade vanilla cream icing or a chocolate whipped cream icing. We made store-bought cake mixes on rainy afternoons in my teens when my mother needed creative ways to keep my sister and me busy. We would make a marble cake, pulling the knife through the blobs of chocolate in the vanilla batter to make interesting designs, our own Rorschach inkblots. Once I was old enough to have birthday parties, though, my mother bought a cake topped with an eight-inch doll with eyes that opened and closed, its hair wavy brunette to match my hair. The doll's dress consisted entirely of icing; when the cake was gone, the doll was naked. You had to rescue her from her nakedness with an appropriate doll dress, after cleaning the icing and crumbs off her. That always struck me as sad somehow, the naked doll having the same fate as the ripped wrapping paper, emptied boxes, unfinished slices of cake. She couldn't even stand up on her own with the icing gone, her full skirt that had once held her upright devoured by my young friends. Now she lay naked amid leftover cake crumbs, flakes even in her once luxuriant hair. She looked like Cinderella after the ball, her stepsisters and stepmother having ripped off her regal clothes.

Before leaving the kitchen, I glance at the treasures I've chosen to take back to Maryland with me: nothing practical. No high-end cooking bowls or utensils. No ceramic salt and pepper shakers. No recipe boxes filled with special desserts. Nothing most people wouldn't throw in the trash without a moment's thought. I realize that the items I saved are objects my mother brought to Ivy Lodge from our more modest home on Gill.

nine

BREAKFAST NOOK: STAND-IN FOR FAMILY ROOM

A few steps from the kitchen, the breakfast nook doubled as our dining area and family room. It functioned as the heart of our home, despite its drab appearance and small size. Walk-in closets on TV shows looked larger.

The breakfast nook seems like an afterthought, tacked onto the bones of the house when the builders realized a family would have nowhere to eat meals except the formal dining room. Or maybe architects discovered a little extra space, an odd outlying angle after they'd factored in the dimensions of the rooms surrounding it: the kitchen, dining room, the L-shaped porch. "We'll create this small room here, and all the other rooms will neatly fit," the architect may have said, forgetting that families need a communal area: someplace to gather, eat meals, have conversations.

A large window looks out on the L-shaped porch, with French doors leading to another part of that same porch. The porch wraps around the outer walls of the breakfast nook, blocking direct sunlight. A second set of glass-paneled doors leads to the dining room. The only furniture consists of the table, six chairs, a small TV console, and my father's low-to-the-ground, green leather easy chair, with a floor lamp next to it. Nothing else fits.

The breakfast nook is where we ate all our meals, the only exceptions at Christmas and Thanksgiving, or when company or the minister from our Episcopal church came for dinner, prompting a move to the formal dining room where we used the fine china, sterling silverware, crystal glasses, cloth tablecloth and napkins. Once my siblings and I had all left home, Sunday dinners moved to the dining room, the result of logistics, of accommodating spouses and children.

The breakfast nook had the only TV in the house. It doubled as the place I did my homework and where my mother curled my hair in sponge rollers each school night.

HAIR TODAY, GONE TOMORROW

Shortly after my sister and I cleared the dinner table and my mother had washed the dishes, I would pull out a metallic chair from the breakfast nook table, sitting with my back to my mother, who stood behind that chair, both of us facing the TV.

My mother would take a section of my chin-length, straight brown hair in her hands, comb it, and wrap it around a pink sponge roller until pink sponge rollers covered my head, snapped into place. I slept in these rollers every night, the next day briefly enjoying curly hair; by noon it had become limp curves. By school's end, my hair had become straight again with only the slightest bend. Somehow, I talked my mother into performing this nightly task of curling it, as though her days weren't already packed with waiting on all of us, as though I couldn't learn how to do it myself like my friends.

Then one night in seventh grade, my mother curled my hair while we watched an episode of *The Fugitive*, one of her favorite shows. Stopping, she blurted out, "Where on earth did this red streak come from?"

"What are you talking about?" I replied impatiently, trying to watch the show.

"There's a red streak down the middle of the back of your hair. Did you dye it? It looks ridiculous, like a zebra."

I had no skill—or practice—in curling my own hair, so coloring it would have been out of the question. I told her this, but she believed I'd somehow bought a bottle of hair dye, using my fifty-cent allowance and walking to nearby Katz Drug Store to buy it, I guess. In reality, my hair must have reacted strangely to the summer sun. I stomped out of the room in a huff, dramatically declaring, "Never mind. I don't need my hair curled."

Unfortunately, this conversation occurred the night before school pictures. In my seventh-grade picture, my hair hangs limply next to my face till it reaches my chin, where the last inch of it juts out at a ninety-degree angle from my face—my unsuccessful effort to curl it—as though trying to escape from my head.

Too late to go back. I stand in the breakfast nook remembering the scene, placing the chair just so, reenacting what we did back then. This beauty parlor time we shared in this room, alone—no more than an hour, the length of two comedies or a drama—was one of the few times just the two of us spent time together. After the red-streak incident, she never curled my hair again. I'm sad I never thanked her, that I let my indignation end the ritual. Funny how you miss those fleeting moments that once felt like nothing—sponge curlers in your hair every night—until years later when those same moments are transformed into special memories, but only when I'm actually here in this room to reenvision them.

It's almost as if the room—the house—has painstakingly recorded everything that happened here. An hour ago, if I'd been asked about the incident, I would have told the story with resentment, indignation. But the room is my time machine; I see it through different eyes. A postscript to this realization, many years later, is that this hair-curling ritual represented a handful of times we had physical contact once I left grade school: my mother brushing my hair, smoothing it with one hand as she used a Fuller Brush to isolate strands of it in her hands, wrapping my hair around pink rollers. It felt almost like a caress, in a house where touching was rare.

Not much in the breakfast nook is worth keeping, in my opinion, certainly not the cheap-looking table with metal legs and six matching metallic chairs where we ate. It's more like a double card table, as though scavenged from someone's basement. Its legs would probably fold like a card table's if they hadn't been locked in place all these years. The chairs' plastic cushions stuck to our bare legs in the summer, making sucking noises when we stood up in our shorts. Nor am I interested in keeping an out-of-date television console, or the small green recliner in the corner, a chair used almost exclusively by my father, so low to the ground it's difficult to get out after you plop down into it.

My brothers are choosier than I am about the mementos they keep; maybe it's just clutter to them, although Sam does lay claim to my father's billy club and brass knuckles from his days in the FBI. Steve will take my mother's extensive collection of memorabilia from the 1904 St. Louis World's Fair. They seem to be more discerning in what they want to keep, as though they had fewer memories to maintain, or less desire to think about what happened.

For me, however, these cast-off items are almost magical, these inexpensive, memory-laden mementos. They're not worth anything, yet for me they represent my parents' lean years, years when they padded their income to the obstetrician who delivered my brothers, making the fee on his sliding scale less embarrassing. My mother told me years later they didn't want the doctor to know how little my father earned back then. I want the little knickknacks going back to those early years, ones evoking memories of time we spent together, time before the money started to roll in.

When we first moved to Ivy Lodge, I think my parents could only afford the grand house because of the aftermath of Brown v. the Board of Education, segregation being dismantled throughout the country, with the subsequent "white flight." Not many people wanted to live in a home, albeit a grand one, when the demographics of the school district where it was located lay in flux. This made it possible for my father to buy Ivy Lodge for a fraction of its market value. Then, as his interest in commercial real estate took off, becoming increasingly profitable, my father's income eventually matched the house in which we lived. He was no longer just an ambitious man who'd made a killing buying a home at a bargain price; he now truly matched that large home. Unfortunately, though, he would rarely allow my mother to have much access to his money, once he became more affluent. With the exception of redoing a few rooms, he decided where and how money would be spent, with little input from her. He bought her a mink coat, a mink stole, a beautiful diamond solitaire ring for their twenty-fifth wedding anniversary, but he funneled much of his money back into commercial real estate or used it for his ever-expanding train collection, an extremely expensive hobby. In addition, a product of the Great Depression, he normally avoided extravagant purchases. You could see this in many of the choices he made. For example, while his friends bought their suits at upscale stores like Saks or Neiman Marcus, my father preferred J.C. Penney's suits. These same friends joined fancy country clubs, while my father (never a golfer) joined a family-oriented middle-rung swim and tennis club in the area, although he attended functions at the upscale St. Louis country clubs.

These seemingly throwaway items I'm finding represent treasures as I begin my search of each room. Clues as to what motivated my mother, pieces of the puzzle allowing me to see her as a multidimensional person, strange as that feels to consider. An inscrutable woman, intent on keeping up a certain image, someone who rarely let emotions rule her. I'm desperate to find reminders to prove she once had a playful, sentimental side. But I am equally desperate to dig up signs that she truly loved me, apart from doing her duty as a wife and mother, signs that I made a difference in her life. The process reminds me of an adolescent girl plucking the petals from a daisy. "She loves me. She loves me not," until the petals are all gone. On any given day, I never know which verdict I'll end up with, what the petals will tell me.

Again I'm reminded of languages, specifically, of dictionaries. If you look up a word in a dictionary, it can have various meanings, many of them differing quite a bit. When my mother told me once in a while that I was a "good" girl, did "good" mean "adequate" in her eyes, or "exemplary"? Or that she was being sarcastic? Big difference. Did it merely mean she was in a good mood that day, that my father had been more attentive than usual, less antagonistic? I frequently did that with her words, put them through my own translator to seek ground truth; it's all I had.

Evidence of my desperation to find proof of my mother's affection occurred in the early 1980s, when she dropped by my home, also in Kirkwood, to visit my newborn son and me. Constantly on the lookout for abandoned treasures, walking in my door she handed me a small, inexpensive, mass-produced tile in the shape of a heart she'd found on the street minutes before, the kind of tile you would use in a large grouping to tile a backsplash in a bathroom, for example. She handed it to me offhandedly— possibly to dispose of—saying something noncommittal like, "Here you go," as she took my son out of my arms. Without telling her, I later took the off-white, quarter-sized tile to a jeweler to have a hole drilled in the one-inch heart, adding a silver jump ring to wear it as a necklace, "proof" of her love for me. I'd translated the moment into a meaningful gesture, into evidence that she wanted me to know she had warm feelings for me. I could just have easily interpreted it to mean that she'd given me trash to throw away, though.

WHEN FOOD IS MORE THAN FOOD

Standing between these two areas where my mother prepared the food and where we ate it—the kitchen and the breakfast nook—I know with certainty that food was never just food in my family, that it was never merely nourishment or culinary enjoyment. It was a way to control us, to keep us seated at the table long after everyone else had left. Or a way for our mother to show how much self-control she had by barely eating, her body the only thing she could control at Ivy Lodge, a means of showing how others at the table lacked such control. It forced us to be together in the same room with parents and siblings, listening to our father speak in what sounded like a foreign language about his day as an attorney at his downtown St. Louis office. It was a time to listen to him argue with my eldest brother, Sam, or to watch as our mother hung on our father's every word. Dessert tempered the atmosphere, softened the blow with its mouth-watering sweetness.

Unlike other fathers I knew, the fathers of friends, my father rarely used an intimate register with us, rarely lovingly conversed with his offspring at their level. Never the softening words of a man who wanted to instruct while expressing his affection. The language he used with us was language he'd use with anyone who worked for him—employees, subordinates. "You'll sit there till I tell you to get up." "Do as your mother tells you." Or, in response to our trying to reason with him, "Because I said so." No one came down to our level, physically or linguistically, used words, gestures, emotions we might have understood as children. He didn't make allowances for the fact we *were* children. No looking at our artwork to comment, "That's a beautiful picture you drew, Linda/Steve/Sam/Janet. How did you do that so well?" Or asking us, "How did your day go today? Did you help Mommy? What did you do to help her?" None of that. Perhaps he viewed us as smaller-sized subordinates. If a stranger closed his eyes, listening to a recording of him speaking, he or she would find it difficult to decide if our father had been talking to a junior employee, a secretary at his law firm, or one of his children. The language and words he used frequently sounded identical.

If I'd angered a parent or a sibling, punishment involved verbal upbraiding (my father's preference) or—more painful—the silent treatment. I'd follow my mother around, a diminutive shadow in her wake, interrogating her: "Are you mad at me? Why are you mad at me? What did I do? Please tell me what I did? Please? I'm sorry . . ." providing her with a blanket apology for whatever I'd done, my voice trailing off as she ignored me, wiping countertops with strong, sweeping motions, washing dishes, preparing dinner, starting a load of laundry, ironing clothes, slamming the quilt down on her bed, even having a conversation with my father, talking over me, through me, as though I weren't there, even mocking me by imitating my whining on occasion. My goal consisted of trying not to anger her—or anyone—of being vigilant about what I might have done to irritate her or my father. In my world, my parents' silence equaled rejection. Worst of all, abandonment.

WARTIME

Sitting down at the breakfast nook table for a moment, the memory of one meal stands out. It happened in the mid-1960s, the middle of the Vietnam War. My eldest brother, Sam, had come home for the summer from college. At dinner one evening he announced he'd enlisted in the Marine Corps. He chose dinner to make the announcement, perhaps knowing the reaction of our father would be swift, angry, and futile, since Sam had already enlisted.

My father slammed his fist down on the table, blurting out, "You what?! Are you crazy? You realize you'll be shipped out to Vietnam, right? What the hell got into you?"

I don't know exactly what Sam said in response, but he might have shrugged his shoulders, replying, "My life, Pop. My choice. You don't have to like it." Or maybe he said nothing. I don't think anyone else spoke up.

We all knew from experience that entering into heated discussions with our father meant running the risk of being knocked down, collateral damage. I learned the lesson slowly, though. Ten years after Sam's announcement, I overheard Janet —then seventeen years old—asking our parents for the combination to the basement safe, allowing her to get information from her birth certificate. She and her future husband wanted to have their horoscopes read. My parents were making their nightly old fashioned cocktail. Our father blew up.

"Absolutely not! I know *exactly* what you're going to do with your birth certificate! You're going to take it to the movie theatre, use it to get into an R-rated movie."

Not able to restrain myself, I entered the room to offer my insight. "Dad, first of all, Janet has never had any interest in seeing any movies that aren't G-rated. Secondly, if she shows the theater staff her birth certificate, it will be proof that she's not old enough to get into the movie. Why would she do that? It doesn't make sense."

At that point, everyone, including my sister, turned on me and told me to mind my own business. I guess that's why they called me "Last-word Linda." The lesson came across loud and clear: if you tried to reason with my father when his anger had been ignited, you would only lose, even if you had logic on your side.

After the conversation between Sam and our father escalated, Sam may have left the breakfast nook, the rest of us going our separate ways: my mother to the kitchen to do the dishes, Steve to his room, Janet and I to help carry the dishes into the kitchen, Dad to read his newspaper in the living room. I'm sure rumblings would have been heard later that night behind my parents' bedroom door when, as always, our father used our mother as a sounding board for his anger. She was ever the good listener, allowing him to vent, absorbing his wrath. This night would have been no exception.

Sam and our father had always had a strained relationship. Early on, my brother may have realized that, in our world, where the role of children was secondary to other matters, he would not be afforded much respect or attention, despite being the eldest son, the eldest child in a patriarchal family.

Unlike our brother Steve, two years his junior, Sam would remain an outsider in our parents' eyes. Not that Steve was smarter or kinder or harder-working or intrinsically better; this was just an inexplicable mystery, our own Bermuda Triangle. In Sam's case, after interrupting college to go to Vietnam, and then graduating Phi Beta Kappa from a prestigious university, going on to earn a law degree, he must have suspected that, in our parents' eyes, his achievements shifted little in the Murphy hierarchy. Nothing external could change how our parents viewed any of us or our place in the family.

Sam's own reaction to the Murphy dynamic set in early, maybe in fourth grade, when he began to go against the grain in school. Maybe he wanted to garner the attention he craved any way he could. Even if it meant being briefly expelled from high school when he taught a fellow classmate how to make a rudimentary explosive device, or sneaking out of our home at night to meet with friends, or tampering with police street barricades, or egging neighbors' homes. Even if it meant signing up to be on the front lines in the Vietnam War.

Maybe he thought, *Whatever it takes.* Just maybe, too, all his acts of rebellion, all the dinnertime arguments between him and our father formed a code, Sam's personal code, a language our father never deciphered, one asking him to pay attention to his eldest son, to help him navigate his life as only a parent can do. But our father never learned this language, never even tried to learn it. What he observed was his child disobeying him, not his son's cry for help. Maybe Sam eventually gave up on communicating what he really wanted from our father, all those years of standoffs between father and son, of harsh words, acting out. Maybe he found a surrogate family in the military, a group of men who would take the place of the family he didn't have back home, men who spoke the same language, who would support him, pay attention to him, value him, lay down their lives for him, remain connected to him the rest of his life.

Even the most innocuous things, paling in comparison to the Vietnam announcement—like being phoned in the middle of dinner—could set our father off. Voice mail and caller ID didn't exist back then; if you didn't answer the phone, it rang till the unidentifiable caller gave up. But if one of us dared to take the few steps from the table to the phone next to the small easy chair in the breakfast nook, the minute we picked it up—when my father realized the call wasn't for him—he bellowed from his place at the table, less than two feet from the phone in that small room, "Tell 'em we're eating!" The catalyst for unleashing his wrath, a phone call for one of his children, ensured that he would raise his voice, his patience quickly disappearing. My siblings and I learned to lean into the receiver, cupping our hands over it to muffle his agitated words, putting our body between the phone and our father to whisper, "I'll call you back," provided the caller hadn't already hung up in fear.

But maybe for all of us, attention was attention, even when it came in the form of explosive, fist-pounding, eardrum-shattering rage from our father. Because in those moments our father's attention laser-locked on whoever had disturbed his equilibrium; those emotions belonged exclusively to that family member. It felt like we might die from the fallout in this breakfast nook, but maybe we privately reasoned we might never get closer to love from our father than we did in those moments.

Before—or after—a meal, sitting in front of the TV in the

breakfast nook provided escape. I watched variety shows like *Ed Sullivan*, entranced by the singers, musicians, dancers, comedians, by the novelty acts like the puppet Topo Gigio, an Italian mouse; Señor Wences, a ventriloquist. I sat glued to the TV the night the Beatles appeared on the show when I was thirteen. But the comedies and sitcoms made me happiest: *Red Skelton, The Dick Van Dyke Show, Andy Griffith, Donna Reed, Leave It to Beaver, Father Knows Best, Make Room for Daddy*, even *Dennis the Menace*.

These shows boosted my spirits: shows about families, families who talked about their feelings, about events of their days. Even at a young age, I knew they weren't real, that the actors read their lines and played their parts. But still these loving parents captivated me, the bond they shared with their children, the way they interacted. I'd pull out a chair from the table in the breakfast nook to watch, transported by the screen. When I watched *Lassie,* the credits rolled at the end with the camera focusing on a closeup of Lassie. Lassie raised a dainty paw halfway through the credits, and I'd rush over to the TV from my metal chair at the table, and place my fingers on the screen to shake hands with the image, long after I became old enough to know better. When my husband and I eventually bought a puppy for our family, I voted for a Sheltie, a miniature version of the Lassie I'd loved as a child, not realizing the connection at the time.

The breakfast nook is a relatively quick assignment to complete without my siblings' involvement, their voices coming to me from deep in the house, the conversations between the couples muffled by distance, maybe also by their desire to speak privately about what they're finding. Standing alone, I am tempted to join them, to learn what they're talking about, be part of the group; but I know they'll close ranks, that the tone of the conversations will change.

It's a lifelong source of deep sadness for me to realize that none of us are close, have never been close, despite what my mother advertised to people, adding to my perpetual confusion of what's real about my family, what's false, what words say versus what they really mean. If she claimed that the four of us had a "close" relationship, what did that word really mean? Not what I thought it meant. More like strangers who've been stuck in the same room for years; there's no base for affection or intimacy or even a sense of very many shared experiences.

Sixteen years after cleaning out Ivy Lodge, in 2016, I will meet my brother Steve for lunch in Washington, DC, after a five-year gap. He will mention how close we used to be as kids, that he regrets we've lost the connection. "We were never close," I correct him, surprised at how calmly I say those words, mustering all my strength to shatter this myth he's promoting, this aberration of the word "close."

Exhibiting courage I have never shown with him, I continue, explaining that while I always wanted to have a close relationship with him, especially since we were nearest in age, it never materialized because our parents had put him up on a pedestal from a young age, rarely encouraging closeness between us. He must know I'm right, that there's nothing he can say, though I hate admitting it. It reminds me of what they tell you when you go on safari in an open-air jeep. You have to remain seated together or the lion or tiger or elephant will not see the group of you as a united, homogenous blob. If one person stands up, it breaks the illusion. It becomes dangerous for everyone.

ten

RATHSKELLER:
TRAIN[ING] GROUND

I head down to the basement to look around the finished portion, the rathskeller, which consists of three rooms: one large room that follows the footprint of the living room above it, and two smaller rooms, each about half the size of the larger room, a deep closet in one. No one has been inside the closet for decades; who knows what's inside? Next to the trio of rathskeller rooms is the unfinished portion of the basement, a large area the length of the home's entire footprint.

In his later years, my father sometimes lamented the loss of the toy soldiers he played with as a young boy, soldiers depicting World War I troops, alongside several to-scale horses. He wondered aloud what could have happened to them, voicing his concerns that perhaps someone had taken them. But now, walking down the wooden staircase into one of the smaller rooms of the rathskeller, I open the rickety, rarely used closet door to have a look inside. Buried in the back, behind all his dusty photographic equipment—one of his hobbies from our years on Gill Avenue— I spot a large, 1950s wooden Kraft cheese box containing several hundred toy soldiers crammed inside, with a few to-scale horses. They'd been here all along. My first reaction is sadness that my father never rediscovered his coveted, long-ago playthings.

After our work is done for the day, I will carefully take them all out and place them in piles: a few for both my brothers, for my sister, for my Murphy cousins whose younger fathers probably played with them, too. I claim a portion for myself, eventually placing them in two plexiglass cases over my family mantelpiece.

I never heard my father mention toys he played with as a boy until these soldiers went missing. Maybe they represented rare moments when he didn't have to be the man of the house in my grandfather's extended absences, didn't have to perform chores or keep an eye on his four younger siblings. Maybe they symbolized a sliver of carefree time he enjoyed. When they disappeared, it must have felt like he'd been robbed of these pleasant memories from his childhood. Regardless, looking at the little soldiers, paint chipped off the metal in places, wobbly legs making it hard to stand some of them up straight, I see evidence of how much he played with them. It's difficult to reconcile my occasionally mercurial father with the innocent boy he must have been once upon a time, sitting on the floor with his toy soldiers scattered around him. But life does that to you, to him, to my mother in other ways. Life knocks you around hard enough, long enough that you forget who you used to be, who you were meant to be, who you are. You become who you must become to survive.

Putting the soldiers aside for the moment, I walk around the dusty rathskeller, sitting on the large, dark red leatherette couch in the largest of the three finished rooms, the couch that used to be in our family room on Gill Avenue. There's no room for it upstairs in the breakfast nook. Nor is it formal enough for the living room. At one point my father contemplated converting the basement rathskeller into a family room.

We had the living room, but it would be years before it had a TV. It had no suitable table where we could play games or put puzzles together, nor a comfortable couch to curl up with a book. The formal room had its couches upholstered in floral prints, wall-to-wall carpet, the Steinway grand piano, a small baby-blue love seat that forced you to sit too close if a sibling or friend or parent joined you, none of it appropriate for family togetherness. We weren't encouraged to lounge there, to read the expensive first edition books in the built-in bookcases flanking the fireplace. The room was primarily intended for company, for show, for sitting up straight in your church clothes when visitors stopped by, although my father liked to read his nightly newspaper there in the winter, the *St. Louis Post-Dispatch*, relaxing in a green leather easy chair, larger than the small one in the tiny breakfast nook.

The idea of converting the rathskeller into a family room soon died out. Maybe because the room was located below ground, its only natural light coming indirectly from a deep, leaf-filled window-well on the west side. Cold, dusty, and damp, with equally cold, cheap linoleum tile, the rathskeller felt cut off from the rest of the family, sounds from upstairs muffled in this dungeon-like space. The floor tile alone is off-putting, its muddy-looking brown base speckled with darker brown amoeba-like designs, similar to the design in the kitchen upstairs, maybe the same, though this never occurred to me till this moment. It always looked dirty, like a viscous substance had been spilled all over the floor and never cleaned up. Years later, I learned from the new owners that the tile contained asbestos. Leaning over to look at the tile, it's impossible to tell if it had ever been mopped. I never saw my mother clean it, nor did anyone else. Then again, maybe the rathskeller wasn't converted to a family room because of the enormous, unfriendly-looking deer heads, their oversized antlers and glassy eyes ominous looking. I can feel their eyes on me now as I sit on the couch. We inherited them from the previous owner, a hunter. They still flank the neglected fireplace, although they could have been moved elsewhere or thrown out.

Maybe the rathskeller wasn't converted to a family room because its three roughly finished rooms are right next door to the oversized, gloomy, unfinished portion of the basement, an even darker area whose only natural light comes from the breadbox-sized frosted pane carved into a heavy, dark-brown door at the bottom of a stairwell leading up to the backyard. When you were in the rathskeller—or the basement—you didn't know if it was sunny or rainy, night or day; you felt cut off from the outside world, as though in your own microclimate.

Another reason might have been the cost; in the early, lean years it would have cost too much to convert the rathskeller to a suitable family room. In addition, by the time my father did have money, Steve and Sam would have been in college, no doubt making it less of a pressing need in his eyes.

Yet another possible reason no one ever dared mention: my father didn't have enough room for all his trains in the unfinished portion of the basement, despite its size. He needed to migrate his growing collection into the wood-paneled rathskeller. This is where he spent most of his free time, where much of his disposable income went. My grandfather had been an attorney for the Union Pacific Railroad for years, and also an enthusiastic train hobbyist. Maybe it made my father feel close to his own father, on the road for chunks of his own childhood, to share this common interest, even after my grandfather's death.

I wonder if this is what I'm doing today. Just like my father, I'm trying to bond with my parents indirectly, wandering through a house crowded with memories of two of the most important people in my life, searching for things that will tie them to me even after their deaths.

What I'm seeing in this gloomy space is the proliferation of the trains, as though one train had given birth to another and another at a steady rate through the years. Our original Ping-Pong table in the largest part of the rathskeller is buried beneath excess train cars, railroad components, building materials; its shape is barely visible.

The room's floor-to-ceiling antique knotty pine paneling has been drilled all the way through at eye level in various places to create slightly asymmetrical tunnels the diameter of a slice of bread in order to accommodate my father's O-gauge trains. The trains traveled through every room in the raths-keller and basement, even crossing into the unfinished, interior fruit cellar. Several of the tunnels extend nearly a foot through solid rock to reach this stone room on the other side of the wall. I never understood why my mother didn't object to the destruction of the decades-old solid wood paneling, not to mention other onslaughts to the original house: painting done by an out-of-work artist in which he depicted mountain scenes on top of this same paneling, a rainbow of colors covering the original wood. Why didn't she object to the explosion of trains throughout this subterranean crypt, throughout their yard, or to the ever-shrinking space she was allotted in the basement to wash and iron everyone's clothes? She actually commented how happy she was, happy because our father could have been off playing golf or frequenting bars like friends' husbands, she said. She was grateful he spent all his free time at home work-ing on his hobby, not elsewhere. But still, she must have cringed as he sawed through the antique paneling, his friend painting over additional panels in the rathskeller on my father's instruc-tions, all in service to the trains.

The trains have fanned out throughout the massive base-ment and rathskeller area like robots taking over turf in a science fiction movie, exiting the house from the top of the ceiling of the basement room closest to the side yard, traveling under the house, then under the L-shaped porch on their way outside to loop around the site of my former Alamo fort, the first of several loops my father eventually built.

What was the point of it? I wonder. It's not like the displays you see in the glossy pages of magazines like *Model Railroader*, beautiful layouts transporting you to miniature cities or mythical places inviting visitors to have a peek inside the hobbyist's fantasy world. No. I've seen those beautiful layouts—public and private—the ones with to-scale mothers, fathers, children, with tiny houses, cars, trees, and dogs, ones where you can imagine the lives of these miniature people. Ones that make you feel like a giant who is privy to a tiny kingdom. Not here.

The large outdoor steam trains my father bought in the early 1980s attracted children and adults alike as they traversed the backyard of Ivy Lodge, but those trains didn't materialize till the four of us were all grown and out of the house. On the contrary, this vast wasteland in the rathskeller and basement was never intended for outsiders or spectators. His personal playground, my father didn't care if the tracks ran through a junkyard of tools, a jumble of wires, excess train equipment, past a table of folded laundry. It didn't matter that the trains looked like they were traveling through the railroad yard of a depressed American city, with orphan tracks, equipment, tools piled up, looking abandoned next to the tracks.

The only proof of human existence in this apocalyptic disarray is that my father ensured nothing impeded the running of the trains. Other than that, aesthetics didn't concern my father. His interest lay in the mechanics, in the degree of curve the train could handle, in the gradient of the cars' climb, in the production of steam for his eventual, much larger, rideable locomotives outside. *His interest lay in the process, not necessarily in the end product.*

Looking around me now at the scattered components in my father's below-ground playground, I know my siblings and I had little chance of competing against all of "this," of competing with our father's own attempt to perhaps recreate his childhood, reconnect with his father. No chance at all. The trains down here were exclusively for his pleasure. It looked like a train-crazed adolescent had been handed hundreds of thousands of dollars and instructed to let his obsession run free. Why would he care what others thought? Why should he?

The only train-related objects I'm interested in taking home as I survey my surroundings are two or three of the boxcars my father made from kits in the mid-1960s with his youngest brother, my uncle Bob, who lived behind us on Gill. They stenciled their initials on each finished car: Santa Fe, Union Pacific, Denver and Salt Lake, Rutland. I'm less interested in claiming the fancy brass engines—more costly than the car I drive—or the few trains artisans custom-made for my father, one-of-a-kind trains complete with dining cars with miniature people inside, eating their meals on teeny-tiny plates, taking sips from minuscule cups, while plastic waitstaff serve them, the only sign of survivors in his apocalyptic train world. These fancier, peopled cars might have been the exception to the rule of scattershot cars, chassis, equipment, but I prefer the trains my father built with his own hands, with my uncle, before he could afford to buy whatever he wanted, before he could pay an artisan to build to his specifications.

I imagine him sitting at a card table with my uncle—ten years younger, an architect—sharing their love of trains, painstakingly following the directions, probably meant for children, like model cars and airplanes. That's the father I want to focus on, especially since the two brothers had a mysterious falling out in the 1970s. I want to think about their times together before they parted ways, the chance for reconciliation ending when my uncle died suddenly of a heart attack at only fifty-two in 1981. A time when happiness was measured by time spent together, not money spent alone. I wonder if that could ever have been me, helping my father put together trains, carefully gluing the roof to the sides of the boxcar, using a magnifying glass to ensure I did it right. I wonder about a connection between my lifelong love of the book *The Boxcar Children*, about four orphaned children who lived in an abandoned freight car, and my father's obsession with trains. It never occurred to me until I began this process in Ivy Lodge.

In my early teens, I approached my father about helping him build scenery using elaborate kits he had bought. Initially he appeared eager for my help. But I showed little aptitude for the intricate projects requiring the combined skills of an engineer and a master origami artist, and his enthusiasm flagged when I turned out to be a slow learner and an inept artisan. I looked for the first excuse to abandon the project. While it lasted, however, he took an interest in my progress, in me.

After a few months of pulling the kit out of the box, reading, rereading the instructions (*Is this truly English?* I wondered), filled with anxiety about the prospect of letting him down, I confessed to my father after dinner one evening that I didn't think I could complete the kit. At the time, he was standing at a worktable down in the basement, working on a train. "It's all right," he replied, not looking up from his work. "Just put it on that table over there. I'll take care of it." "I'll take care of it" translated into his having given up on me, his low expectations now confirmed. I hated hearing those words. Somehow, I found his anger easier to stomach than his resigned disappointment.

"Why am I down here?" I ask out loud, sighing as I absent-mindedly pick up a stray train chassis from the Ping-Pong table, eyeing the stuffed deer like I did as a child, still expecting one or both disembodied heads to leap at me from the wall, their bodies miraculously restored. "There's nothing for any of us here," I say to no one, or maybe to the ghosts of my parents. It's no accident neither of my brothers nor my sister came down here with me to sort through everything. The truth is, of the four of us, no one has ever shown much interest in the trains: in building them, in watching them chug around the tracks in the house, in talking about them, in asking our father about them, in attending train meets with him . . . in being anywhere near them. Absentmindedly examining the train part in my hand, I know it would have been our ticket into his world. But with the exception of a few short-lived attempts, we've all distanced ourselves from the trains, thus assuring our isolation from him.

I'm curious, though, if life would have been different if he'd taken the time to include us in his train-world, if he had involved us in the building of the tracks, or the planning of the layout, or the intricate interior work of the trains themselves, or taken us to train meets or to his train clubs. He eventually included my much younger cousin—his nephew—in that world, after the premature death of Ruel's father in 1981, long after my siblings and I had left home. Ruel's father, my uncle Bob, had been the brother my father worked on train kits with till they had their falling out. Janet's husband would also share a keen interest in the trains, but that came in the late 1970s.

The generation-hopping silver lining to my father's trains occurred in the early 1980s when my father offered to hold my young children's birthday parties here at Ivy Lodge. By then he could afford large, live-steam, rideable trains—the train cars traveling all over the back and side yards on larger tracks—the kids piling on, thrilled as my dad acted as the conductor on their journey, the children wearing smocks to prevent the soot from staining their clothes, my father in striped coveralls with a train-themed cap. Thirty years later, the now-grown kids—including their parents—still talk about those one-of-a-kind birthday parties.

I haven't done anything productive since I stopped bagging trash upstairs in the kitchen. I feel powerless to make decisions about what should or shouldn't be thrown out down here. It seems a sacrilege to throw out things that had a special role for my parents, things they loved. Things they worked on or with, or bought for themselves, even though most of it should mean little to me, these things they loved. But who am I to decide what stays and what goes?

My mind is pulled back to the years we lived here, to memories of my family, to what happened in the various rooms of this old home. So far, my grandfather's miniature coffee pot and a few kitchen items are the only things of interest I've found, plus my father's toy soldiers. Since I'm already in the basement area, though, I cross from the rathskeller into the large unfinished portion. I might as well revisit the largest section of the house.

eleven

BASEMENT:
WORKING ON THE RAILROAD

*I*n order to pass through the door between the rathskeller and the unfinished rooms in the basement, I have to duck under train tracks bisecting the main doorway at chest level. For my mother, this meant she had to be vigilant when carrying a load of laundry, or just walking between the rooms, doing a modified limbo to avoid being smacked down by the tracks. A hinge to lift the railroad track intersects the doorway, but one or more train cars normally sat on top of the tracks. It saved time to just duck, particularly if you didn't plan on staying too long, always the goal for everyone but my father. We all became accustomed to ducking.

The rathskeller and basement haven't always been this cluttered, this jammed with trains, tools, disembodied train parts, equipment. When we first moved here in 1960, I could roller skate the entire length of the unfinished portion, a space the size of three or four good-sized rooms. I'd strap my silver skates onto my penny loafers or saddle shoes, tightening them with the special metal key, gliding across the slick cement floors. The area spread before me like a miniature public skating rink. But that was years ago.

PUPPY LOVE

This unfinished part of the basement is where our German shepherd Heidi had two litters of puppies. I don't know why my parents decided to breed her, since my father didn't show much interest in our dogs. My mother already had her hands full with four children, one dog, and the care of a large home. Whatever their reasons, my father built a large box-like structure with a shallow interior wall running around the perimeter—six feet by six feet—to ensure no puppies suffocated.

After the first litter was born, I gave the puppies temporary names before my parents sold them, using the names of planets: Venus, Jupiter, Saturn, Neptune, Mars, Mercury.

Heidi gave birth to her second litter several years after the first, when I was twelve. One puppy remained from the litter; no one had expressed an interest in him, maybe because he didn't have the classic German shepherd markings—more beige than dark brownish-black—or maybe because they thought him less handsome than his litter mates. I loved him, though, played with him, taught him tricks while we waited for him to be bought. I felt a kinship between us, wanted to give him the life he deserved, at least while I could.

As time passed, I felt emboldened to ask my father if we could keep him. Obviously, no one wanted to buy him as he got older. I longed to have my own dog. To my surprise, my father agreed. I was thrilled. It marked the first time I'd been responsible for a pet that wasn't a hamster or parakeet. It meant a chance to change my disastrous luck with all the wild bunnies and baby birds that had died on my watch.

I named him Specks, had a dog tag made for him at Kirkwood Hardware Store with his name, my name, our address and phone number engraved on it, and then began training him. We were inseparable.

When Specks was about six months old, all legs and heart, his training progressing, a farmer who lived several hours from us in rural Missouri stopped by our suburban home one weekend afternoon to talk to my father. He watched how Specks moved, how fast he ran, explaining to my father that he needed a working dog for his farm, an outside dog—not a pet—to act as a watchdog on the farm. The man was a friend of a friend of my father's, and had heard about the litter's leftover puppy. After a brief conversation, my father agreed to sell Specks to him, ignoring the promise he'd made to me several months before. A deal was a deal for my father. Money was money. I was devastated.

Standing alone in the basement now, even though the wooden crate my father built for the puppies is long gone, I remember quickly realizing that this stranger was not just a visitor, that my father would sell Specks to him. I pleaded with him not to go through with it. Desperate for my father to listen to me, I grabbed his sleeve as though that would stop the transaction, not caring that this man in overalls was watching me as though viewing a specimen under a magnifying glass. "Don't you remember you told me he could be *my* dog, Dad? You told me I could keep him, train him. Don't you? You promised. Please, please, don't do this. He can find another dog; this is *my* dog. I've been training him. You gave your word!"

My father's initial reaction to my begging was embarrassment, nervous laughter soon building to anger. Meanwhile, the farmer stood by, uncomfortable, trying not to stare at me, at this spectacle. But I was inconsolable, tears streaming down my face, my nose running as I tried to make myself heard. At some point my father must have signaled my mother—as always—to deal with me. He didn't like messes with children. He didn't like emotional outbursts.

After cash changed hands, the farmer pulled a loose piece of rope out of his deep overall pocket, placed it around Specks's neck, pulled him to his pickup truck, and put him in the open back. I watched, sobbing, as Specks craned his neck to look back at me, whimpering. I never saw or heard about Specks again. This marked the last time my parents bred German shepherds.

FISHING FOR COMPLIMENTS

For a while, my father kept tropical fish in the basement. The fish are long gone; all that's left is an enormous tank that looks like an empty glass coffin, accented by fading ornamental rocks shoved into corners, bits of glass confetti left out in the sun too long.

This was my father. With the exception of the trains and commercial real estate, his forever interests, he threw himself into the pursuit of a hobby—tropical fish, photography, breeding German shepherds, bridge construction, collecting specialty tools and Franklin Mint sterling silver replicas of old cars, or expensive, to-scale replicas of classic buildings. But once he'd invested a substantial amount of money into the hobby, his interest would usually fade. Then he'd move on to another interest.

Gazing at the vacant fish tank, I wonder if the problems between my siblings and me weren't also rooted in this idea. Like the rest of his hobbies, he made investments in our lives, but couldn't sustain his interest in us, or maybe he decided he hadn't seen enough return on his investment, leaving the heavy lifting of raising us to our mother while he pursued his other interests in the few hours available outside his office work. Thinking along these lines seems harsh, yet I detect at least a kernel of truth in my theory. My father wanted to see return on his investment, but his expectations remained low, at least with his female children.

Once, when I was a teenager, my parents took a trip to Mexico. My father asked me to take care of the fish while they were gone. The care of tropical fish had become an all-consuming hobby before his trains crowded them out of his life. He had tanks, filters, specialized food, colorful rocks, books, everything necessary. The fish he kept in the tank on this unfinished side of the basement—neons and guppies—darted all over the large tank, colorful streaks of movement, animated when they saw anyone approach with a container of dried fish food.

My father sometimes assigned me tasks, but rarely asked me to do favors for him, so I was thrilled. This was new. I could contribute, make a difference in his life. I'd been selected for an important mission.

Looking back on his fathering style, I think he preferred being around people who had mastered whatever he needed from them, a philosophy that spilled over into being a parent. We never played tennis together, nor did he ever ride in a car with me when I was learning to drive—or even after I got my license. Nor did he show any interest in listening to my piano playing until recital day. He avoided being around half-formed people, people in training or, for that matter, those struggling, broken, maybe even needing counseling, tutoring, or therapy, a helping hand. He preferred being surrounded by bright and shiny, competent, ready-to-go, at-the-top-of-their-game individuals, particularly in the case of family members. This might have been because, as the eldest in his Depression-era family of five children, no one had time to apprentice, to learn through their mistakes, to try, try again. You had to get it right, at least in my father's family of origin. You had to get it right, right now, the first time.

That may have been why raising children created problems for him; he had no patience for the large swath of in-between years between birth and adulthood that required parents' involvement, understanding, patience. A dearth of such qualities had existed in his own Depression-era childhood. He understood only competence, obedience; no halfway or halfhearted performances, no displays of improvement along the way to mastery, no gradations on the path to success, and no "lip," as he put it, no back-talking. Certainly, no whining about personal struggles or fears.

In the case of the tropical fish, however, he probably reasoned, "How hard can it be? Surely she can handle sprinkling fish food into a tank once a day; no dog running off the leash or swallowing pesticide. No helpless baby to contend with. Just a few fish. Easy." Besides, no one else could take on the assignment: my eldest brother, Sam, had left for college, Steve had friends, schoolwork, college applications. Janet was too young.

I'm sure he must have given me instructions, although they would have been verbal, not written. He may not have seen the need to write anything down: give the fish food from this can—ten flakes—once a day, don't overfeed them. But whenever my father spoke to me, I became anxious—anxious with anyone, truthfully, but most of all with him—never sure what would come next, afraid I'd get it wrong, as though I'd been given an important test. In many cases what resulted was impatience or condescension, never the goal. If he gave me instructions, I probably repeated to myself, *OK OK OK OK OK. I've got it. Please don't act impatient with me. I'll feed the fish. OK OK OK,* basically missing everything. Even if he'd barked at me afterward, "Did you get that?" I would have lied, said yes, but would have shut down even more. By then his voice would have increased in volume, taken on a slight edge, an edge serving only to increase my anxiety, the more questions I asked, at which point he might have made a comment about my slowness. "What exactly do you *not* understand about my instructions? This isn't rocket science, after all." Better to pretend I knew what he needed, to figure it out on my own, later.

My parents left on their trip. Marzie came to stay with us while I jumped into my job. After each feeding, I lingered by the tank, wondering if I'd given the fish enough flakes. I had to do the job perfectly. *What if this isn't enough food to share among themselves?* I wondered, scrutinizing every movement of their tiny bodies, their perpetually wiggling gills. *It looks like one fish is hogging the food,* I noticed another time, trying to count the number of flakes the piggish fish had consumed.

It came as no surprise, then, that I fed them two, maybe three times the number of little dried flakes they required, twice as many times a day as they needed it. If one shake of the food into the aquarium sufficed, two would be even better, three best, I reasoned. If feeding them a little made my father happy, think how happy he'd be when I spoiled his prize guppies and neons, I told myself. Why, who knew what might follow this? He might trust me with his trains, might want to play tennis with me. Might invite me to go for a walk with him if he thought I had half a brain, though I'd never seen him take a walk with anyone.

I sprinkled a bit of food on one side of the tank, then the other for balance, watching the fish dart from one side to the other to gulp down the flakes. I enjoyed watching them congregate whenever I approached with their food. I thought I had them trained. They looked happy to see me, almost tame. I loved feeling needed, needed by the fish, by my father.

Since they gobbled the food up every time, I thought I'd been giving them just the right amount. What I realized too late is they weren't eating it all; they spit much of it back out. The uneaten food lay in the bottom of the tank, clouding the water, making it toxic.

The last day of my parents' trip, I raced down the basement stairs to feed the fish one last time before school, confident my father would be proud of me, perhaps give me more challenging tasks in the future. But I came to an abrupt halt when I reached the large fish tank, gasping at what I saw. Most of the fish floated belly up at the top of the tank, while a few others flopped around sideways, a last-ditch effort to swim, to survive. They'd all died—or were dying—because of my overfeeding, my hovering, my overzealousness, my obsession with pleasing my father, of doing more, to elicit more from him. More what? Attention? Love? Respect? More of something was all I could verbalize. But look at the results. Disastrous.

His reaction when he returned from his trip is hazy, going downstairs, seeing for himself that all his fish were dead or dying, after being greeted by his near-hysterical daughter. A brief burst of words, followed by agonizing silence when my mother stepped in to referee. Nothing he could say could make me feel worse. But he never asked for my help again with his fish, or with any of his other hobbies or projects. I felt worse when my mother showed me gifts they'd gotten for me: a tiny jumping bean from Mexico; a seedpod the size of a lima bean filled with microscopic, carved ivory creatures inside; a doll for my foreign doll collection. How could I have been so stupid, I thought. But seeing my distress, it must not have occurred to my father to remind me that, despite what I'd done, he still loved me. That only magnified the crime in my mind. What I'd done haunted me for years. Still haunts me, even though I think he probably forgot about it . . . eventually.

The fish incident, coupled with my maternal grandmother's accusation that I'd killed my parakeet through my negligence, coupled with my bad luck with the wild birds and baby rabbits I tried to rescue, instilled in me a belief that I had a reverse Midas touch when it came to pets. Even now I have a nightmare several times a year that I've been entrusted to take care of a pet, usually a hamster. Suddenly it occurs to me that I haven't fed it in days or weeks. I rush to its cage, shoving aside shavings to see if it's alive. That moment in the dream between remembering I have a pet and checking on the pet feels like a lifetime, my emotional state hanging in the balance.

Lost in my sad memories in front of the basement fish tank, I realize I learned a lesson with my father's fish, one I keep on learning, namely, the pitfall of trying too hard, with pets or plants or people. The more time, energy, or emotion I put into a relationship—friend, family, teacher, business, or casual—the greater the return will be, I believe. But more often than not, this backfires. I'm like my adolescent self, reasoning that if a little fish food is good, how much better would double the amount be? If a little attention/flattery/eagerness to please is good, how much better to try harder? I even do it with plants. If I love a certain plant, if my son or daughter gave it to me, I water it three times a week instead of once a week to ensure it has enough water, till it inevitably dies from root rot.

MAKE ROOM FOR MOMMY

My mother spent hours in the basement every week, but not by choice. This is where she washed and ironed all the family laundry. The washer and dryer are in a small area near the door leading to the outside stairwell. Forming an ever-shrinking corral of washer, dryer, ironing board, a large table for sorting laundry, and two sizable double sinks, her designated parcel of real estate lay here, a single bare lightbulb hanging from a flimsy cord over the ironing board, a film noir scene from the 1940s.

A boat-sized wooden hamper in the shape of a V still stands in the middle of the basement. Chutes lead to it from two of the upstairs bathrooms—the one my parents, sister and I shared, and another from Steve's former bathroom on the first floor, directly above the large hamper. Clothes still lie in the bottom of the V. Draped over the side are frayed hand towels, a negligee, a few flannel shirts, three stray socks, along with old blouses my mother wore metal-detecting.

I lean over the hamper and twist my head around to peer up into the chute's narrow shaft. We tossed our dirty laundry down that rectangular metal tube each day, waiting for it to fall into the hamper below, listening till we heard the thud at the bottom when it reached the basement. We had to wait to ensure the clothes had made it all the way down, hadn't hit a snag. Sometimes my siblings and I dropped other things down it, though—shoes, pencils, balls, dolls, books—Newtonian experiments in determining how fast objects of different sizes and weights made the downward trip. They clanged and banged their way down its metal sides, sometimes getting stuck. When that happened, careful thought had to be given as to what to throw on top of the item to dislodge it, allowing it to continue its downward journey.

My mother's laundry area in the basement shrank periodically as my father continued to expand his train layouts. More train paraphernalia called for more card tables, more floor space. A simple case of supply and demand; space had to come from somewhere.

Walking over to my mother's large black laundry table, I see the trademark items she kept down here. A small, inexpensive black transistor radio rests on the table's corner, its antenna always raised because of the poor reception in the basement. She tuned in to the Cardinals baseball game if one was playing, or to a talk show on popular KMOX. An old-fashioned boom box stood on the table with an array of cassettes. If she couldn't find anything interesting on the radio she could always listen to Frank Sinatra, Bing Crosby, or classical piano cassettes.

I recognize the miniature four-by-six-inch binder my mother used to record every undershirt, handkerchief, sheet, and pair of underwear she ironed, with the date. Everything had to be ironed. The notebook is still open to a page dated December 14, 1999, the last day she recorded her work in hash marks: four straight lines, then a slanted line for the fifth, the lines running across the page. Day after day. Week after week. Month after month. Year after year. Each page has the category of the item, "handkerchief," for example, followed by the series of hash marks across the page to denote how many she completed on any given day. The next line is "undershirts," with hash tags, followed by a new line with "sheets." In addition, she kept track of outer garments: shirts, blouses, dresses, pants. If it came out of the dryer or hung on the line over the ironing board, it had to be ironed, even after the invention of permanent-press clothing. No exceptions. She had control over this tally, unlike most parts of her life, unlike the unfinished parts of the house, the disrepair of many rooms, the trains taking over much of the house and yard, family financial decisions. This, she could control.

Her laundry tally goes back years. Flipping through it now, I wonder if it also provided her with positive reinforcement when no one—certainly not my father, my siblings or me—thanked her for her numerous, frequently unrewarding, contributions to the family's well-being, tasks completed in less-than-inviting spaces.

I decide to take the little notebook with me, though I'm not sure why. Because it's evidence of all her hard work down here? Because it held importance for her? Or because it symbolized one of only a handful of things not overlapping with my father's world, proof she existed apart from him? Maybe the notebook— seemingly insignificant—gave me a glimpse into what made my cryptic mother tick. Hard to read, to understand, always intent on playing the role of the devoted wife, saying and doing what she thought appropriate; I never penetrated the façade. But this tiny notebook is off script, an almost secret way to perhaps let a bit of her true identity peek through.

I will keep it next to another little notebook, the same size, one she kept with the names of personalized license plates. She carried that notebook in her purse because she had to be ready for recording them.

My mother began keeping track of personalized "vanity" license plates shortly after they started appearing in the late 1960s. Knowing about her little notebook, I would help her by writing down ones I spotted while driving, entries to add to her collection. Each letter of the alphabet has its own page in the tiny three-by-five-inch loose-leaf notebook. The book also includes a page for each digit, one to ten, along with a separate page for license plates she found in California, inexplicably.

"A" in her notebook has AZALEA. "B" has BIG-MOI, BUY

FUR, and BY-4-NOW. The entries B4-WIFE and HOT-ICE both refer to license plates on Corvettes, according to her notes in the margins. She noticed C-WITHME in an Optometrist's parking lot (noted in parenthesis). Even "Q" is represented with Q-TEE, QUICHE. The letter "X" has XOXO, XCEL-NT, and two radiologists' cars (also noted in parenthesis) have X-RAY-1 and X-RAY-2.

In all, she recorded nearly a thousand personalized license plates. To me, the list offers another series of clues as to what made my mother tick, what mattered to her, just like the innocuous laundry tally. They signaled that she existed beneath her wardrobe of tiny skirts and dresses, behind her perfectly coiffed hair. That she'd been imprisoned despite her predictable comments about having a model marriage with my father.

My father had an impatient or angry switch, a sullen switch, and a charming switch, the latter usually brought out for social or business events, although sometimes he revealed it to extended family members, or in later years when we'd moved out and he saw us less frequently. He—and my mother—subscribed to the unexpressed philosophy that praising anyone for a job well done risked an unwanted outcome, that this person would become spoiled, full of him or herself, selfish, complacent, difficult to live with. Better to keep everyone guessing, wondering if the work they'd done met their threshold, even downplaying the quality of whatever they'd done. I don't know that my father ever told my mother that often that she looked pretty, or that he'd enjoyed a meal she'd prepared, or that he appreciated all the chores she did for him, errands she ran for him, many of them thankless tasks performed by his intelligent, college-educated wife.

When still in my teens, one job I helped with was the ironing: handkerchiefs, sheets, undergarments, but no tricky outer garments I could scorch. My mother paid me five cents for each small item (handkerchiefs and underwear), a dime for undershirts, a quarter for sheets. I enjoyed the ironing itself, but not being in the basement; even now it's unpleasant. Damp and musty, it smells like electricity, grease, mildew. Dark like a sepia-tone painting, it has become even darker over time. An old house, Ivy Lodge is alive with creaks, unidentifiable sounds. I wonder what passed through my mother's mind during the hundreds of hours she spent in this basement.

Back when I helped with the ironing, occasionally a sibling or parent dropped a pile of dirty clothes or sheets down the clothes chute, a large blob of clothing or towels or sheets falling without warning like dead weight into the hamper only a few feet from me. It never failed to startle me. But I did enjoy watching the wrinkles disappear from whatever I ironed, much more rewarding than other minor chores my parents asked me to do: setting the table, clearing the table, sweeping the front steps, washing the dishes in the summer, making dinner salads for the family, babysitting for Janet. But I hadn't been sentenced to doing these chores—plus a hundred more—for the rest of my life like my mother.

As my father's income increased, my parents hired Marzie to help out with the ironing. A wonderful chunky African American woman, she occasionally stayed with Janet and me when our parents traveled. Marzie hummed while she ironed. Even upstairs, above the dungeon-like basement, you could hear snippets of her happy tunes from down below. She came on Thursdays, her husband Joseph dropping her off in his late model, cream-colored Cadillac. Susie, the "cleaning lady," came on Wednesdays, taking the bus from nearby, segregated Meacham Park. Coming through the back door after the two-block walk from the bus stop, Susie would walk into the breakfast nook where I was finishing up my breakfast, reminding me to drink my orange juice as she affectionately mussed my hair.

When Marzie babysat for us during our parents' trips, our diet changed from our mother's blander fare of peas, tomato aspic, creamed corn, and roast beef, to fried chicken with a typical dessert of angel food cake smothered in two inches of chocolate frosting. We loved the time we spent with her for that reason alone. She put my hair up in rollers each school night—just like my mother did when she was in town—but she wound it so tightly my curls looked unnaturally curly the following day, at least in comparison to my normally poker-straight hair. The next morning, I would wait till I left the house for school, tugging at my hair all the way to school, frantic to have the curls relax before I arrived, not wanting to invite mocking comments about my transformation into a brunette Orphan Annie. I didn't want to look different, tried to avoid anything that made me stand out negatively, any change that might prompt snickering from my classmates.

A clothesline is draped twenty feet side to side, just over my head. A few stray nightgowns remain, a pair of pants, one of my father's flannel shirts. My mother also used the line for delicate items she didn't want to put in the dryer, as well as jeans, worn only when she went metal-detecting, panning for gold, or arrowhead digging—favorite hobbies—or when they stayed at their country place in the Missouri Ozarks.

Clothes Call

During my senior year in college, I gained about twenty pounds. Returning home after graduation, I made progress losing the weight but still carried a little extra. Down in the basement, talking to my mother about something unrelated, I noticed a pair of my dark red bell-bottom pants drying on the line, attached with wooden clothespins. I confided in her how relieved I felt to finally fit into those same pants again. "I'm feeling good, Mom. They didn't fit in June, but now they do! Isn't that great?"

Without saying a word initially, she grabbed the pants off the clothesline in a single movement, clothespins flying onto the cement floor. She held them up at their widest point, one hand on each side of the waist. Next to her tiny figure they swallowed her up, resembled pants that could have belonged to an Amazonian woman.

"Are you serious? Are you talking about these? They're huge! What are you talking about? I'm not sure what makes you think fitting into *these* makes you slim." Pausing to make sure I had heard, taking note of my crestfallen expression, she added in a quieter, yet still condescending tone, "Come *on*, Linda." In my mind's eye, I ballooned to three hundred pounds on hearing her words. I had no response.

Several years later, married and living a few miles away, I stopped by my parents' home, unannounced. Walking in the back door to the kitchen, I stopped when I saw my mother. She was wearing one of my former outfits from thinner days, lime-green wool pants with a matching cable knit lime-green sweater. "Mom, are those my clothes?" I blurted out, without thinking. My mother had an extensive wardrobe, had no need for my castoffs. Unlike my situation, losing and regaining the same twenty or thirty pounds over the years, her weight never varied more than two or three pounds; she could theoretically fit into every outfit she'd worn since high school.

Before she had a chance to answer me, I heard my father slam his newspaper against the table as he barged into the kitchen from where he'd been, in the breakfast nook. Staring daggers at me as he waved his newspaper in the air he roared, "Why do *you* care? You'll *never* fit into them again! She can wear whatever she wants; it's *my* money that paid for these clothes in the first place!" He then shook the newspaper back into shape and returned to his green easy chair.

My mother didn't say a word, but I caught the remnants of a faint smile when she saw my father both silence me and take her side. I didn't say anything, never mentioned my clothes again. He'd been right, after all. His money had paid for everything in that house, including my former clothes. And he was accurate that I'd probably never fit into those small pants again.

TEAM OF RIVALS?

Darker thoughts emerge here in the basement, the dark and dampness serving as a petri dish for episodes in my life. It's like those fortune-telling Magic 8 Balls, with predictions cloudy at first before popping up through the inky background. Or foreign words on a page, their meaning slowly starting to make sense after I've read them, reread them, coming up with an accurate translation.

It reminds me of a language identification class I taught once. Based on the concept of bird calls, students had to identify various languages based solely on characteristics of the sounds they heard. Did it sound guttural? Staccato? Harsh? Did it seem heavier on vowels than consonants? Did it sound similar to a language they already knew? Were certain sounds repeated more than others, say, a final "a" or "o" (meaning it might be Spanish)? Using an inverted triangle, students narrowed the field down to a handful of languages, the bottom tip of the triangle, making a guess based on the fairly unscientific method they'd used.

It seemed like that with my parents. I heard the words they said, but the meaning eluded me. When my mother asked, "Are you still eating?" I knew she didn't want to know if I'd had enough to fill me up. It signaled her indictment of my eating too much or weighing too much. But I knew this only because I listened for the tone in her voice, the looks she gave me when she made it, the context of her words, her body language. The meaning carried more weight than the stand-alone English words. I had to put all the clues together and try to come up with the real significance behind her words. Or when my father told me I was "something else." That had to be interpreted in the context of other words that surrounded those two words, as well as his tone, his facial expressions. "Something else" translated—for me —into "I'm displeased with you but I'm not going to tell you why." I had to work to find the meanings, though, and never take the words at face value. It wore me out.

Starting at a young age, on occasion I had the fleeting thought—but soon dismissed it—that my mother considered me more of a rival than a daughter. When talking to me about my father, she never referred to him as "your father," or "Dad," or "your dad," the way other mothers did. She called him "Sam" in conversations with me, as when she announced, "Sam and I will probably be out of town when you have your baby," or "Sam can't talk to you right now; he's working outside. Call later."

Memories continue to overtake me in this netherworld, this railroad crypt. For instance, when my father was hospitalized in St. Louis following the strokes he'd had on our Mediterranean cruise, I would call him from Maryland. After talking a few minutes, I'd tell him I loved him before hanging up. Once he got back from Barcelona, he had become kinder, more demonstrative, as though the strokes had shuffled the contents of his mind, rid it of his anger, aggression, standoffishness. But my mother didn't appear to like how this transformation manifested itself in our relationship. During one call to the hospital, I overheard her in the background complaining to my sister-in-law, mocking the words I'd just spoken to my father. "I love you," her singsong words rang out, adding, "He tells *her* he loves her, but not *me*," as though we were competitors for his affection, as though he had a finite amount of love to give, making us rivals for that love, not a mother and daughter.

At my father's visitation, the day before his funeral, I stood next to my mother with a small group of her friends. My husband, children, and I had crammed our suitcases with photographs of my father and, along with pictures my mother and siblings had furnished, we placed them around the perimeter of the room at the funeral parlor for the benefit of my father's friends, for relatives. Half listening as she made small talk with her friends, most of whom I had known all my life, I remained silent at her side. Unexpectedly, at one point she glanced over at me, as though she hadn't noticed me before. Fluffing her hair, straightening her dress, she launched into making comments that were completely out of character. Donning an almost coquettish air, she boasted to the group—while looking straight at me—about how "compatible" she and my father had been, "if you know what I mean." I had the horrifying impression she'd decided to share this personal information to signal that she—not I—had won the contest for my father's affection. Embarrassed that her friends had witnessed this bizarre behavior, I attributed it to the stress of losing her husband of fifty-six years. Now that I reflect on it, though, alone in this depressing basement, I view it in a different light. She chanted a refrain to me growing up, a warning, I guess: "As Daddy [my grandfather] often told Jane and me, look long and hard at whom you marry because once you're out of the house, there's no coming back." Visiting my Aunt Jane—her sister—years later in Arizona, I asked her if my kindly, tiddlywink-playing grandfather had ever spoken those words. They seemed out of character. Laughing as though I'd told a joke, my aunt told me how ridiculous that was, that their father would never have made such a mean-spirited comment. Regardless, I got the message from a young age that, once I graduated from college, time would run out; I would no longer be welcome in their home.

Trying to think about other topics, shake off the possibility my mother considered me a rival, I considered that whenever my parents lashed out at me, maybe their words weren't based on reality. I've never been obese or stupid or lazy or friendless, or any of the other traits they ascribed to me, although I usually had to convince myself of that fact, even as an adult. Maybe my mother was frustrated with her own life when she humiliated me. I was her surrogate. Maybe her lack of choices, coupled with what she considered to be my charmed life in comparison, made her angry. For my father, perhaps he was disappointed I'd defied his traditional expectations for a female member of the Murphy family in nearly every way possible. If only I could hang onto this insight. If only my default reaction to my worth, my baseline self-concept, hadn't been rooted in seeing myself through their eyes. If only I could stop viewing my life through the arbitrary lexicon my parents devised and could build my own.

I'm sad for the little girl I used to be, a child who knew no other way to understand language besides literally, for whom every utterance coming from either parent was gospel. Added to that is the fact that, for the most part, my parents behaved inscrutably, each in different ways "impossible to understand or interpret." Especially my mother. Again those words: translation, interpretation. I rarely felt I'd solved the riddle of who she was. When she criticized or lashed out at me, it felt like another piece of the language puzzle I longed to solve. Realistically, too, part of me is still that little girl, combing through all their words, searching through all their possessions, walking through all the rooms of their home, as though secret compartments could be released from the walls, explaining my parents and my siblings to me.

BE PREPARED

One special evening back in high school, I spent time in this basement with my father. The night before retaking my college SATs. I followed him through the maze of train paraphernalia as he drilled me on possible vocabulary words while simultaneously working on a train project.

I made my way through the card tables, the train tracks, stepping around all the unidentifiable gizmos and gadgets on the floor, avoiding the original steel support beams jutting up to the ceiling from the cement floor, all to grab a few minutes with him. But I'll never forget that special evening: he told me about the Latin roots of certain words, about the trick of figuring out words from cognates. It represented an unusual, special circumstance in my life, allowing me to have quality time with him as father and daughter.

My father was the smartest person I'd ever known, with a vocabulary to match. In my teenage eyes, that night in the basement took on special significance, hearing him talk about words —my passion—how to retain the difficult ones, dissecting each one to get at its root, its meaning, how to make guesses as to what the test words meant.

My love of words began at a young age. I used dictionaries to pin reality, hold it in place, make the meanings stand still, be less confusing than what I experienced at home. In elementary school, my third-grade teacher introduced us to headwords. She held contests where we flipped through our abridged dictionaries to see who could find the designated word the fastest. For instance, she'd say "emerald," signaling us to look for the page with the headwords "emblements" and "emergent," the first and last words on the correct page. We waved our hands to get her attention when we found the actual entry for "emerald." I rarely raised my hand first, but not for lack of trying. It was my kind of game.

I was intrigued when this same elementary teacher informed us that the longest word in the English language—then—was *antidisestablishmentarianism.* A magical twenty-eight-letter word. My obsession with words continued as I made my mark in school spelling bees in fifth grade, out-spelling most of my classmates.

Getting personal help from either parent was rare in our family, to prepare for the SAT or otherwise. They either instructed us to figure out whatever it was on our own or sent us off with a surrogate deemed suitable to do the job. No time to bring the four of us children, or even one of us, up to the level our parents considered appropriate in any given activity. Better to be a spectator, a sideliner, or have someone else train you rather than risking their impatience or—worse—anger or rejection when you couldn't quickly master whatever the skill was: train construction, sewing, math, science, cooking, tennis, photography, gardening, fish care, driving, typing. In fact, the best plan, in my mind anyway, involved branching off into areas in which they had little or no expertise, which is why I ended up studying foreign languages.

I think that might have been my unconscious plan: to go as far afield as possible from my family members' areas of interest and expertise. Once I realized that, unlike my experience with math and science, I had an aptitude for learning other languages, I felt unfettered, free, almost good about myself when immersed in speaking Spanish or Portuguese or French while still in college. It was tantamount to having my own private room, a room no one else in my family had the key to enter, even if they tried.

A SIGN OF THE TIMES

The last thing I do before leaving the basement and rathskeller comes in a flash of insight: a cardboard sign is down here somewhere—maybe I spotted it when my father helped me prepare for the SAT test—but where? Finally I spot it in a far corner, scotch-taped to a metal pillar, hidden from view unless you're standing right next to it. "CAUTION: ADULTS AT PLAY." For some unknown reason, this is what I want from the tens of thousands of belongings in this wasteland of gold-plated, custom-made trains, tools, empty fish tanks, expensive photographic equipment, orphaned laundry. In a sense, this is all evidence that, when his own children were growing up, my father exchanged our childhoods for his lost one, swapped much of his free time for hundreds of hours with his trains as well as his other hobbies.

Carefully removing the sign from the wall, I dust it off with my sleeve, roll it up, and push it deep inside my oversized bag, nervous my siblings will see it and want to claim it for themselves. As it happens, a few weeks later a cousin who lives in the area asks me about that specific sign, wants to know what happened to it. I explain to him that I have it, that I'm planning to put it in a special place in my home. When I get back to Maryland, I tack the "ADULTS AT PLAY" sign on the wooden ceiling beams of my loft study, over my desk, next to a homemade "HAPPY MOTHER'S DAY" sign my children made for me. The sign is private, visible only if you're standing right next to my desk and look up. It's a comfort to me when powerful memories have me in their grip, a reminder that my father had a playful side, a wonderful, almost childlike sense of humor, a counterpoint to more frightening aspects of his personality.

twelve

FIRST-FLOOR BATHROOM: UNWELCOME VISITORS

I head upstairs and check the main first-floor bathroom, the bathroom down the hall from the kitchen, used by occasional visitors to Ivy Lodge. Overnight guests used a second bathroom, a smaller one a few steps down the hall outside Sam's old room. The bathtub—the only one in the house—is what I recall about this larger bathroom.

I would soak in the bathtub, pretending to be Doris Day singing a favorite song, "Que Será Será," "What Will Be Will Be," using a hairbrush as my microphone. Being in the bathroom represented a rare chance to have privacy, soaking in the soothing warm water. But once in a while, I'd spy little black feelers poking out from the overflow drain in front of me, as though conducting me in my singing, *tap tap tap*, one tiny antenna and then the other, up down up down, probably checking to see if it was safe to come out. Seconds later, a cockroach would plop down into the water in front of me, swimming in circles, its hairy-looking legs spinning this way and that, ever closer to me. I couldn't get out of the bathtub fast enough, screaming as though a mass murderer had been let loose in the bathroom. It's a wonder I ever took baths.

Ivy Lodge is an old house, an ideal breeding ground for cockroaches and water bugs, though how they climbed up one or two stories is a mystery. As a child, I wasn't interested in how they made the journey, just in their presumed goal of upending my sanity. Looking at the old bathtub now, making note of the cockroaches' former diving board, I reconsider my bug phobia. Maybe it had more to do with the feeling that, once again, I had little control over my world. Even in the midst of a relaxing environment, I never knew when an unexpected incident would darken the skies. Though cockroaches ranked high on my list of phobias, the presence of other unwanted things made me anxious as a child and adolescent. The list was ever-growing, to include the fear of being dunked while at a swimming pool, having my face washed with snow, swimming directly over pool drains, being stuck in small spaces.

This bathroom is evidence of Ivy Lodge's pockets of neglect, juxtaposed with the glossier areas located in the front of our majestic looking home. This lay in sharp contrast to my mother's meticulous appearance, her detailed lists, her high standards for her children's appearance, their behavior. Her overarching focus, though, remained our father. That focus, coupled with her lack of financial control over much of anything in Ivy Lodge, may partly explain her turning a blind eye to what probably would have been apparent to anyone else.

Thorstein Veblen referred to showcases of wealth evident in the nineteenth century as "conspicuous consumption," namely, the open—in many cases ostentatious—display of wealth. Here in this first-floor bathroom at the back of the house, however, large sheets of wallpaper are peeling off the walls like the sails of a ship. The bathtub has no shower curtain, has never had a shower curtain. Frosted windows in both first-floor bathrooms feature thick, opaque glass blocks letting virtually no light—or air—into the small rooms. The windows look like they were nailed shut when Ivy Lodge was first built, although I have no proof of that. They resemble windows in the home of a chain smoker, yellow, uninviting.

I peek under the vanity at the clothes chute and then at the bathtub, the peeling wallpaper, the yellowed window. Another memory comes to me, a ritual between my mother and me. Beginning in high school, every Tuesday morning we'd pull out the old white scale kept in this bathroom to see who had lost more weight the previous week, despite the fact that neither of us carried extra pounds. My mother wore a long silky, delicate beige slip, while I wore the lightest pair of pajamas I owned. I never won.

thirteen

FIRST-FLOOR BEDROOM: THE TEENAGE YEARS

*T*he bedroom I inherited when Steve left for college, adjoining the bathroom I just visited, no longer bears any resemblance to my former green-and-yellow room. After I got married, it became my father's study.

When this was still my room, my narrow desk had a pulldown writing surface about nine inches by twelve, too small to put more than a single book or notebook on. It had two bookshelves above the desk itself where I displayed my foreign doll collection: a hand-painted Spanish señorita with a lace mantilla, a straw woman from the Bahamas whom I named Toccatina after the Kabalevsky composition I played on the piano, and a doll my parents brought me from Mexico. I had a pair of Greek dancers in traditional costumes; a French doll dressed in a short frilly skirt; an Irish doll wearing a silky green peasant dress with a white apron, her auburn hair pulled back in a bun; a Japanese geisha doll with eight interchangeable wigs; a larger, foot-tall Asian cloth doll wearing a kimono, to name just a few. I even had two American Indian dolls my parents brought back from trips to the Missouri Ozarks, dolls with beautiful brown braids, wearing intricate beaded dresses and moccasins.

I had no way of knowing it back then—or of even imagining it—but I would end up traveling extensively for work and for pleasure after I moved from Kirkwood to the East Coast. Maybe these dolls helped me envision a different life, helped me think of adventures abroad. Maybe they represented an eventual shift within me, let me see the folly of my quest to be pretty, to be thin. Maybe they planted a seed inside me that there were many ways to live in the world. Whatever the reason, I loved the dolls, expanding my collection through the years. They survived my periodic room purges when I'd decided I had to let go of certain toys, was too old for them. I brought the dolls with me when I moved to the East Coast.

Another thought pulls at me, standing in my former teenage room, or its absence, I should say. My mother had the habit of commenting on my weight, even though I didn't have a weight problem till college, threatening to install a full-length mirror on my closet door, concrete evidence of what I looked like from every angle. Nowhere to hide, no escape. "If you could just *see* yourself from the rear, you'd know what I'm talking about, Linda!" she'd remind me, as though trying to be helpful, as though I needed to be reminded of my shortcomings. Fortunately, she never followed through with her plan, but the fear of a life-size mirror being put in my room loomed. I fully expected to come home from school one day at fourteen, fifteen, sixteen years old, confronted with the dreaded "proof" of my reflected imperfections.

MIND OVER MATTER

My mother admired certain aspects of Christian Science. She wasn't a bona fide, card-carrying Christian Scientist, though. She came from a long line of Episcopalians: parents, grandparents and beyond, dating back to their roots in Anglican England. But she cherry-picked that part of Christian Science in which the church looked at sickness as an illusion, a mental mistake better treated by prayer than by medicine. Tweaking it somewhat, she turned it into our family credo, although mental power replaced prayer power.

The whole idea of Christian Science baffled me because it sounded like a contradiction in terms. Wasn't Christianity mysterious, based on faith, believing in the unseen, the unproven? Whereas science consisted of empirical data, provable, logical. This was an oxymoron if I'd known what the term meant back then. This philosophy prevailed in our home when one of us became sick. It formed part of my mother's world and had no other context in my life. It felt more like her hobby than her religion.

My mother's admiration of Christian Science touched us the summer between my freshman and sophomore years in college. I'd been resting in my bedroom when I started having bad stomach cramps. I hoped the pain would subside, thought maybe I'd eaten too much or consumed something tainted. By evening the pain had grown worse. I couldn't get out of bed. My mother—occasionally accompanied by my brother—checked on me once in a while.

Doubled up from cramps, I wanted to call the doctor, who still made house calls back then. My brother tried to downplay my pain, confiding that he'd had similar symptoms at college, yet look, he'd had no health issues; I probably had the same problem. As usual, my mother assured me I'd feel better if I got my mind off it. But the pain continued to worsen, regardless of my mental gymnastics and the encouragement of my mother and brother. I panicked.

I asked again if we could call the doctor. "We are not hauling Herman Ross out of bed at this hour," I could hear my father snap. On his way to the living room to read his *Wall Street Journal*, my mother had interrupted this nightly ritual to give him an update on my worsening condition, her mind-over-matter ideas proving increasingly ineffective. But Herman Ross wasn't just the family doctor; he'd been a friend for years as well as a member of our church.

As my mother retreated from the living room, I could hear my father saying, "We'll see how she is in the morning. I'm going to bed." Twenty years later, I might have broken with family protocol, dragged myself to the pink princess phone on my bedside table, dialed 911, but 911 wasn't an option yet.

In the middle of the night, I spiked a high fever. My mother and brother drove me to the hospital, thankfully disobeying my father's previous instructions. The hospital lay twenty miles from our suburban home in an unsafe part of the city. I had appendicitis. Acute appendicitis.

Once we arrived at the hospital, I heard my mother downplay my condition, tell the nurses that no emergency was involved, not to disturb the surgeon on our behalf, that I could wait. I lay on a hospital cot, floating in and out of consciousness, too weak to counter her comments.

My mother didn't like to bother people she held in high regard: doctors, ministers, politicians, for example. The medical staff finally deemed my condition an emergency when they pressed on the tender, inflamed area around my appendix, eliciting my cries. The staff summoned the surgeon to perform an emergency appendectomy, but it was too late. My appendix had already burst, probably hours before when I still lay in my bed at home.

I remained in the hospital for a week, as toxins had been released into my body. After I'd been home a few days, I had to return to the hospital when I developed another high fever. Poison from my ruptured appendix remained in my system, necessitating a second operation, ten days after the first.

Walking over to the window of my former first-floor bedroom, I look out at a spot just outside, where I sunbathed on a chaise lounge in the backyard after my initial surgery, still feeling unwell. My mother came outside to report the news, her tone stern, somewhat accusatory, as though I'd brought this on myself, somehow willing my illness to continue. "Get what you need for the hospital ready. We have to take you *back*. Your fever is too high."

I wondered back then if this stemmed from negligence on my part. It must have been my fault, I reasoned. I'd brought it on somehow, but how? Something I'd eaten? I'd inconvenienced everyone, taking up their valuable time to have another operation. It reminded me of what had happened more than a decade before. Only six, I'd been seriously ill with infectious hepatitis. My mother had pulled me aside in our kitchen on Gill Avenue when no one was around, shortly after I'd returned from my week-long stay at the hospital to begin my long convalescence at home. Stooping down to my level, careful to lower her voice, she placed a firm hand on my shoulder to stop my squirming and sternly told me the cause of my illness had been my poor hygiene. "You brought this on yourself," she whispered. "You never wash your hands after you use the bathroom; this is what happens. You have no one to blame but yourself. Don't you *dare* tell anyone this was my fault, do you hear?" In my six-year-old naïveté, I believed her, shook my head in silent assent, guilt-ridden for what I'd done to myself, eager for the conversation to end. A dozen years later, I'd somehow made myself sick again, this time with appendicitis. At least that's what I feared.

The second operation took place on a Saturday. My mother stayed with me at the hospital long enough for me to be checked in, then she left. Alone in my hospital room, waiting to be prepped for surgery, I called home, nervous: what if they couldn't get all the poison? What if it had traveled to other parts of my body? What if I had the same surgeon who didn't do it right the first time, the one my father threatened to sue for malpractice? My stomach already looked horrible from the first emergency surgery; wouldn't this make me even more disfigured?

Lying in bed, the phone propped against my head, I spoke with my mother. In the background I could hear activity at home, at Ivy Lodge, as everyone went about their day: my little sister listening to cartoons in the breakfast nook, the laugh track in stark contrast to my anxiety.

My mother, preoccupied with household matters, barely registered my words. My older brothers had left the house with friends. My father had chores to do. It was a normal day for them, not their problem I'd had to return to the hospital, at least that's what I imagined them thinking, maybe even saying. That same night after the second operation, I lay in my hospital bed alone watching *Laugh-In* on the hospital TV, holding the site of my incision when Goldie Hawn popped out of the web of boxes, and when Rowan and Martin cracked jokes. It hurt, but it made me laugh, helped lift my spirits.

My burst appendix left a gash that looked like I'd dueled with a master fencer who'd slashed me diagonally from my lower waist to my groin, instead of the textbook hairline appendectomy scar. Six inches long, raised, red, puffy, oozing pus for weeks, it looked like a gigantic caterpillar had burrowed just beneath the surface of my skin and died trying to escape. Because of the medical emergency, the rush to operate, no one worried about cosmetic concerns. But I put the situation in perspective several years later when a friend in the medical field told me I'd been lucky to survive my burst appendix. It could have been worse.

In a postscript, years after my ruptured appendix, my father sometimes brought up the incident, telling friends and family members he blamed the surgeon. "That quack let her lie in the admitting room far too long, should have operated immediately," he complained. "I should have sued him for malpractice when I had the chance." I didn't contradict him, pointing out his role in the delay. What would have been the point?

RUNNING ON EMPTY

Besides her mind-over-matter tactic, my mother used another strategy to deal with her occasionally uncooperative children: divide and conquer. One quiet summer afternoon, my brother Steve approached me to ask if I wanted to go running with him. An avid runner, he always ventured out alone; I was thrilled he'd thought of me, a freshman in high school. I had this fantasy we'd someday grow close. After all, at only three years my senior, the closest to me in age of my three siblings, this was exciting in my world of this-is-what-girls-do v. this-is-what-boys-do. But, over-hearing Steve's invitation, my mother followed me.

I'd scurried off to my bedroom—the same first-floor former bedroom where I'm now standing—and changed into my version of running clothes, nervous he would have second thoughts about his rare invitation if I took too long. Closing the door behind her, my mother quietly spoke, careful not to let her voice carry beyond the walls of my room.

Adopting a confidential air, lowering her voice, she said, "Linda, do you think this is wise? I know you're excited about your brother's invitation, but when boys run, they become leaner, while women runners develop unattractive, muscular thighs. Do you want to blow up, have no clothes that fit? You know how hard you've worked to try to have a slim figure, how you struggle with your weight." An insincere pained look accompanied her words.

The threat of looking muscular—hence, overweight—trumped my desire to go running with my brother. I bowed out of running, killed the possibility of a tradition being established between us, a bond, because he never invited me again. As much as I wanted to be looked at as an equal in my brother's eyes, to be friends with him, it wasn't worth the risk of looking fat, unattractive, which translated into being unpopular, even though I would eventually learn that what my mother told me had no basis in fact. But I didn't realize it then. My mother said this. Why would she lie? What possible motivation could she have had for discouraging me? But later, when I'd become an expert anthropologist in observing the ways of my mother, in decoding her words and actions, I realized she couldn't risk us forging a bond, becoming close, just as she couldn't risk my sister and me developing a close relationship, or my brothers, only two years apart. She fostered dissent among us, and it worked. Together, we might have changed the paradigm, especially when my father thrust his commercial real estate deals into our world, but that would never happen because we remained four independent agents, wary of the motives of our respective siblings.

Her discouragement at my attempts at athleticism extended into my adulthood. After I'd been married five years, but before we had children, my then-husband and I went to Florida with my parents, along with a number of other Kirkwood families. One morning when the men had gone fishing, I left a note for my mother saying I'd gone to swim laps in the condominium pool. I'd been swimming regularly for about a year. It had helped me lose weight and feel good about myself. When I returned to the condo, my mother looked frantic, said she'd been looking all over for me to give me a key because she and my father had decided to take a walk. Regarding me with disdain—still in my swimming suit and dripping wet—adopting her singsong voice, she asked, "Have you been swimming all this time, honey?" When I said I had, she shook her head, saying, "That's *too* much." Although she'd criticized me for years for being overweight, when I finally decided to adopt a healthy lifestyle, she hated it. I couldn't win.

MOTHER TONGUE

Whenever my siblings and I made any attempt to strengthen the tenuous bonds between us, my mother put a damper on our efforts. She compared Sam, Janet, and me unfavorably to Steve, made Janet feel inferior to all of us, I found out later, since my mother liked to remind her she was the only one without a graduate degree. Our mother capitalized on any real or apparent differences between us, blowing them out of proportion, drawing attention to these so-called differences when she spoke about my siblings, sowing disagreements. She also had the habit of inserting herself into any activities or conversations or interests we had—board games, friends, school outings—snooping around to spread discord, start rumors, get information. Knowledge equaled power in her world.

When we were growing up, any hint of conflict brewing between my siblings and me meant the involvement of our mother. When I moved an inch over the imaginary line in the car and Janet blurted out her objections, when Sam punched me in the arm causing me to cry out, when Steve argued with Sam about who could use the car, she silenced us. "Stop it!" our mother hissed. "We don't *talk* like that." We had to remain polite, even when she was the one stoking the embers of discord.

Everything had to be "civil," in my mother's words, at least superficially. For the benefit of everyone outside the family, our behavior had to remain placid. But this meant nothing ever got worked out, and not just between Janet and me, either. Issues were never tackled, grudges never dealt with, arguments never resolved, spats between any of us rarely discussed. We embodied the lithograph our parents gave us: it all looked nice enough on the outside, on the surface, but the inside held dark, pent-up emotions, secrets. Actors in a play, a genteel play containing no harsh words (except from our father) prevailed: no slamming of doors, no crying, no whining, no complaining. But this meant no closeness, no secrets, no struggles, no true emotions, no sibling to turn to as a confidant, no calls for help from a brother or sister.

fourteen

FOYER:
MAKING AN ENTRANCE

*L*eaving my first-floor bedroom, I bypass the living room and dining room, and enter the foyer. The foyer is located in the center of my parents' home, where my siblings and I congregated when we first arrived to sort, throw out, box up, tally.

The layout of this house is a testimony to poor planning as I look at it through the filter of having lived in five homes since I moved out of Ivy Lodge, two of them in Missouri and three in Maryland. Criticizing a foyer is unpopular to history buffs since guests were welcomed in the foyer; hosts took their coats, made introductions, exchanged pleasantries. Maybe in the nineteenth century. But to me, it's wasted space between the living room and dining room, the first room you enter when you come through the front door. A counterpoint to the basement and rathskeller immediately beneath it, it's empty space with a chandelier hanging from a high ceiling, a tall, solid, domed wooden front door, a spiral staircase leading to the half-finished second floor on the far side, with an eight-chime doorbell embedded in the stairway wall, an enormous, nondescript space heater against a wall beneath the stairs. That's it. Nothing to see here but dead space, in a home where livable space was already at a premium.

No one—in my family at least—regularly used the front door when we lived in Ivy Lodge, just the occasional traveling salesmen selling their wares: Fuller Brush combs and brushes, vacuum cleaners, lightbulbs, World Book Encyclopedias, to name a few, with a gaggle of trick-or-treaters on Halloween. The mailman might ring the doorbell occasionally to deliver a package. Even the milkman came to the back door, along with most of our friends and relatives, and Marzie and Susie.

Something a bit intimidating happened when you made your way down the sidewalk from the front driveway, crossing the wide flagstone porch, up the few steps to the oversized domed doorway, ringing the eight-tone doorbell, and waiting. You had to ring the doorbell, or no one would know you stood outside the front door. Most people probably didn't want to make a grand entrance, sought to avoid creating such an impression. As soon as people got to know us, they parked at the back of the house and entered the back porch to ring the deafening single-toned bell outside the kitchen door.

The foyer represents a misuse of space, at least in this home where giant swaths of unfinished areas lie abandoned on the second story, where equally massive, poorly or underutilized areas lie just below, in the basement, where the formal dining room remains largely unoccupied, more like the repository of the home's supply of silver, crystal, and lace, a diorama of sorts.

I ring the doorbell, calling out in advance to my siblings— still scattered throughout the house—to prevent them from coming when they hear the sound of the classic eight-note chime. Pressing the outside button, the sound stirs an ancient— thirty-four-year-old—memory specific to the foyer, one I'm sure my mother would be able to recreate with eidetic precision if she were still alive. Odd that I think of it after all these years.

WAR CHIMES

In the winter and spring of 1966, my brother Sam was twenty-one, a Marine serving in Vietnam. Sam was the radioman for his unit, a position the Viet Cong targeted. Destroying the soldiers' communications meant isolating troops, getting an upper hand in battle. Long stretches of time passed between Sam's letters from combat areas. Life became even more tense at home. With Steve off at college, there was one less person to run interference with our parents.

I was a sophomore in high school, naïve about the danger Sam faced, or maybe I chose "not to dwell on it," as my mother would have advised, in order to discourage obsessing about problems. Maybe I thought my teenage issues presented more pressing problems. Am I popular? Will anyone invite me to the prom? Does Bruce Smith like me? Am I fat? Will that ugly blemish ever disappear?

In my diary, I mentioned Sam in passing, and then moved on to more mundane topics, unable, or maybe unwilling, to hold the image in my mind of a brother on the front lines of a war in the remote jungles of Southeast Asia. I didn't have the vocabulary, imagination, or emotional depth to identify with my brother's life, or my parents' lives in response to Sam's situation.

But on March 24, 1966, when a friend dropped me off after school, everything changed. I could no longer skirt the issue of Sam serving in Vietnam or limit it to my brief diary entries sandwiched between my teenage obsessions of boys, school, weight, my complexion, not to mention the elusive goal of being popular. The war came right up to our front door and rang the doorbell.

Walking into the kitchen through the back door, plopping my schoolbooks on the counter, I glanced at my mother doing the dishes. I noticed she was scrubbing more aggressively than usual, exerting such pressure it looked like the dishes might break. Approaching her, I could see she'd been crying, her eyes rimmed in red, her face blotchy. Had I ever seen my mother cry? I didn't know if I had. She had little patience for showing weakness. When she caught me in tears, her frustration grew; she'd accuse me of being "weepy," or announce that she'd wait till I was "done," comments that had the opposite effect on her emotional daughter.

"Mom. What's wrong? What happened?" I said, peering at her face like a scientist into a microscope. "Are you crying?" Setting aside the dishes she'd been washing in the sink, still holding the wet dishrag in her hand, not stopping to turn the water off, she turned to me and got right to the point. "Sam's been shot."

I felt like I'd been punched in the stomach. She continued, "I was doing a load of laundry in the basement when I heard the front doorbell ring. The dogs wouldn't stop barking, so I came upstairs to see what was going on. On my way to the door, through the living room window I saw a car in the driveway with the official Marine Corps insignia."

At this point she paused, catching her breath, still emotional but intent on composing herself. "I thought they only made official calls when your son had been killed," she said. "I ran to the door, tried to get it open, but it was locked. Even after I unlocked it, it jammed."

"When I finally managed to get it open," she went on, "I saw these two men in uniform, standing on the front porch, official looking. Before they could speak, I blurted out, 'No! No! No!' because I was scared to death he'd been killed. Why else would they make an official visit?"

"Facing their palms outward," she went on, pantomiming the soldiers' movements for me, "shaking their heads to signal I was wrong, they told me that, no, he'd been shot but would be all right. They'd airlifted him to a hospital in Japan. I've never been so scared yet relieved in my life."

I didn't know which shocked me more, my brother having been shot in this faraway, doesn't-seem-real-to-me war, or my mother crying, letting her vulnerable side show. By the time my father came home from work, she'd regained control, her steely demeanor snapped back in place, but for a while my worldview flipped from all sides: my brother lying wounded in a faraway hospital, my mother crying. My father made a few phone calls that afternoon and learned that Sam had been transported to a hospital in Japan, where our father had friends from his FBI days. They would check on Sam while he remained in the hospital, reporting back to my parents. Fortunately, Sam actually phoned us that same night. He'd hoped to reach us before the Marine Corps' official visit to our home. My parents were so relieved to actually hear his voice, I know, even if just for a few minutes. That marked the end of active combat for him; the Marines transferred him back to the States when he became stable.

This served as a turning point in how I viewed my mother, how I translated her words, her actions. Till then, she'd been almost like an actress to me, never deviating from the role she'd chosen, the persona she'd assumed. She wouldn't depart from it unless she became angry with one of us, briskly leaving "the stage" to restore order. Suddenly, though, she had gone off script, letting her true emotions show, speaking words I'd never heard, ones that reflected her vulnerability.

The doorbell chimes have long since stopped ringing, although if I listen carefully, I hear tiny echoes of the sounds. It's a reminder that everything that happened in Ivy Lodge is still here, maybe at a higher frequency than any of us can hear, and invisible to the naked eye. It's all contained within the walls of the rooms, rooms we lived in, slept in, fought in, ate in, cried in, even laughed in. It's captured in the DNA of Ivy Lodge.

BRUSH WITH DEATH

Following my parents' deaths, we divided everything of value in the house systematically, equitably, except for one item: my father's hairbrush. My mother owned a sterling silver dressing table set with a comb, two brushes, and a handheld mirror, all originally placed on a silver tray. It may have been a wedding gift when my parents got married the summer of 1942.

The man's brush has a short, nubby silver handle, a little knob with a silver Ping-Pong-ball-sized handle to grip the brush at the end, with soft, thick, inch-long bristles attached to an ornate, sterling silver top, three inches wide by four inches long. The woman's hand-tooled brush is more ornate, and its long metal handle has a smaller silver brush head. The handle itself is nearly eight inches long. The comb has a thin sterling silver cap running the length of the comb on the side.

Back in its prime, the set would have been found in the home of a woman of means, placed on a dressing table with a tall, segmented mirror, located in a separate part of the marital bedroom, somewhere she could sit on a small bench to fix her hair or apply makeup, a boudoir. Nowadays such luxuries exist primarily in 1940s movies where the women wear long, diaphanous dressing gowns, staring into an oval-shaped mirror as they brush their hair one hundred times before bed each night.

I walked around the table at my brother's home, looking at the array of expensive items my parents owned, items brought to Steve's home after our parents' deaths. All of them had been sorted, catalogued, appraised, and displayed in his spacious dining room before we went through the more mundane items contained in Ivy Lodge. I observed that we had more than enough items to open our own high-end jewelry and silver antique store. But conducting her own inventory, Janet had noticed a missing item: the man's brush. A mate that belonged to the brush and comb set. "We're missing Dad's brush," she announced, sounding somewhat alarmed. "Does anyone know where it is? We should keep everything together."

I knew the exact location of the brush. I had it. I'd claimed it after my mother's hospitalization the month before. Two of her guilty pleasures in life consisted in having her hair brushed and her scalp massaged. She sometimes referred to herself as a "cat." A paragon of self-control, she never admitted to needing anything; even eating an entire serving of dessert bordered on excessive for her. ("I can't eat another bite. It's just too rich," she'd remark, pushing herself away from the table while I secretly wondered how to pilfer her mostly untouched portion.) You couldn't tempt her with many of life's frivolities, except for hair or scalp massages. Once in a while my father indulged her; even less frequently my sister or I did.

Staying at her home during her last weeks at the hospital, I'd looked in her bedroom for an appropriate brush to take to the hospital each day, hopeful that I could lift her burden somewhat. The hairbrushes she regularly ordered from the Fuller Brush man felt coarse. I thought they'd be rough on her already-fragile body. The hand-tooled silver woman's brush in the vanity set felt unwieldy with its long handle. But testing my father's much smaller brush against the palm of my hand, the bristles felt soft, Goldilocks "just right" soft.

I put it in my purse for my daily trip to the hospital. Every day I brushed her hair with the silver brush. My mother would never again be able to speak for herself after her tracheostomy, but I watched as her eyes closed, maybe not from depression or fear or pain. When I brushed her hair, it was different. I could tell it had a soothing effect on her.

I did it the way she liked: slow, deep strokes, pulling her hair away from her forehead, always brushing against her natural part. Knowing she couldn't answer me, I asked her anyway, "Is this all right? Is this how you like it? Do you want me to keep brushing?" She never nodded or gestured, but I knew I was doing it right. I had years of trying to guess, of anticipating my mother's moods, forced to interpret expressions and gestures when no words had been spoken.

I knew I'd never relinquish the brush because this marked the closest we'd ever come to bonding. No hurtful words launched in either direction as I pulled the brush through her short, salt-and-pepper permed hair. She lay on her hospital bed, with tubes, vials, fluids, bags arrayed around her, in her, like a tangled spider web. No interference from my father, who'd died a little more than a year before. No orders being barked at her, no constant interruptions. Life had been reduced to basic nonverbal communication, silence.

This turned out to be the closest she ever came to needing me, to accepting love from me. At some level I realized this. But only while brushing her hair. After I'd been in town for three weeks, her condition grave but stable, I asked if she wanted me to extend my stay, continue visiting her each day at the hospital, or if I should return to my family in Maryland, come back later.

All I needed was a nod, a sign, a smile, a squeeze of my hand, a flicker of assent in her eyes. I would have done anything to make it happen, stayed as long as she wanted, forever. But she opened her palms face up, shrugged as though to say, "It makes no difference to me." Even in the last days of her life, she wouldn't allow herself to appear needy; she had to be strong.

Another explanation for the importance of the brush exists, one that occurred to me after I'd returned home from helping to clean out our parents' home. Just maybe, I thought, my mother and I had something important in common. In both of our cases, but for different reasons, maybe we'd had our fill of language, of thousands of words being hurled at each other over the years. In my case, I felt like I'd been drowning in a sea of words, words that, more often than not, bore no resemblance to their dictionary definitions. What was the point of communicating if, inevitably, a subtext bubbled up, one I had trouble making sense of in my naïveté, in my confusion? What was the point if a word's meaning had been distorted to fit secret agendas, flip-flopped for unknown ulterior motives, withheld for other reasons? Translating what anyone said had become impossible for me, my work with languages, my love of words failing me when it came to my own family. All my dictionaries proved useless in trying to decipher a lifetime of communication fraught with subtexts buried beneath more subtexts.

She delivered infrequent proclamations of love in a singsong voice. They somehow never rang true, the occasional "I love you!" uttered just after she'd subtly conveyed one of my imperfections, as though providing a counterweight to the negative comment. Who knew where the truth lay since instances of her putting me in my place abounded, of comparing me unfavorably to a friend, a smarter, prettier, more popular, more successful, kinder friend? What to believe? Whom to believe? I had the impression these artificial compliments originated in other events in my mother's life, rare occasions when she was feeling good and deigned to pass on her good mood to me, regardless of the words' connection to reality. As a result, I had difficulty weighing the sincerity of her words.

During my mother's final days, she kept her eyes closed, as though to block out words, anyone's words. After all, my father had probably spoken millions in her presence—most directed at her—during their marriage. Now the only words she heard in the hospital consisted of comments made by the steady stream of doctors, nurses, social workers concerning her dismal future. Having her hair brushed translated into a silent, almost pure way to communicate at the end of her life. We behaved like mutes having found another way to express ourselves, maybe even a better way, one not warped by the years, twisted out of shape by ulterior motives.

Responding to my sister's original query I answered, "I have the brush. The set will have to remain incomplete because I used it to brush Mom's hair at the hospital. I'm keeping it." I added a defiant look, daring her—or my brothers or sisters-in-law—to contradict me, maybe even to bolster my resolve. No one said a word, but they exchanged meaningful, wide-eyed glances, as though to say, "Wow. Here goes Linda again, causing trouble."

EYE OF THE BEHOLDER

If they'd wanted to make sense of my behavior with the silver brush, my siblings might have remembered a few years earlier when my mother decided to rethink her decision to have her two daughters and daughters-in-law designate pieces of jewelry we'd like after her death. She had instructed us to compile a wish list, presenting the four of us with a complete inventory of her jewelry. Janet and I picked sentimental pieces our mother had let us look at as children, pieces she kept in her old, beat-up, green faux-snakeskin jewelry box: a gold garnet ring her parents gave her on her eighteenth birthday, a tiny tourmaline ring, thin sterling silver bands, each of our beaded blue and white birth bracelets, our names spelled out in these beads; a few other modest items. Our brothers' wives obviously had no such sentimental leanings and chose more expensive items.

My mother never mentioned the wish list again. Maybe she realized her plan had flaws, or that it would be a nightmare trying to sort out everyone's choices, given the differences in value. Consequently, after she died my sister, sisters-in-law, and I took turns going around the table in the breakfast nook, picking from the large pile of her treasures till they were all gone. My first choice was an elaborate necklace that looks like a knight's chain mail, an armor of tiny charms spaced with beads streaming in separate strands from a clasp made out of a large rectangular Carnelian cabochon. It's the most personal piece of jewelry she owned, an unusual, beautiful piece of wearable art containing tiny mementos from all four of my grandparents, from her parents and my father's. My mother had a large part in creating the necklace. She selected more than sixty charms from her own collection, ones she'd bought or been given over the years. They came from our grandmother's charm bracelets, from pins and other random items she'd collected from relatives' estates. She then selected the size and color of the accompanying filler beads, the clasp, devising the design, the shape of the necklace. She commissioned an artist in Arizona to create it with multiple strands of semiprecious beads of various sizes—blue lapis, orange carnelian, red coral, yellow tiger's eye, green jade—to link the sixty-eight charms. It has her imprint, reveals her creativity, her personality, whereas other items in her estate were generic pieces or came from upscale stores or from the early years of her marriage to my father.

Nothing on the carefully crafted necklace, none of the sixty-eight charms hints at her role of mother. No baby rings, charms with our birthstones, beaded birth bracelets, profile charms of a baby or a mother, of a girl or a boy, nothing to reflect schools we went to, interests we had, trips we all took together. Not even charms we'd all given her through the years, for instance, the gold heart charm I presented her with to thank her (along with my father) for letting me spend my junior year of college in Spain. The picture of my mother as reflected in her necklace is that of a wife, daughter, daughter-in-law, sorority member, daughter of a sorority member, a woman with collections, hobbies, and interests, a woman who visited many states, countries, cultural sites, but who, when putting together her intricate necklace, chose not to reveal her role as a mother. Our mother.

In fairness, maybe she calculated that between the years of 1944 (the year my eldest brother was born) and 1977 (the year Janet left home to get married), a thirty-three-year period, her life revolved around the four of us, plus our father, like it or not. Maybe she decided to scrape off the jelly-stained, clutching fingers of her four time-sucking progeny. But, still . . . thinking about it when I looked at the necklace again, it reminded me that, even when prompted, I never heard her relate amusing anecdotes from any of our childhoods, tell the cute stories most parents or grandparents delight in telling and retelling, boring others in the process. She could tell you with encyclopedic precision who all of our teachers and friends had been and, if quizzed, would have gotten 100 percent on such a test, but seemed to avoid unnecessary, sentimental reminiscing. On the few occasions when I dared to ask her about such-and-such a childhood event, she'd look at me blankly and shrug her shoulders as if to say, "I don't know; why are you asking me this?"

Maybe her choice of charms also paid tribute to times before her role as a wife began. After all, she didn't have the grand wedding she'd planned, even though invitations had been engraved and mailed, plans made, caterers hired, the Episcopal church in Webster Groves, Missouri, reserved. It all came to a halt at the last minute when the FBI canceled my father's leave. He was stationed in San Francisco during World War II in June of 1942, making it impossible to leave the area. My mother took the train from St. Louis to California, inviting strangers she met on the train to be witnesses at their small church ceremony.

I never heard her complain about the sudden change of plans, about missing out on her dream wedding, but I remembered it when she was hospitalized shortly before her death. Going through her papers and photographs I came across her original wedding invitation, an invitation engraved with the "wrong" date, the original one. Early evidence of having to twist her life around to accommodate my father, even though the change in plans hadn't been his fault.

fifteen

ATTIC:

GONE AND FORGOTTEN

I need to move on, go upstairs to the second story, from one cluttered area (the basement/rathskeller) to the next, the unfinished swath of the house we called the attic, even though it wasn't actually an attic. I dread this, knowing it will be cold since this oversized area has no heat (or air-conditioning). Winter is keenly felt within its sweeping, cold, dark spaces; I'm not sure I am dressed warmly enough.

The attic is at the top of the curving wrought iron stairs ascending from the foyer, inside the first door on the right. It's safe to assume that, after seeing the front of the house, visitors imagined elegant rooms lay upstairs. Their expectations would have been dashed if they'd opened the door off the second-floor landing. But no one but immediate family ever did. Even first cousins growing up just a few blocks away expressed disbelief when they learned about the layout of Ivy Lodge after my parents' deaths. Guests never went upstairs, even extended family members. I never heard my parents reveal that the second story was largely unfinished.

"Nothing but two bedrooms and a half bath up there? How is that possible?" The reality that more than half the second floor is a faux attic is a little-known fact. I think maybe—like the rathskeller—my parents had plans to finish it someday, but like many other plans for the house, they never materialized, or they took a backseat to the trains or to other financial considerations like college for four children.

Raw wall studs rim the perimeter of the attic, and bare wooden planks stand in for floors. Unfinished ceilings reveal exposed beams, with batt insulation panels lying between the studs where walls should be. The insulation panels make it look like oversized, overstuffed paper bags have been wedged between the building studs, many torn, spilling out from the wall, their contents exposed.

The only source of artificial light in this large space consists of two bare, low-watt lightbulbs hanging from the rafters on long wires. There's a third light inside an interior closet, the closet also unfinished. The lightbulbs have accumulated decades of dust, creating an eerie, otherworldly, film noir atmosphere, sepia tones complementing the basement schemata.

The attic is a graveyard of sorts for belongings that would never—or rarely—be seen again. Shivering in the attic's frigid spaces, I briefly wonder why we ever called it an "attic," if maybe that label somehow made it easier to justify this depressing area. How did we all fall into that trap? To me, it represents the death of illusion, of the idea of this wealthy, up-and-coming family. It's as though this mountain of discarded "stuff" had been cast out from the rest of the house because it didn't fit with our sparkly Ivy Lodge image, not like the living room and dining room. It's where the family secrets came to die, the main secret being that we weren't that well-off, weren't any better-off than our former neighbors on Gill Avenue, at least initially.

I wonder what my mother thought about it, having a waste-land next door to her bedroom, a dumping ground of papers, furniture, old toys, clothes, Christmas decorations. My mother with her organized lists and tallies and ledgers of coins, license plates, laundry, arrowheads. I doubt the situation with the attic made her happy, but I also doubt she ever expressed those feelings to my father. The secret remained safe with her. She didn't want outsiders to see that the habitable part of Ivy Lodge was far smaller than it appeared from the exterior, that our family probably couldn't afford to finish it, at least not until my siblings and I had left the nest, graduated from college.

A fairly large closet occupies a section of this unfinished expanse. It's more like a walk-in box, where cracked and abandoned suitcases, old coats, scouting uniforms, and my mother's out-of-date, frilly chiffon party dresses have gone to die. Unfortunately, someone mistakenly installed the lock on the outside of the door, which automatically swings shut. If trapped inside, your cries can scarcely be heard from the rest of the house, if at all, particularly since the door to the attic is kept closed to prevent the frigid or stifling temperatures from permeating the rest of the house, depending on the season.

I personally fell victim to this closet's faulty locks one Sunday when I was eleven or so. I'd been searching for an item in the closet when the door automatically shut behind me. My parents had company over and were sitting outside on the screened-in porch. They couldn't hear my frantic cries. I remained locked inside till a sibling heard the faint sound of my voice.

The house appeared to have a mind of its own, a dark soul ready to ensnare you. I had to be careful. Doors slammed behind me, trapping me. Giant cockroaches leapt out at me when I took a bath or put my head on my pillow. Statues in the yard looked like they came to life at night. A sinkhole garden sank year after year. Bats clung to the walls of the house. A stone room in the basement looked, smelled, and felt like a miniature dungeon. Who knew what else remained hidden inside and outside the house?

The attic housed three sets of front-facing double windows with another set on the north side of the house. When viewed from the outside, they looked like eyes into the elegance found elsewhere in the home, not portholes into a barren expanse of discarded memorabilia and dust. They served as props from a play, attractive shells concealing piles of junk just on the other side, reinforcing my belief that we were all just actors playing at being a family, with a script expressly written and directed to hide our flaws from the outside world. A script intended to disguise real people forever being reminded of our lines.

A GIFT FORGOTTEN

As I start to leave the attic, too cold to go through anything, I stop, remembering an early spring day more than twenty years ago when the temperature in the attic was more moderate than usual. On my way out of the attic that day, I'd lingered over an enormous cardboard packing box near the door, the type people use when they move.

The box had been crammed with a hodgepodge of uninteresting-looking, ancient papers, but partially hidden under a small stack, I'd caught a glimpse of an old crayon drawing that had somehow withstood the test of time and other enemies. The colors weren't too faded. Largely intact, it showed just a few small stains.

Judging from its appearance, along with the inclusion of my

sister's name on the card, I probably made it at six or seven years old, using a horizontal perspective on a plain five-by-eight-inch piece of paper to create a small, makeshift greeting card by folding it in the middle.

On the left side I'd written a poem with "WE LOVE MOM" carefully added in bold letters on the right-hand side using crayons. The front of the card had a little drawing of two clouds with "To Mom" added. Three colored flowers fringed the bottom, a bigger one in the middle, flanked by two smaller ones, possibly representing my younger sister and me, with our mother. These same three flowers appeared on the right side of the card, the focal point of my drawing. In addition, the right side of the card featured green curlicue lines around the perimeter, creating a makeshift frame to the blue sky I'd added. In the bottom right-hand corner, in small letters, I had painstakingly printed: "From Linda."

My poem read:

To Mom who's always nice and kind,
Who picks up our toys right after us,
Who spoils us with birthday
Cakes of every shape and kind.
Who prettys [sic] us up for the talent show,
And puts up our hair in curls.
Who tells us a story at night
So to sleep we'll go,
Who I think is the best mom on earth!!

I'd stood in the attic that spring day two decades ago, looking at my former artwork, marveling that it had lasted so many years. I was filled with emotion for that little girl—me—who had created a special card for her mother. I was grateful I'd also done it on behalf of my younger sister, then only two or three years old. Although I wasn't yet a mother myself, I knew how much it would mean to me to be given such a thoughtful gift by my son or daughter, and I wondered how my own mother had reacted initially. I wished I knew.

That's when I had the idea to take the card and give it to my mother again, give it a second life. She'd probably forgotten all about it. This would be like giving her a new gift. I reasoned that it would perhaps be the best gift I could give her. My parents posed a challenge when it came to birthdays, Christmas, other holidays. I liked the idea of making gifts, of creating a treasure out of nothing for a person you loved.

With Mother's Day coming, I decided to take the card to a local frame store. I hoped this would be a chance to connect with her—always my goal—to act in such a way that it caused her to look at me with love, maybe even see me with new eyes. I don't think I realized back then that I wanted to rewrite the past, though, perform a do-over. It's only in hindsight I've come to this conclusion.

A few weeks later, we all met at Steve's home, presenting our mother with gifts after brunch. I watched as my siblings all gave her beautiful store-bought presents, much like the ones I'd given her in years past: a decorative music box, a wooden flower, a glass figurine. When one sister-in-law presented her with a wooden tulip on a stand, my mother nearly leapt out of her chair. "This is just exquisite! I love it! You shouldn't have! Oh, thank you so much!" she gushed.

As she opened my gift on the heels of opening the tulip from my sister-in-law and brother, my anticipation was high, my eyes locked onto her every expression, every gesture. She opened it slowly, but when she realized what it was, her frozen smile transformed from joy left over from the tulip to the briefest flash of annoyance, settling into a controlled mask of polite gratitude. If I hadn't been looking at her intently, I'd have missed the spark of disappointment buried in the fast forwarding of her emotions.

"Why, thank you, Linda. Wherever did you find this? How thoughtful of you," she flatly commented, cranking the words out mechanically as though to get them out of the way. Immediately after speaking these emotionless words, she went on to the next gift without examining the framed card I'd given her, without asking questions about its origin, gradually pushing it as far away as she could, as though she couldn't bear to have it remain in her line of vision.

Listening to my mother I'd been reminded of my Spanish studies, of the choice to use the formal *Ud.* form for "you" versus the more informal *tú*. Even though English was her first—only —language, when she was around others, my mother normally used formal speech, creating a distance between herself and those to whom she spoke, even family members. I knew that, if Spanish had been her language of origin, this exchange would have been in the more formal *Ud.* register, even though I was her daughter.

Except for the out-of-character private, more familiar lexicon she occasionally used with me to express her displeasure, her default language choices in front of others sounded quite formal. On the rare occasions when I dared to vent at Janet for being a tattletale—even told her to "shut up"—if my mother heard (or Janet told her), she would react as though I'd released a string of expletives at my sister. "We do *not* speak that way in this house," she would caution me. "Wait till your father hears about *this!*" The discrepancy between my mother's various ways of speaking was jarring.

For a moment I sat there, numb. Then I attempted to salvage the moment by giving her the history of the gift, explaining how I'd come across it in the attic and taken it to the framer to be restored, along with his positive reaction. I droned on, but my words fell on deaf ears. The moment had ended, she'd flipped the switch, moved on to the next gift. Meanwhile, my siblings sighed, staring at me as though to say, "Time's up, Linda. You had your ten seconds. Our turn."

Standing here inside the attic door, the memory of my disappointment on that Mother's Day comes back to me: how confused I felt, wondering why nothing I bought or made or wrote or did for either parent ever seemed to measure up in their eyes. Following their deaths, it could never be right. Yes. Time was up.

sixteen

MY PARENTS' BEDROOM: MY MOTHER

Mystery Solved

I close the attic door behind me and walk next door to my parents' spacious bedroom. I head to a wide window ledge, a window looking out over the side pillars where I sat a few hours ago. Making room to sit down, I push aside large, messy stacks of bent, torn magazines and out-of-date brochures. That's when I spot a familiar shape in the heap, the corner of the framed card I gave my mother so long ago, buried under copies of *Coin World, Live Steam, Model Railroad, Numismatic News*, a copy of the Grace Episcopal Church publication, *The Messenger*. I lift it out from the stack, not sure what to make of my discovery. I vow not to let this be its final resting place, even though the "why" of it being placed here will forever elude me.

Wrapping it in a thin, worn-out towel I retrieve from the small bathroom my parents, Janet, and I shared for nearly five years, I place it next to my father's "ADULTS AT PLAY" poster in my bag. I will take it home, find a place on my bedroom wall, ensure it's never lost again. Unexpectedly, it brings to mind the time I overfed my father's fish. *If only I'd tried harder, done more, surely their attitude toward me would change*, I'd thought. If only my little crayon drawing had been more beautiful, reflected more talent, the outcome would have been different. If only my poem had been more clever, more professional sounding. But looking at my artwork now, I know that none of that would have mattered. Had I been a prodigy, painted like Matisse or Picasso, written like Emily Dickinson or Sylvia Plath, played the piano like Horowitz or Van Cliburn, been fluent in a hundred languages, none of it would have changed anything. I finally realize this.

But still. I'm looking down at my little framed drawing, secure in my bag along with the papier-mâché bowl my mother kept all these years, the ceramic ashtray, the chipped angel candle holders, my grandfather's old coffee pot. Why did she keep these random items? How did they make the cut? Maybe she felt it had to be her decision what to keep, what to discard, just as it's my turn now, my decision as I go room to room, playing God with my parents' possessions. Maybe I'd gone too far when I rescued my drawing from the attic. I'd temporarily toppled her world order.

COLLATERAL INFORMATION

More than a decade later, I will discover a document corroborating part of what I'd been piecing together, a new discovery, years after the contents of Ivy Lodge had been sifted through, thrown out, saved, or sold to the highest bidder. In 2016, doing a search on the internet, I will come across an interview my father gave to the Missouri Historical Society in 1996.

Most of the interview revolved around my father's stories about his experiences in the state legislature, political colleagues, the state of governmental affairs in Missouri, but once in a while the interviewer directed his questions at my normally quiet mother. Reading the interview, I could picture her sitting attentively on the edge of the living room couch, hanging on my father's every word, trying to look interested, enthusiastic, supportive. This, despite the fact she'd spent a painful day at the dentist the day before, according to what my father shared at the outset of the interview. Reading her brief remarks, comments in which she hints at how difficult life could be during the eight years my father served in the legislature, from 1950 to 1958, it struck me how oblivious I'd been to this growing up. Those years had been magical, more carefree, for the most part—for me, that is. I spent more time with my mother in his absence. Even though she had to handle the household alone, she wasn't running around waiting on him, could accomplish more. She acted less tense, less stressed. But eight years of dealing by herself with children who ranged from infancy to adolescence had obviously been difficult. Too late, I would look at it from her vantage point. After all, what did I know, only eight years old when his four terms ended in 1958? My mother rarely displayed her emotions directly. I had no idea what a burden it must have been, not to mention the sour mood my father sometimes exhibited after he made the long trek back from Jeff City to Kirkwood, forever trying to catch up, be so much: legislator, attorney, husband, father. I wonder if my grandparents—my father's parents— pitched in during my father's absence since they lived close by. I don't remember.

During the period my father was in Jefferson City, Missouri, my mother and the four of us led more casual lives, although my mother's workload increased. We went to the popular fast food restaurant Steak 'n Shake once in a while. I dug into their wonderful hamburgers and skinny french fries with my siblings, drinking delicious orange freezes. Or we frequented the nearby Parkmoor Drive-In, where carhops came out to our car, resting a large metal tray on the driver's side window—my mother's—when the order was ready. We called in our order on a small metallic box on the side of the car, trying to decipher the operator's staticky voice on the other end. The carhop delivered the food right to our car, where we ate it on the spot, ignoring the mess we made in our normally ordered world, excited to be breaking out of our routine. My father didn't care for fast food or drive-ins, probably a throwback to his lean years growing up during the Great Depression. We usually ate at these more casual places when the legislature was in session, when he was out of town.

As nice as these periods could be for my siblings and me, in the 1996 interview my mother admitted how difficult those years had been for her, being alone with four children. As she told it,

"He [Sam] went into politics when our third child [Linda] was two weeks old, and our fourth child [Janet] was born while he was still a member. The two years that he was floor leader [House Speaker] he was gone far more; really Monday through Friday. . . . It was simply that he was not home very much. He'd laugh when he'd say he went up to Jeff City and he was practicing law the first day he was up there. His heart was back here. And then he'd come back here and he's back in the legislature his first day here. I think to do both was hard to juggle."

Concluding her remarks, my mother added—just the slightest hint of a complaint evident in her words—"He was away a lot at a time when the children were small. And then he would come home worn out."

These stood out as out-of-character, candid comments for my mother to make, particularly to a relative stranger, a journalist she'd just met. A private person, she rarely opened up to outsiders, or even to people she'd known for years. She rarely challenged my father. Reading her words, I knew I'd never heard her speak that openly. In essence, she admitted she'd been a single parent during his long absences. Too late, I could identify with her. I knew the life of a single parent; we had this in common, even though she was still married to my father, would remain married to him. But I had left my marriage, painstakingly creating a completely new life for my two small children and myself, whereas my mother's situation had been worse in many ways. She was alone eight years to my four, she had four children to my two, and she was completely dependent on my father for her income while I had a steady job. Maybe, most importantly, my father dropping in and out of our lives hadn't been helpful, her life perpetually swinging out of balance, tipping first this way, then the other.

Censoring herself in this same interview, perhaps realizing she'd said too much, she backpedaled: "But I'm glad he was in it [the legislature]. I think it was an interesting experience."

She wanted to be perceived as a good sport, an exemplary, capable wife of the 1950s, standard-bearer of her generation, her gender. She continued:

"I went up to Jeff City maybe three times, or four times. A couple of times with the children. They would be honorary pages. That was interesting for them, young as they were. So I think the only disadvantage was the fact that when he came back home, his mind was back there still. It was hard to pitch right in. . . . He didn't have a lot of time to participate in stuff back here."

The interview served as a catalyst for me to think back to an incident when she confronted my father. A rare instance of witnessing her challenge him—on any topic—in the more than fifty-five years of their marriage, to even hint that his behavior had affected her adversely.

My second husband and I were in town and had joined my parents for dinner at a local restaurant in the St. Louis suburb of Webster Groves in the late 1980s, a decade before the interview. My father was reminiscing about his days in the legislature, regaling the three of us with interesting anecdotes only he could tell, a master storyteller.

My mother sat listening quietly, as she usually did when my father launched into his stories, rarely interjecting her own thoughts unless called on, nervously gnawing on the cuticles of her fingernails in the background. But then she unexpectedly interrupted him long enough to comment that it hadn't, in fact, been enjoyable for her during his years in the legislature; that he hadn't been available, for example, when I'd been hospitalized with hepatitis, leaving her to carry the load alone. After his initial shock at both her interruption and unflattering comment, he glowered but said nothing in response, no doubt surprised at her candor. His storytelling had ended for the night, the lighthearted atmosphere snuffed out.

She was referring to the events of 1956. I'd just turned six and had been hospitalized for a week, diagnosed with infectious hepatitis. I had to remain in quarantine at St. Luke's Hospital in St. Louis. Then I convalesced at home, missing several months of school, gradually returning part-time, then full-time. Copies of my report cards for those months reveal extensive absences from school. At one point my mother warned me I would have to repeat first grade if I couldn't catch up with my classmates. In the car with her when she broke that news to me, I slammed my eyes shut as the words "held back" left her lips, the brightness of the early fall days right before the start of second grade penetrating my eyelids, a red haze. I wanted to block her words out. That one sentence branded me like nothing else, ensured I forever thought of myself as "slow," always playing catch-up, even when it wasn't warranted. It didn't matter that I'd been sick, had missed months of school. My interpretation of her words: I was dumb, slow. Surely anyone else would have been able to keep up with her classmates. Now I see it differently. I had caught up with my classmates despite my extended absences, partly because my mother worked with me on the daily mimeographed sheets the teachers sent home, partly because I worked hard, fearful I'd have to repeat the first grade.

The jobs of nurse and home-school teacher complicated my mother's already busy life when I became sick. My teacher sent home stacks of mimeographed worksheets, their purple ink with the distinctive smell permeating the air. Steve—in fourth grade —brought the papers home with him, the pile filling the family room table on Gill Avenue where my mother and I worked. Years later, on the back of the envelope in which my grades had been sent home I found a note my mother wrote to my father before forwarding all of our grades to him in Jefferson City. She wrote, "I'm particularly pleased with Linda's [report card]. Notice the days present on the card (she missed about half of the third term and one fourth of the fourth term and even then, only went half of the day)."

In retrospect, her words seem formal, as though she'd written a note to her supervisor, not her absent husband. Then again, my father might not have been with us in person, but she knew she had the responsibility of reporting our progress to him. The point she made that night at the restaurant in Webster Groves, though, was that he hadn't come home from Jeff City when needed during my sickness, hadn't been there for the family, even when one of his children had been seriously ill. She'd had to carry the load alone.

My mother normally didn't reminisce about our childhoods, making that evening in the 1980s stand out. I listened to her talking about those days, weeks, months I'd been so sick; she rarely complained about my father's absence. It helped me see that period through her eyes, not from my own vantage point as a scared young child, worried I'd be held back in school, a mouse on a treadmill trying to catch up with my smarter classmates while also enjoying the special treatment I received at home.

When you're translating a document or a speech, if you don't have all the words, you don't have all the meaning. I'd only had *my* words thus far, *my* thoughts, not hers. That had given me an incomplete picture, one with pockets of omissions . . . until the day I read the Missouri Historical Society interview. Translation also involves more than just words, after all; even if you do have both people's words, you need to add context, gestures, facial expressions, the tone of what is being said, the input of other people, if available. When my mother repeatedly told people what a "close" family we were, this had to be put into the context of evidence to the contrary. I couldn't take her words at face value, even when I looked up the word "close" in the dictionary.

Once, maybe ten years before that dinner with my parents, when I'd been with my mother in Bronxville to help take care of my ailing grandmother, she confided in me that she often found it difficult to deal with my father's demanding ways, particularly when he openly resented time she spent away from him, hours she spent doing volunteer work, for example, her altar guild work for the church. She rarely let herself complain about him. I felt needed, flattered she'd confided in me. But minutes after opening up, the gates slammed shut again; she'd returned to playing the role of the dutiful wife. Nothing to see here. Almost a physical transformation, she changed from her rarely seen vulnerable side back to being in complete control.

Knowing what I know in 2000, the 1980s dinner incident, along with others scattered throughout my life, would have made more sense if I'd had access to the 1996 Missouri Historical Society Interview sooner. It would have given me a window into how she felt, what she had to deal with. But I had to put it together piecemeal, even after everything I uncover in 2000 as I continue to search through the house.

When I finish reading the interview, adding the information to what I learn inside Ivy Lodge in 2000, it will feel like I've been reintroduced to my mother. It reveals—at least partially—what her opinions were, how she viewed my father's years in the legislature. I'm both surprised and grateful, at long last, to have more pieces of the puzzle at my disposal, serendipity throwing information my way every once in a while.

METAL DETECTOR AND THE REAL TREASURES

My crayon drawing safe in my bag, I head to the small alcove of my parents' bedroom, a tasteful little niche with a small bay window overlooking the front of the house (the only second-story front window without the bare-bones "attic" behind it). I spot a small wooden chest of drawers on the floor, one my brother Steve made for our mother to keep her most cherished metal detecting treasures in. I know he'll want to keep that. It looks like the miniature dresser of a large doll: originally white drawers painted in dark, rich colors, greens and blues, with six drawers revealing the best of what she found with her metal detector through the years: sterling silver religious medals, crosses, crucifixes; signet rings; wedding rings; high school graduation rings; earrings, pieces of necklaces, bracelets. Whenever possible, she returned rings to their original owners, tracking them down through their initials and the schools featured on the insignia. This is what's left of what she didn't throw out. The lesser "finds" are kept in various tubs, catalogued by type: religious medals, crosses, rings, cufflinks, earrings, pins, loose pieces of metal.

I sit down on the plush carpet, opening each drawer, hoping my brother doesn't appear while I'm having this private moment. An impressive haul, some might say. Many would probably think—erroneously—that this is a normal yield for metal detecting. But my mother's treasures represent more than thirty years of dedication to her hobby. Endless false beeps back in the days when aluminum foil and metal bottle caps covered the earth, when she had to dig thousands of shallow holes, turn over tons of dirt with her spade as she searched, buckets of sweat pouring from her brow. In my own way, maybe that's what I'm doing here, searching this home for anything that is evidence of my parents' love for me, for clues to the puzzle, translations of their behavior toward me. But most of what I have found is like the hundreds of bottle caps and scraps of aluminum foil she unearthed; it proves nothing.

As I finger the treasures, I know how happy metal-detecting made my mother. I pick class rings out of the little drawers, Clayton High School, Class of 1959; a sterling silver St. Christopher medal; several yellow gold wedding bands, their inscriptions no longer visible; one silver earring with a garnet. *There's a whole world beneath our feet*, my mother communicated through her hobby, digging below the earth's surface. She wanted to make a dent in uncovering it.

My mother took up metal detecting in the late 1960s when three of the four of us had left for college. Janet was well into her teens. I could spot my mother with her metal detector from a distance, in a park or on the beach, in a friend's yard, her petite frame leaning into her work. The rhythmic sweeping movement of the metal detector's pole-like shaft made her look like a diminutive farmer scything his crop, back and forth till the control box pinged. In the late 1960s, more metal had been tossed out or lost; metal detectors weren't as high-tech. She became adept at interpreting the language of the beeps, at anticipating what caused them. This extended beyond the obvious loud or soft sounds; she broke down the metal detector's beeps to fairly sophisticated levels. Other 1950s housewives might have been able to correctly second-guess the meaning of the doorbell chimes at their homes on any given day: is it the Fuller Brush man, the Encyclopedia Britannica man, or another traveling salesman? Is it a Girl Scout selling cookies, the mailman, the milkman, a neighbor, or a child? My mother, on the other hand, had a sixth sense about her metal detector's beeps, the clues they announced.

Regardless of what the beeps revealed, she heeded their call, unearthed the unidentified object with her trowel, carefully dropping it into a small cloth bag she carried. Much of her enjoyment lay in the fact that even after it had been unearthed, she had to scrape off the sand or caked-on dirt to determine what she had, decide if it was worth keeping. Should it be tossed into the trash or taken home for a second look? She removed the outer layer as if unwrapping a gift, confident something wonderful—or at least interesting—lay beneath. Just like me, I think, as I analyze each object, each tchotchke, each bauble, each treasure in Ivy Lodge to see if it speaks to me, communicates information I need to know. Maybe we're not as different as I've always believed.

People in the parks, churches, schools she frequented became curious, interested in what she did and why she did it.

When she started in the late 1960s, people still thought of it as a novelty. Curious onlookers followed her around like the Pied Piper, plying her with questions, many endlessly repetitious, even annoying. "What are you doing?" "What have you found?" "Can I see it?" "How do you know when you've found something?" "What does it sound like?" "Why are you looking here?" "Where did you buy your metal detector?" "Is it heavy?" "Can I lift it?" "How much did it cost?" "Is that real gold?" "Can I try it for a minute?" "Why not!?" "How much money have you found?"

The more questions they asked her, the more it slowed her down. In her mind, a finite supply of potential treasures lay just beneath her feet as well as a finite amount of time to spend with her hobby. Her task entailed finding as many treasures as possible within a narrow time frame; questions diverted her from the job at hand.

In addition, my mother was a true introvert. She didn't welcome this invasion into her private world by the curious set (no headphones back then to block out unwanted voices). These all-too-short mornings or afternoons represented rare opportunities for her to escape the demands of my father: listening to him talk about any number of topics, taking care of their large home, taking care of the four of us growing up, not to mention our pets.

I imagine she craved solitude, punctuated only by the occasional beeping from the monitor, or by the scraping sound her trowel made as she unearthed what lay buried beneath her feet. Perhaps it doubled as a kind of meditation for her, though she would never have admitted that. She made an effort to be polite to the enthusiasts trailing her but limited her answers to the fewest words possible, probably avoiding eye contact, hoping her unspoken message would be Greta Garbo clear: "I want to be alone."

Little in my mother's daily life belonged to her alone, despite the exodus of my brothers and me by 1968. The overlapping and competing needs of others monopolized her energies. But her favorite hobbies—limited by the narrow windows of time available to her—lay almost exclusively in finding things: those that lay outside our home, had been overlooked, forgotten, or were not visible to the naked eye, those that hid beneath the ground's surface that others might not have wanted. These included the arrowheads she dug up on the banks of the Meramec River, the tiny gold nuggets she found panning for gold, her metal detecting treasures. It also included her rare gift of finding treasures above ground: four-leaf clovers, for example, or coins, even pieces of jewelry on the sidewalk, spotting what others missed. Whenever any of us misplaced anything at home—a watch, a book, a small piece of jewelry, a pair of sunglasses—we turned to her. She had a sixth sense.

Back from college, I witnessed my mother returning home after her metal detecting outings, bearing no resemblance to the woman I normally saw: carefully coiffed, makeup in place, hair neatly combed, designer clothes clean and ironed, the ideal woman. That may have been who she'd been the day before, but not after a metal-detecting afternoon. In the span of a few short hours, my prim and proper mother had been transformed into a woman who'd lost track of time, who'd been digging up treasures, enjoying herself immensely. The contrast was dramatic in my eyes. I looked at her happy, disheveled state, longed to get to know *this* woman, this imperfect person. Here stood a woman who—with her metal detector, her alter ego—temporarily forgot about her appearance, allowed herself to get dirty. Fingernails chipped, caked with mud, she wore old pants along with a cast-off, half-tucked-in flannel shirt. With her diminutive figure, in an outfit more befitting a field hand, she reminded me of a toddler after an hour of unbridled fun in an old, abandoned sandbox, mud smeared across her face, hands, clothes, and strands of hair that had escaped their permed helmet.

She bore no resemblance to the woman who'd headed off to Washington University's Quarterly Dance Club the night before with my father, decked out in diamond rings and necklaces like Queen Elizabeth, wearing a silk dress and mink coat, her hair styled that afternoon by "Mr. William." This person looked different, unrecognizable. But she looked utterly happy, maybe like the person she'd been with her own father, spending time outdoors with him, immersed in nature, during the years before her indoctrination had begun into how young women needed to behave once they got married.

Peering inside the drawers of the delicate chest my brother made for my mother, I'm reminded of her complexity, of her dislike of any of us going barefoot in the house ("Put your shoes on!"). But there she'd be, transformed after a metal detecting expedition, encrusted in mud, yet happy as she would ever be. She was a woman of contradictions, someone who habitually referred to herself as a "softie," or "Pollyanna," but who could cut you to the quick, rattling off a few well-placed words rivaling a drill sergeant's when she told you to "Get a hold of yourself!" or "Snap out of it!" or who admonished you to "Keep your shirt on!" if you let your emotions get the best of you. Someone who kept up with investments by reading detailed stock reports, tracked complex numismatic spreadsheets to check the value of her coin collection. But also someone who left behind a small army of children's stuffed Beanie Babies when she died, ones she'd bought for herself as though still a grade-school girl. She didn't buy these as investments, either; their original boxes had been thrown out. She lovingly placed them together on the twin bed in my sister's and my former bedroom, next to the bedroom she shared with my father. They served a deeper, more mysterious purpose. For my part, I never knew who she'd be on any given day. Now that she's gone, the mystery remains unsolved, part of my untranslatable life.

MORE BURIED TREASURES

Arrowheads hold untold stories she sought to uncover. When my father purchased land on the Meramec River outside St. Louis in the late 1970s, building a home up on a bluff, my mother found a Native American Osage Indian campsite near the river, just below the bluff where they'd had their country home built. She spent hours digging for arrowheads on that patch of land, finding hundreds during the last twenty-five years of her life, many of them museum quality. In fact, one was a rare Clovis point, thought to date back almost fourteen thousand years.

Panning for elusive gold flecks buried in mine tailings (the flecks referred to optimistically as "nuggets") was another physically demanding hobby that appealed to her. Yet another way to look beneath the ground's surface for treasures. When she learned about a gold mine in Dahlonega, Georgia, in the early 1980s, she began driving there from St. Louis with my father once a year to buy fifty-pound bags of mine tailings, transporting them back home. She would then singlehandedly dump the sandy contents of the bags into a full-sized wash basin and fill the basin with icy cold water. Next she began the time-consuming, back-breaking task of panning for gold, kneeling beside the large basin as she shook the metal pan. The specks of gold could have passed through the eye of a needle. On a good day she might find ten microscopic nuggets, but this didn't faze her. She lovingly dropped each hard-won gold filing into a miniature vial the size of a thimble, careful not to breathe too deeply to prevent the tiny flakes from blowing away in the transfer process. All of us—plus her grandchildren—have at least one or two of these inch-high vials filled with the products of her work, fueled by her love of this hobby.

Unlike the more sedentary hobbies of my friends' mothers, most of my mother's unusual interests entailed considerable physical effort, hard-core calorie-burning, not the traditional variety. Although she played the piano well, she usually did it in private, avoiding the spotlight. But crafts, knitting or sewing, stamp collecting, scrapbooking, other more common pursuits popular back then failed to hold her attention. The actual return on the physical labor expended to perform her hobbies was relatively small compared to the investment she made with metal detecting (not to mention lugging the cumbersome machine around) or digging for arrowheads, or panning for gold, thus adding to the effort she exerted. She didn't need a gym; exercise was programmed into her hobbies.

Still sitting on the plush carpet of my parents' bedroom alcove, I realize that all these objects my mother found underground—the metal detecting objects, the arrowheads, the gold flecks—share something with her. An air of mystery surrounds them. Their identity—their existence—lies dormant underground, much like my mother's, partly as a result of the generation into which she was born. Like these objects, she often twisted herself out of shape, her spirit pounded to meet my father's and others' needs, her true self and identity buried underground by everyone else's demands.

In the spirit of this idea, I select several second-tier pieces she kept—all of them 14-karat gold—none deemed worthy of keeping in the special chest Steve built for her, but too special to throw out, although a less observant person might have catalogued them as scrap metal. I choose a tiny heart, a charm of a hand in the Corona gesture, several children's rings, a high school ring, a signet ring, an old wedding band, a baby ring, a smashed earring. Placing them all in the palm of my hand, I decide I'm attracted to these old, beat-up, or misshapen pieces because they give me hope my mother could love what was riddled with imperfections. When I return home to Maryland, I will loosely string all of the misshaped gold pieces together on a long chain, wearing them in memory of my mother.

LADY OF SPAIN

Something else about this bedroom reminds me of my mother specifically: the Spanish señorita costume she made for me here, using her sewing machine. It was my fourth grade Halloween costume when I'd just begun studying a little Spanish in school. I still have the dress, with a photo of myself wearing it that Halloween, its long red skirt trimmed with three rows of white lace at the bottom, a black velvet bodice with crisscross ties in front. I wore a gypsy-style blouse under the sleeveless dress, and a mantilla she created using only a headband, wire, a little lace. I felt beautiful. Spanish.

My fourth-grade teacher—Mrs. Stivers—introduced us to Spanish that year, first by having us answer "*aquí*" or "*presente*" when she took attendance. Then we learned a few more words, putting on *The Three Bears* in Spanish. The shortest girl in class, I played the baby bear.

Graduating from Pig Latin to Spanish had been exciting for me, so when I told my mother I wanted to be a *señorita* for Halloween that year, she agreed to make me a costume. Spanish—

along with other foreign languages, eventually—made me feel like I'd entered my own private world, a world my parents and siblings weren't privy to. Languages became a window into other cultures, other ways of being in the world; my family members didn't have the key. That feeling persisted. When my parents visited me in Spain my junior year in college, I realized they'd been cut off from what I experienced, had only glimpsed a thin sliver of my new world.

On Halloween night, my best friend, Michele, went door to door with me in my neighborhood. Michele explained to our neighbors that I'd come to the US on an exchange program. I pretended to be fluent in Spanish, speaking gobbledygook with a few Spanish words thrown in to make it sound authentic. We fooled no one, but they treated the strange *señorita* kindly, went along with the charade. It stands out as my favorite Halloween. Decades later, my own daughter wore the same costume, also in the fourth grade.

CLOSETED TREASURES

On an impulse, I open my mother's closet, to the right of the small bed she shared with my father. I want to see her clothes again, imagine her wearing them. I want to catch a whiff of her perfume to hold in my mind forever.

Her clothes affect me more than I'd anticipated, hanging at attention, waiting for her to return: tailored, tasteful silk suits, blouses, A-line skirts, a few pairs of plaid wool pants, and a number of jackets. If we'd been the same size, I might be tempted to take a jacket, but my mother was three inches shorter and much more petite.

I've already spotted a small bottle of perfume from her dresser that I'd like to take with me. Only about half an inch of liquid remains, its name rubbed off years ago, but they say smell is our strongest sense, and it's like breathing in the essence of my mother.

As I open the door of the closet, my eyes are drawn to the carpeted floor. A small plastic card lies in front of her shoes. I gave it to her a few months ago on her eightieth birthday, November 25th, nearly three months before her death. It's a plastic credit card-sized poem I found in a Hallmark store. On the front, the little card reads:

Mom, no matter what I do today, or where the future takes me tomorrow,
I promise to remember all the things you've taught me, and how very much
You love me.
And, in case I don't always say it,
And sometimes I forget to show it,
I wanted you to have this
So you know
I love you, too, Mom.

On the back, I had written, "For Mom, From Linda. 11-25-99."

The words on the card, the part about remembering how much she loved me, at least, aren't really true. That represented wishful thinking on my part. I did that quite a bit, usually with greeting cards. I'd pick one reflecting the relationship I longed to have with her but didn't. These cards served more as my prayers to the universe. Or maybe I thought she might be so moved when she read the card that she'd become the warm, accepting, empathic mother depicted in the cards.

But seeing the plastic card I gave my mom on the closet floor, I'm wondering why it's there. Next to it, no more than an inch away lies a 14-karat gold loop, the tool of serious coin collectors. Why are these together? It reminded me of the child's game where you decide if two objects are alike or different, and how. If she caught me doing this, my mother would chastise me for analyzing life/people/events/words too much. I'm forever parsing what people say, what people do, what they don't say, what they don't do, how they look at me, how they don't look at me, hunting for possible ulterior motives. Translating. It's exhausting.

I search for the underlying meaning, the hidden truth, seeking what undergirds the untranslatable. But I rarely get answers, nor will I have future chances for answers. I pocket the plastic card. Maybe she dumped the contents of her purse as she undressed at the end of the day. Maybe this fell to the floor.

OLLIE, OLLIE, OXEN FREE/
COME OUT, COME OUT . . .

My mother's behavior confused me as a child; I had two—or more—mothers. One, stern, cold, businesslike. The other, child-like. Still another presented a forced smile once in a while—usually in the presence of other people—telling me how much she loved me. But the voice of that affectionate woman never rang true, making me feel like I was watching a TV show, but a show with an actress unskilled at delivering her lines.

After she'd washed the evening dishes, sometimes my mother would join my father in the living room. Every once in a while, she sat on the arm of his green leather easy chair, cooing an old nursery rhyme to him in a singsong, half childlike, half seductress voice:

ABCD goldfish?

LMNO goldfish!

OSAR2 goldfish!

ICM2 goldfish!

My ears would perk up at hearing this almost unrecognizable voice in the house. I'd go stand in the wide archway leading from the foyer to the living room to witness it. I watched as my stern mother transformed herself from standoffish to childlike, delighting in using baby talk with my father who, for his part, laughed at my mother's performance. Because that's what it looked like to me: a performance.

I heard the words but knew something was missing. It felt like walking onstage in the middle of a play. I'd intruded, gone where I didn't belong; I wasn't supposed to be there. Something had gone wrong, but the lines still had to be delivered. My father's impatience toward me felt real, palpable, unambiguous, as much as I dreaded these emotions, but my mother's infrequent declarations of love sounded false, hollow. I didn't know this person in front of me delivering the child's poem. I couldn't drill down to find the meaning. She was an actress delivering her lines.

Once, at the end of my father's life, at the hospital with my mother, we were sitting in the waiting room as the nurses performed a procedure. Deviating 180 degrees from her normal behavior toward me, she suddenly became animated, childlike, grabbing my arm, putting her face close to mine, asking if we were friends. I felt like a child who'd been kicked across the room only to be hugged tenderly afterward.

When I hesitated, she asked again. "Linda, we're friends, aren't we?" "Sure," I replied. "I guess so." She wanted to swap the paperback art book my sister-in-law had given her for the more desirable hardcopy version she preferred. I had no objections at all, especially since I was receiving a beautiful art book in the process, but the way she was acting baffled me, her sudden switch to behaving like a child, referring to me as her friend, especially when I normally considered myself *persona non grata.*

Instead of being relieved that my usually aloof mother had a fun-loving, warm side when she launched into these playful episodes with my father or me, I found it unnerving. It felt like another woman had taken over her mind, someone I didn't know . . . or trust. She spoke a childlike language I didn't recognize. *Who is that?* I wondered, although she looked the same.

As a child, my mother seemed unattainably perfect in my eyes. I never saw her watch TV during the day, rarely even at night unless it was a televised baseball game with her beloved Cardinals, or a favorite show like *The Fugitive* or *Perry Mason.* I never saw her take a nap (a "siesta," as my father called his own habit of taking short naps) or read a fashion magazine or a book of fiction. I never saw her get cozy on a winter night in a robe or pajamas, curled up on the couch to watch a trashy TV show. She didn't cry, swear, raise her voice, or talk back to my father. I was aware of just a few times she criticized him: the brief moments at my grandmother's home in New York when she confided in me, dinner at the restaurant in Webster Groves that night when she interrupted my father's stories about serving in the Missouri legislature. One of the few times I felt close to her was that night in New York. I thought I could support her just by listening.

I went through a period in elementary school when I confessed everything I did wrong to my mother, most infractions minor, even inadvertent mistakes: teasing my sister, stealing a cookie from her kitchen stash, telling her a white lie, using her special cream. I might have thought it would bridge the gap between us, improve our relationship the same way secrets sometimes do. But that never happened. She grew weary of my obsessive confessions, prompting me to discontinue the habit. In the case of her frustrations with my father when we talked in New York, the closeness didn't last long then, either. "You have a right to have your own activities, Mom," I'd told her. "Dad has all his train groups, business meetings; you should stand up for yourself." My subtext was intended to show her she could count on me, that I would support her, take her side. But no sooner had she finished criticizing my father than I knew she regretted having spoken, of having confided in me. She pulled back. She had inadvertently crossed a line, and quickly changed the subject. It had felt good to be needed during those brief moments, though, to feel close to her, but I soon floated out of reach, always out of reach, on my own, untethered, never able to latch hold of her, make her see me, make her care about me, make her realize that I'd do anything for her.

Even now, after her death, sorting through piles of magazines with my siblings, loose papers in every room of Ivy Lodge, I keep hoping I'll stumble across a journal or a notebook my mother left behind. In my fantasy, it will be a handwritten confessional, expressing her complicated feelings for me, for all of us, maybe even regret at what she said and did through the years. Why not? She kept the little notebook with personalized license plates, along with the one recording the clothes she ironed, why not a few heartfelt phrases about her children? I think she may have wondered what ran through my mind, too, because I kept diaries throughout my childhood and adolescence using inexpensive daybooks my father's business associates had given him. But in high school, the diary I'd kept disappeared from my room. I found it years later, stashed underneath a stack of forgotten papers in the attic. I never said anything about it to my mother, but I suspected she'd been the one to take it from my bedroom, where I'd kept it tucked under a pile of clothes. Now, though, I question if, in her own way, she wasn't also trying to figure out what made me tick.

In cryptography, the term "plaintext" refers to data that can be understood without knowing a special key, or a foreign language; it doesn't need to be decrypted or translated. That's what she found if she read my diary, pure plaintext. No translation would have been necessary on her part. My diary contained all my ups and downs, what I'd done that day, with whom, as well as my thoughts and fears. I used it as a way to express feelings that had no outlet. For instance, when I was a sophomore in high school, I wrote the following:

"Mom is in one heck of a bad mood. I've about had it, anything that happens she takes out on me. She is constantly cutting me down, too. Before I got rid of my bangs, they were too long, and you couldn't see my face. Next she is always telling me what a bad complexion I have, how lazy I am, how dumb in school I am, how I never practice the right things on the piano, how rude I am to her, how fat I am, how skinny she is, how I'm always picking on [that] poor little defenseless sister of mine, Janet. I guess I should be reborn!"

There I was, right on the pages of my diary. Plaintext. Vulnerable. Although I didn't understand my mother, she couldn't have failed to understand me when she read my words.

Immersed in the stacks of papers in Ivy Lodge, I had become briefly optimistic I'd find imaginary confessionals from my mother when I came across a stash of loose Post-it Notes with her distinctive handwriting, a rainbow of pastel-colored slips of paper tucked in ceramic dishes with loose buttons, cufflinks, commemorative coins from the various hobby-related conventions my parents attended. Enigmatic phrases are written on each small square of paper using her elegant loopy handwriting;

she no doubt planned to consolidate them into their own little notebook someday. Initially, I was hopeful, thinking these bits of paper might be a code, her messages to me from beyond the grave. I carefully smoothed out the wrinkles from each one, fanning them out in front of me like playing cards, looking for clues, connections, secrets to unravel about my mother. But then I found one note with a book title on it, *The Verse by the Side of The Road.* I realize with sadness that all these scraps of paper with the cryptic messages are Burma Shave jingles she collected, much like the personalized license plates. They're road signs she saw on trips with my father, miniature billboards with clever jingles advertising a shaving cream popular the first half of the twentieth century, not encrypted love notes to me, her daughter.

Before her death, I made numerous attempts to confirm our linkage, prove we weren't mother–daughter in name only. Notably, the handmade card probably stands out as my earliest attempt, but I made others. Years after I moved to Maryland, I found a tiny, green hinged ceramic box in the shape of a pea pod with "Two Peas in a Pod" painted on the side. When you opened the whimsical container, two smiling ceramic peas were tucked inside. My mother collected small decorative boxes and loved peas (a staple at family dinners). I thought I'd hit the jackpot with my gift. Opening it, she paused, and using a slightly theatrical voice said, "Why, thank you, Linda. It's a wonderful symbol for my relationship with Sam [referring to my father]." I never had the nerve to correct her, to tell her I'd meant it to symbolize us, our mother–daughter relationship.

My mother rarely admitted to being sick all the years I knew her, even though many times I knew she must be suffering. I never saw her lying in bed with a headache or the flu or a sore throat, or even when she'd been diagnosed with a rare neurological disorder, blepharospasm, in her early sixties. The times she did admit to being sick—major health crises: heart attacks, bleeding ulcers—it inevitably led to emergency hospitalizations, the last one when she was dying. In each case, she went to the hospital only because one of us had insisted on it. Being sick meant admitting defeat, going against everything she stood for.

Except for her bridge club friends (women she had met as a young-married wife when my parents first moved back to Kirkwood from the West Coast), she didn't spend much time with girlfriends. She didn't seem to have anyone to call up, chat with, vent. No one to compare notes with or go out to lunch or dinner with. I never witnessed a close support system of female friends, no network of women she could rely on for advice or empathy, people to listen, but that may have been more a sign of the times in which she lived. Most of her friends were the wives of my father's friends. In a real sense, she had to act on her own in figuring out how to navigate life as the wife of a demanding man, as the mother of four complicated children.

Frugal, she believed that spending money on herself—like overeating—to be an act of self-indulgence, even selfishness, at least for a woman. Even after my father died, she wrote me a long business letter once, reporting in great detail how she'd returned money to her bank account, paid herself back. She'd earmarked the money to buy a bracelet for herself. But now she wanted to make sure I knew she'd restored order, had been "good" in not wasting money, even though it was hers to spend, even though she could well afford to buy whatever she wanted. It wasn't surprising, then, that her church attendance record was impeccable, that she criticized people who only attended services on Christmas and Easter. "What could possibly be more important?" she complained.

I saw her cry only a handful of times. In addition to learning that my brother Sam had been wounded in Vietnam, the second time occurred after she'd had a heart attack while visiting me in Maryland in 1991. Having said goodnight to her at the local hospital after visiting hours, I walked out of her room, looking back at her over my shoulder. I saw her eyes welling up, her chin quivering. Unnerved by her tears, I went back to her bed to comfort her, but by then she'd recovered her composure, assuring me she was fine. Six years later, suffering from a urinary tract infection in Avignon, France, during a side trip we took before departing on our last family cruise, her tears stemmed from fear as she implored me not to tell my father, nervous about what his reaction would be if he learned of her sickness. Even when my father was dying, I never saw her cry. Nor did I see her cry after he died or at his funeral. Crying equaled weakness.

Following his strokes in Barcelona in 1997, my father circulated in and out of the hospital in St. Louis: in rehabilitation, and then returning after more strokes and setbacks. Through it all, she visited him every day, sitting attentively in the hospital room like a diminutive soldier, showing little emotion, doing her duty, her hands on her lap next to what she referred to as her pocketbook, steadfastly at his side. After my father died, without any prompting she explained her lack of tears to me several times, reminding me that her own mother hadn't cried at my grandfather's funeral, either. "Who am I to cry after losing my husband, when other women have lost their spouses, too," my grandmother had apparently said. My mother had followed suit, as though a hierarchy existed for displaying sadness.

Compared to her, I was a mass of insecurities, a panoply of imperfections spilling out into the world. I overindulged in sweets, my weight fluctuating twenty or thirty pounds from adolescence to when I first married, ranging from near anorexia levels to unpleasantly plump, and everywhere in between.

I cried a lot, or at least became emotional with little provocation: watching sad movies, seeing a child in distress, hearing sad stories on the news, reading books with ailing animals; spotting a dying deer, squirrel, ground hog, or bird by the side of the road; after real or imagined slights from friends, siblings, teachers, or my parents; hearing second- or third-hand stories about tragedies that had befallen people I'd never met. In short, it didn't take much to bring tears to my eyes, even random things like half-dried worms on the sidewalk, Broadway musicals, sappy TV commercials, a warm greeting card from a friend, a well-timed hug. Reflecting on this major difference between us, I decide that maybe I cry or become emotional because of a surfeit of emotions, of sadness, just below the surface. Maybe all these feelings are lying in wait, a floating vault of secrets, truths too painful to acknowledge, but present all the same. The slightest unsettling of my emotional equilibrium is enough to tap into this dark, deep well of melancholy. Is that why I'm reduced to tears with little effort, standing at the edge of that cliff, balancing on one leg until a puff of air bumps me over the edge? Maybe the tears arise from a larger truth I'm unwilling or unable to examine. A truth too devastating to ponder that would change my worldview as it relates to my family. It leaks out at every opportunity, tiny clues for me to explore when I feel emboldened.

Throughout my life I've proven myself to be much more impractical than my mother, devouring novels and fashion magazines, snatching snippets of soap operas as a young mother at home with infants, marveling at the excess of emotions the characters showed. She didn't permit me—or my siblings—to watch "trash" growing up, but I managed to steal moments of this decadent pastime when I could, later.

Unlike my mother, I frequently became ill, especially in elementary school. My threshold for wanting to avoid school was low. I suffered from anxiety attacks, had real (and imagined) illnesses I used as excuses to avoid school. My parents finally took me to a psychiatrist at six or seven. After meeting with me, he assured them I suffered from a standard case of school-related anxiety, nothing to worry about. Ironically, the fact they'd sent me to a psychiatrist produced as much anxiety in me as the underlying cause of the anxiety, especially since I came to understand that neither parent believed in counseling, in baring your soul to strangers, expressing your emotions. Because of this, I used to follow my mother around the house as she performed her many chores, badgering her well into my teens, asking why she and my father had sent me to see a psychiatrist, pleading with her to reveal what was wrong with me.

In my mind it all translated into being inferior, sick-in-the-head, even more of an outlier. But my anxiety was real. Every year I sat at yet another wooden desk, anxious about being called on by my teachers, looking stupid, being humiliated or laughed at, being rejected by my classmates. I wanted to stay at home and hide. On those days when the thought of going to school became too much, I'd stand outside my parents' closed bedroom door, near tears, asking if I could please stay home from school that day, claiming to be sick, sick with ailments I thought up on the spot.

I'm sure I didn't fool my parents. Usually they instructed me to pull myself together, get ready to join my siblings at school, that nothing was wrong with me. But I believed that untold dangers awaited me at school. Staying at home—sick or not—although not enjoyable, was preferable to the alternative. TV was off limits except game shows (no soap operas), and only if I was well enough to get out of bed. "If you're too sick to go to school, you're too sick to do anything else," my mother would tell me.

Another striking difference between my mother and me was that I sometimes confronted my father—both parents, actually—

raised my voice, behaved in an antagonistic manner, argumentative, confrontational. I argued, whined, complained, protested, pleaded, cried. But my behavior didn't achieve the desired effect, usually eliciting anger or ostracism by one or both of my parents.

PEANUTS

When I was eleven or twelve, a seemingly insignificant incident occurred, yet it revealed another side of my mother. Following her around after school, I was brimming over with stories I wanted to share about my day. She was busy, though, always busy, going from task to task with the efficiency of an accountant, barely aware of me. My father was due home soon. She still had a long list of things to do before their nightly cocktail hour.

Leaning against my parents' four-poster bed, I'm transported back to this day in the early 1960s, a day my mother stopped her activities, sat on the edge of the full-sized bed my parents shared, patting the bedspread to invite me to join her. She began by asking if I could help her with a quick project. She rarely needed anyone's help, certainly not mine. I climbed up on my parents' smallish marital bed, careful to remove my shoes first.

After I'd settled in, my legs neatly off to the side, my two-piece blue-and-white-striped seersucker outfit modestly covering my always-scuffed knees, my mother pulled out a pencil from behind her ear along with a little spiral notebook she carried around with her. She wet the tip of the pencil with her tongue to signal the start of our mysterious project. Looking over at me, yet providing no context, she asked how many calories I thought a jar of Planters Peanuts contained. Initially, her question threw me off balance; I hadn't anticipated this topic, despite her expertise at calorie-counting. I answered that I didn't know for sure—math was my worst subject in school—but guessed, well-trained by my mother in the science of calorie counts for major foods. "A thousand? Maybe six servings per jar?" I replied, excited to be part of this mysterious project.

"Let's say someone eats an entire jar every day, then he would consume at least seven thousand extra calories in one week, right? That's just the peanuts, too! That's not even considering all the other calories he would eat during the day!" She briefly looked over at me, lost in her calculations. I could see the calorie count we'd come up with simultaneously thrilled and horrified her, as she rapidly drew columns in her spiral notebook, adding numbers, wetting the pencil tip in her mouth again, adding more food intake to her tally, occasionally consulting with me. "What if we add Kentucky Fried Chicken to the count? Say, a bucket?" Gradually it became clear when she added, "Sam can finish off a bucket all by himself, right? You've seen that, haven't you? It's *loaded* with calories because it's fried! No wonder he's overweight!" she concluded gleefully, not waiting for my answer, lost in her reverie as though she'd just solved a math problem worthy of Einstein. "How can one person eat that much, do you suppose?!"

A rhetorical question, but I wondered, *Does she want me to answer? What happened?* The glow I'd been feeling just minutes before had drained from me. I wanted to get off the bed, disappear. I felt like an accomplice to a crime I'd never intended to commit. But my mother had needed a partner, confirmation of calculations she could easily have made without my help. I also knew—and she no doubt knew—that I was just as capable as my brother of eating a jar of peanuts or a bucket of chicken; not everyone ate like a bird in our house.

This was my mother. Her presence still keenly felt in every room, in every object. A thin veneer of respectability on top of a shrewdness below. Thinking about her now, I realize maybe she wasn't as perfect as I thought, that the idea I held fast to my entire childhood and much of my adulthood lacked credibility. So much of what she did, she did for effect, a façade to lead others to believe she could do no wrong. Acting in a friendly manner with others, while letting pieces of her truer nature escape with my siblings and me. Like steam escaping from a boiling tea kettle. Nowhere else for it to go: the frozen smile, the starched clothes, the blind loyalty to my father, the ladylike demeanor and language. Maybe others needed to see her best side because no one would ever imagine that, behind the scenes, she could wound her children with words delivered with exact precision, or with a well-placed grimace. People adored her because no one really knew her. This prompts the memory of how she came out of the shadows once my father fell into a coma, shortly before his death in 1998. She no longer needed to hide anymore; the play had ended, the man she half-jokingly referred to as her lord and master lay dying.

TABLES TURNED

Thinking about the period leading up to my father's death, the point when my mother's behavior underwent a major transformation, I'm reminded of a book I read in graduate school by the Brazilian philosopher Paulo Freire: *Pedagogia do Oprimido*, or *Pedagogy of the Oppressed*. A principal theory maintained that, unless the "oppressed" are educated, and achieve what he termed *conscientização*, critical consciousness, there's a real danger these oppressed individuals will turn the tables, repeat what their oppressors did to them, when and if there is a power shift, because that's all these formerly oppressed individuals know. Freire stated, "The oppressed want at any cost to resemble the oppressors," adding that, "the oppressed, instead of striving for liberation, tend themselves to become oppressors."

My mother started to become that person when my father died. For fifty-six years she'd been married to a man who sometimes belittled or ignored her, who wouldn't allow her to work outside their home until their children had left home (and then only part-time), who rarely let her finish a sentence, running roughshod over her attempts to get a word in edgewise. Occasionally he lost his temper with her, or at least became impatient. Even the luxury of being sick was taboo. When she did become ill, it had to be an illness serious enough to warrant hospitalization; otherwise it was business as usual in the Murphy household. For fifty-six years she stood at the beck and call of a man who criticized her dinner if he'd had the same meal for lunch in town that workday, who let his model trains crowd her out of virtually every room in the house. He rarely complimented her, listened to her, or showed her much affection, at least in public. No wonder then, that once she could, she became more assertive, outspoken. Her turn had come. At long last.

Although she would never have admitted it, even to herself, I know she was sometimes fearful of him: of his temper, his outbursts threatening to break through the surface. She would tremble, behave almost like a child on occasion. The catalyst for his outburst could have been getting the car stuck in the deeply rutted road leading from their country home down to the landing on the Meramec River, or a meal she'd served him, or her urinary tract infection in Avignon, or something one of us had done, or nothing at all. But his moods had such a powerful effect on her that she would anticipate what could set him off.

Still leaning against their bed, lost in these memories, I have an insight I've toyed with before but quickly dismissed, chalking it up to amateur psychology. Maybe the four of us functioned as an outlet for our mother, the teapot metaphor again, a way to do and say what would have been unthinkable in front of our father, a way to talk back to our father without saying a word to him, a way to redirect her own feelings of frustration through us. The feelings flowed in a torrent from him to her, and then from her on to us. After all, it had to go somewhere. Steve and Janet usually got out of the way of either parent's emotions, whereas Sam or I would stand in the line of fire, for different reasons, the full weight and velocity of our parents' anger coming at us, through us. In my case, I sought to connect with my parents, to "fix" whatever had angered them, although other times I couldn't bear to remain silent about what I perceived to be irrational ideas. I had to have my say, the last word: Last-Word Linda. Regardless of my motivation, I got mowed over in the process.

CRYSTAL BALL

That winter of 2000, looking around my parents' bedroom, through drawers, closets, sitting on their bed, in their alcove, I would never have imagined that Janet, the youngest of the four of us—nearly eleven years younger than Sam, the eldest—would die of heart disease complicated by diabetes a little more than a decade later.

If I'd had a crystal ball to see ten years ahead, what would I have done differently? I wonder. What would I have said to her?

Tried harder to break through barriers we'd each built, reminded her I loved her, invited my only sister to visit me in Maryland? I hope so. Would I have made my way to the part of the house where she was working, just to check on her? Initiated plans to go out to dinner that night? Maybe. But thinking about it later, I realize that being close to any of my siblings was probably just a pipe dream. The relationship I had—have—with them, especially after our parents' deaths when the glue holding us together had disappeared, resembled that of colleagues who no longer work in the same office. If necessary, we can hold a conversation or socialize on rare occasions, maybe even go out to lunch or dinner when I'm in town. But using this same work metaphor, once we left the office behind, we had nothing much left to say to each other. Once our reasons to be together—our parents, our childhood years—had been removed, not much linkage between us remained.

Hesitating on my journey around my parents' bedroom, I expand on that thought. It seems curious that the four children, all of us gathered together here in our childhood home, have little in common except our biology. We spent years together within these walls, yet we're reenacting our childhoods today, scattered throughout the house. Aristotle's theory that the whole is greater than the sum of its parts works in reverse in our family. When isolated, each member possesses innate talent, drive, intelligence. Together, we're a sinking ship.

seventeen

◦♣◦

MY PARENTS' BEDROOM: MY FATHER

Spit Shine

*J*ust like the lithograph of Ivy Lodge, my father posed a striking figure: pillar of the community, attorney, success-ful businessman, former FBI special agent, former state senator, commercial real estate titan in his later years, church leader, model railroading expert, a self-made man all rolled into one. But husband needed to be added. Father. My father. This man was my father. The father of four children.

I picture him in the monogrammed cufflinks on top of his dresser, the curlicue *M* on each one. I feel his presence in the business cards stacked inside: Samuel B. Murphy, Attorney at Law. I take a few as mementos. I see him in the fine cut of his nice suits hanging in his closet, in the wooden shoe protectors he inserted into his leather wingtip shoes each night. Pushing aside the handful of suits and shirts still hanging here, I wish my mother had let me claim a piece of clothing after his death, maybe a flannel shirt or two, those soft, print shirts he loved to wear working on his railroad here at Ivy Lodge or at their coun-try place in Steelville, Missouri.

There are a number of belts with sterling silver buckles he bought in the Southwest. I take one with an eagle, another with turquoise chips accenting its eyes, a small piece of coral in its beak. My father loved the Southwest, devouring Tony Hillerman novels about the Navajo police, although I don't know the origin of his interest in the region. I wish he'd done what he long promised, recorded himself on cassette tapes, stories of his youth, of growing up during the Depression. In the end, my mother gave most of his clothes to charity, claiming none of us wore the same size. She got rid of the clothes—as well as most of his more expensive trains—shortly after he died.

When we were growing up, he told a story about his teenage years. He'd been small; his classmates enjoyed mocking him for his size. One day they put him in a trash can so his arms, legs, and head stuck out of the top; then they hoisted the trash can up onto a shelf in the chemistry lab. The teacher, who'd left the room on a brief errand, discovered him a few minutes later when he returned, and blamed my father for being up on the shelf, as though he had managed the feat himself. My father never forgot the humiliation, revisiting the story from time to time. When he retold it, his lips became pursed, nearly disappearing in his frustration. He shook his head back and forth as though trying to dislodge the ever-present memory of this embarrassment.

DEPRESSION DAYS AND THEIR AFTERMATH

In the 1996 interview he gave to the Missouri Historical Society, my father shared information about the Depression-era days of his childhood. Each week during the Great Depression, beginning when he was just eleven years old until his late teens, one of myriad chores he had as the eldest of five children consisted of walking to the grocery store to do the family food shopping. He'd been left in charge when my grandfather was working out of town as an attorney for the Cotton Belt railroad. My father commented: "[A]s soon as I was old enough to do something, I was expected to work. I used to buy the family's groceries on the basis that I would get half of what I could save. Would you believe it? Under sixty dollars a month. Seven people. They used to get an awful lot of mush."

This might explain why, once he married my mother, eventually earning a decent living, he turned up his nose at leftovers, barely tolerating those from the Thanksgiving feast. He had eaten too many reconstituted meals growing up and wanted no part of warmed up food from the night before.

He notes in the interview that, once he'd reached his early teens, his parents expected him to have a job each summer. One such job involved loading dry ice onto trucks in north St. Louis; another, driving a truck. In yet another he worked as a laborer on a signal gang in Arkansas for the Missouri Pacific Railroad. As he told the reporter, "I still can't believe I did what I did down there. Like, have three hundred sixty-five pounds of wire in a coil loaded on my shoulder and walk across six railroad tracks and dump it. When I tell people today that I could carry three hundred pounds, they just don't believe it. My father believed it, though, because it would get my shoulders bloody on both sides."

My father may have been a small man, but he was strong, "mulish," to use a favorite term of his. From my vantage point as a child, hearing a smattering of these stories about his summer jobs while seated at the dinner table in the breakfast nook—the only time all six of us normally congregated—it reminded me of accounts I'd read in school about prisoners doing forced labor on chain gangs. But my father had continued in this same Missouri Historical Society interview to say he believed these types of grueling, backbreaking jobs had given him the necessary skills to establish connections with a variety of people. "When you associate with these people [from different socioeconomic backgrounds], you learn to develop rapport with them," he said.

There's a line from the Rudyard Kipling poem "If" that reminds me of him: "Or walk with kings—nor lose the common touch." That personified my father. He joked with Willy, the tall, talkative Black man who waxed his car in our backyard for fifty cents as easily as he conversed with the then-governor of Missouri, Christopher "Kit" Bond, a friend.

Given the degree of success he ultimately achieved in life, my father possessed extraordinary resourcefulness, learning from an early age how to navigate his environment using intelligence, ingenuity, charisma, persistence, as well as a strong work ethic. When cornered, however, he could become aggressive, impatient, or angry without warning. After his childhood years of being bullied, not to mention the occasional harsh treatment by his own father, who depended on him to act as the surrogate man of the house, I imagine my father believed no one would ever get the best of him again, physically, emotionally, or intellectually.

FATHERHOOD: HARDER THAN IT LOOKED

If forced to, after the birth of all four of his children, my father may have admitted to himself that fatherhood complicated his life, adding layers of financial, emotional, and physical obligations that translated into less time for work, for activities he loved. Being a father prevented him from working on his hobbies such as model railroading, photography, tropical fish. He enjoyed marriage since it freed up his schedule, our mother taking care of the home, the four children. She did everything he didn't want to do (cleaning, washing dishes, running errands, shopping, taking care of holiday preparations, paying the bills, doing most of the yard work, managing the social calendar, taking care of the pets, packing for trips, raising the children) or didn't know how to do (cooking, sewing, laundry, clothes shopping).

Having children could be messy and expensive. I imagine he considered children poor subordinates, rarely grateful for what you did for them, for all you sacrificed, especially in light of his own childhood, different from ours. If given the chance, he might have occasionally fantasized jumping into a time machine and gone straight to having grandchildren: all the fun with none of the obligations, financial or otherwise.

Prompted by my discovery of the Historical Society interview, I pull out old black-and-white photographs of my father I found in my mother's bedroom dresser drawers, photographs dating back to early days with my eldest brother, Sam, born in 1944 before the end of World War II. None are "action" pictures, casual ones taken to capture a special moment. None show him doing anything but posing. None show him playing catch with any of us, or basketball, or whiffle ball, or croquet, or board games. None show him on his knees playing with toy cars or Erector Sets or building blocks, or reading books to us, all of which we owned, generously paid for by him. I have no memories of such activities, nor photographs.

I do, however, have photographs of him wrestling with his young grandchildren; spontaneous, joyful scenes from a trip to Rehoboth Beach, Delaware, in May of 1987. I have photographs of him when we held my children's birthday parties at my parents' home, my kids and their friends all piling onto my father's rideable steam-engine train that snaked its way through Ivy Lodge's grounds, my father enjoying these occasions with little people, wearing coveralls and a railroad engineer's cap, his "costume," as a friend of mine put it. But I can find no pictures of my father roughhousing, playing games with any of his own four children. It wasn't till I had my own children that I looked back at his fathering style, realizing it had been primarily that of a hands-off parent. He either occupied himself with work, or with his own childhood-reenacting activities, avoiding physical contact with us, more embarrassed by it than anything. Our mother idealized him, though, so maybe he thought it wasn't fitting to come down to the level of his children, except once in a long while. One of my brothers—in a rare moment of candor to me— once asked if I had any memories of our father playing with us, tossing a ball, engaging in board games, cards, or helping us with our homework, with potential school issues. No. Neither did he.

Occasionally, flashes of connection occurred. In the late 1950s, my father briefly shared my brother Sam's love of go-carts, taking him to meets at a local shopping center to race through the empty parking lots (malls were closed on Sundays back then), even helping him build a go-cart in the back of the house. But that ended up being short-lived. About the same time, he put up a basketball hoop in the driveway for both my brothers, but when someone accidentally backed into it, knocking it down, it was never repaired. I never saw him shoot a basket. We had the Ping-Pong table in the finished part of our basement, but before any of us got used to having it in the house, he took it over to use as a staging area for excess model trains, a nine-by-five-foot flat surface on which to pile train parts. No use wasting good space suitable for his trains, he must have reasoned, especially if his children didn't play Ping-Pong every day.

I can hear him telling us, "Well, you kids don't use it; why let it go to waste?" I never witnessed him playing Ping-Pong.

Once he invited my then-thirteen-year-old son to build a birdhouse with him, several years prior to his death. The two of them disappeared into the basement of my parents' second home outside St. Louis, on the Meramec River in the Ozarks. He spent several happy hours with my son, measuring the wood, sawing it, painting the structure bright red, nailing the pieces together. It was like watching another man, not my father. I took numerous pictures to capture the moment, as though I'd spotted a rare bird I might never see again, listening to their joint laughter coming up from the basement, as though I could go back in time, imagining it as time spent with me. It wasn't just that he'd had little time for us, but I think it was also awkward for him with his own children, though I never understood why.

WORKAROUNDS

My siblings and I devised strategies to bypass our father's domineering personality, although as a female I faced pushback from both parents since I disliked acknowledging "my place" as a woman. Paraphrasing a theory of the twentieth-century psychologist Raymond Cattell, I believe I was punished for deviating from what my parents thought of as culturally expected patterns. At a minimum, I pushed the boundaries of what they considered acceptable behavior for a woman living in Kirkwood, Missouri, in the 1960s. I liked to express my opinions, wanted a career, wanted to be independent, longed to be respected. I wanted the same rights and privileges as my brothers and my father, and rejected my mother's life, one where she exercised scant control over her destiny. As a small child, I didn't realize my occasionally outspoken behavior would ultimately be viewed negatively, though, a liability to my relationship with family members. My conflicting goals—goals that canceled each other out—consisted of carving out my own identity, but also of connecting with members of my family, belonging. To that end, when still in grade school, at bedtime each night, I ran from the bottom of the stairs to the easy chair in the living room where my father relaxed after dinner, reading the local *Post-Dispatch* newspaper.

Arms extended to each side, angled slightly behind me like angel wings, I called out, "I love you!" as I ran toward him, tripping over my two-piece yellow cotton pajamas with white ribbing, each word filling the air for two or three seconds, stretched to fill the time it took to reach my father's chair. "IIIIIIIIIIIIII LOOOOOOOOVE YOOOOOOOU!" I cried out as I ran, throwing myself onto his lap when I reached his chair, nestling my head into his neck, wrapping my arms around him.

He didn't encourage this. Embarrassed, carefully extricating himself from my needy clutches, he peeled me off his body one appendage at a time, nervously laughing at the scene. "All right, Lin. That's enough. Time for bed. Be a good girl." But I didn't care if he acted less than welcoming; this constituted my entire physical contact for the day, unless you counted being bathed by my mother as a young child, having the stubborn knots pulled out of my hair after she washed it or, later, when she put my hair in sponge rollers each school night. "It hurts!" I would cry out as a young child, placing my hands on my scalp to lessen the pulling.

"Sit still! I need to get these out! It can't possibly hurt that much," she'd tell me, no doubt anxious to be done with all the tasks on her list.

Those nightly sprints to my father offered the only exchange of affection with anyone in my family. I didn't want to give them up. He became my captive audience, if only for a moment, only till I became an adolescent, when he became increasingly uncomfortable with my overtures.

Touching rarely happened. I can think of numerous people in my life with whom I had more physical contact than anyone in my family: my orthodontist, when he tightened my braces every two weeks; the woman in the shoe store who measured my feet; the woman at the shopping center who cut my hair; my grade school teachers who patted me on the back occasionally to encourage my efforts; my piano teacher, who called me "kiddo" as he patted my shoulder for a piece I'd played well. Photographs of me at Jones Beach the summers we visited my maternal grandparents show me clinging to my grandfather's leg.

My mother gave me a peck on the cheek when she tucked me in bed every night, carefully leaning over my bed. Her breath smelled of black licorice from the wafer lozenges she loved. I loathed black licorice, though, wanted the ritual to be over, turning my face away from her. After she left my room, I heard strains of a popular musical from the 1960s playing on the stereo downstairs. *My Fair Lady*, *The Sound of Music*, and *Camelot* were favorites. Listening to Robert Goulet sing "If Ever I Would Leave You," I somehow found the music more soothing than my mother's good night ritual. I stayed awake as long as I could, soaking in the sound of his voice.

Music remains a principal source of comfort in my life, makes me feel less anxious whenever I hear certain songs I like. In a way, it's like yet another language, the voices and melodies flowing over me, telling me, "You're OK. Everything will be OK." If it's quiet, slow-tempo music, it's as though I'm being told through the music that I'll be all right. It's a hug, a pat on the back, a kind word. If it's rousing, upbeat music, it feels like a pep talk, encouragement.

My brothers laughed at me, did what older brothers do, shoving me into the nearest wall whenever I tried to hug them, or they punched me in the arm. In principle at least, they wholeheartedly rejected any display of affection, unless it came from a teenage girlfriend.

My father believed that a male exhibiting affection beyond a certain point, past a young age, might be a homosexual. No more damning label existed in his eyes. During my junior year in college in Spain, when my parents visited me, this philosophy was reinforced. We sat at an outdoor café one afternoon when my father noticed two men sitting close to each other at a nearby table, lost in conversation, touching each other discreetly, looking into each other's eyes. He could barely contain himself. "Just look at that. Disgusting. What's wrong with a world where behavior like this is tolerated?"

Nevertheless, my father stood out as the most approachable member of my family. The most accepting of my displays of affection, provided I managed to catch him at the right moment, in the right mood.

Unconditional love in my family was rare; you had to earn love, but it proved to be an elusive goal, the artist's vanishing point, unreachable in the distance. The more I tried to earn my parents' respect, the more it backfired, having the opposite effect. *Who do you think you are?* they seemed to ask whenever I shared one modest achievement or another, wondering, *Will this be enough? Did I do enough? Have I tipped the balance, or do you need more proof of my worthiness?* But their unstated answer remained obvious: Why don't you know your place? Are you trying to outshine your siblings? What are you trying to prove? Why are you telling us this?

Dance with Me?

❦

Combing through my father's bedroom dresser drawers, I spot more cufflinks, ones engraved with the distinctive insignia of the Missouri Athletic Club, the MAC, a men's club in downtown St. Louis, specifically, a dining, social, and athletic club. My father had no desire to belong to any of St. Louis's elite country clubs—Old Warson Country Club, St. Louis Country Club, Bellerive—even after he could have afforded to become a member when he eventually became successful in commercial real estate.

He had numerous friends with memberships at these fancier clubs, but he didn't play golf. He didn't care for people who put on airs, avoiding places where he observed such behavior. His theory was that, when he met someone who had attended an Ivy League college, that person would make a point of slipping it into the conversation within minutes.

The MAC had a good reputation. Stan Musial, Charles Lindbergh, sports announcer Jack Buck, astronaut Alan Shepherd, and Harry Truman had all been members.

Once a year my sister and I put on frilly new party dresses, flouncing and twirling around the house beforehand in our excitement. We had our father to ourselves for one magical evening at the MAC's father–daughter dance. The highlight of our year. We not only ate a special dinner with him, we also took turns dancing with him, carefully stepping on top of his shoes to add to our height, straining to reach up to his arms as he waltzed us carefully across the floor to the live music of the orchestra playing Glenn Miller, Frank Sinatra, Tommy Dorsey songs. We knew he had to be the most handsome father at the party with his jet-black hair and dark eyes. The highlight of the evening, though, happened when we did the Hokey Pokey and the Bunny

Hop with our father, who acted much more spontaneous than at home.

During the Bunny Hop, I was sandwiched between my father and my sister. I put my hands on my father's hips, while Janet put hers on mine as we wove through the enormous ballroom along with a line of fathers with their daughters. Right foot out, right foot out again, left foot out, left foot out again, jump forward once, jump backward once, jump forward three times, and then start again as we moved forward, listening as the band leader helped call out instructions. Heaven. We laughed so hard we were doubled over, had to catch up with the others, get back in sync with the music and our fellow dancers. I didn't want the dance or the evening to end.

The Hokey Pokey brought equal enjoyment. Standing in a circle with other fathers and daughters, we listened to the words of the song, being instructed to put our right foot in, take our right foot out, put our right foot in and shake it all about. Every part of our body was called out, until we nearly collapsed with laughter when we reached the part of the song where we put our whole body in, took our whole body out. I will always cherish those evenings, not just because of the fun we had, but seeing our father like this, acting silly, happy, almost carefree, not having to share him with our mother or our brothers. He looked like he might even have been enjoying himself.

We were princesses at the ball in our matching pink tulle party dresses purchased with our mother especially for this party. We looked forward to this once-a-year evening with our handsome father, evenings away from our normal routine. Maybe one of the only times when being dressed up translated into fun, my sister and I loved not being wedged into a church pew between our parents, counting the minutes till the service ended.

The MAC ballroom had impossibly high ceilings, glimmering crystal chandeliers dripping with shimmering drops of glass, fancy sconces on the walls. The floors had been buffed to a mirror-like sheen; I could see my black patent leather Mary Jane shoes in the reflection. A special dance floor with intricate inlaid tiles fanned out from where the orchestra played. Even the ladies room looked like it had been inspired by a princess: soft white towels with an *M* engraved on them, surrounded by the distinctive tilted red square on the insignia; brass fixtures; porcelain sinks; faucets. The antique faucets had been labeled *H* and *C*.

My sister, my father, and I sat at a table for eight with two other fathers and their daughters, all the daughters in frilly, pastel dresses bought especially for this once-a-year occasion, bows in our shiny, freshly brushed hair. Our mother regularly rinsed our hair in vinegar after washing it to make it shine, and this night proved no exception. I hated the smell of vinegar but wanted my hair to sparkle. Janet and I each had our own name tags, with special place cards at the table, our names carefully written out in beautiful calligraphy indicating where to sit. Attention to detail added a special touch to everything. We felt like royalty.

Even the engraved silverware, delicate dishes, and glassware all looked like it had come from a princess's coffer. We enjoyed a delicious meal of fried chicken, mashed potatoes, and a small salad, a hard roll, a pat of engraved butter chilled in a small bowl of ice, followed by miniature sundaes. We were careful not to spill any on our beautiful outfits. But the highlight of the evening consisted of dancing with our father. I didn't have to share him with anyone but my sister. He didn't talk about work with the other fathers. Instead of being pulled in a dozen directions, my sister and I shared all his attention, if only for a few precious hours. Reducing it to its most basic, it meant a chance to be touched by him, to have him hold both my hands during our few dances, to have him look at me, listen to me, talk to me, to hear him laugh at what I said, trying to be funny. It meant connecting with him.

The cufflinks from the MAC are still in my hand, as though they could magically conjure up those precious nights with my father again, but I inexplicably shudder at the memory of this same father who had a much harsher side. If that person had shown himself to me at an MAC dance when I'd still been a child, I would have run from the ballroom in terror. Maybe, though, his rage had to do with me growing up, coming into my own. At those MAC father–daughter dances, I continued to be an innocent little girl whose world revolved around my father. The special night gave me an opportunity to be noticed, maybe even loved. The woman I grew up to be remained desperate for his love, for his respect, but by then I'd carved out a life of my own, independent of my parents, thinking he'd be proud of me. Along the way, between childhood and adulthood, something shifted, the magic created at those yearly MAC balls snuffed out.

Once safely back home in Kirkwood following his strokes in Barcelona in 1997, the softened edges of my father's personality surfaced. Affectionate for the first time, he acted openly warm to me, maybe even respected me. Once, I'd flown back to St. Louis to visit him in the hospital following yet another stroke. He was out of the room when I arrived, so I introduced myself to his roommate, who asked if I was "the one who speaks all the languages." Such an innocent, ordinary question, but till then my father had shown little interest in my love of languages or career as a translator, at least in my presence.

"Yes, I am," I'd replied.

"Well, he talks about you a lot," the man continued. I could feel my eyes fill with tears. At the end of his life, my father had unwittingly given me a small gift. This marked one of the only

times he ever told me—or someone else told me on his behalf—
that he was proud of me.

A little more than a year later, while looking through my
mother's family pictures the nights I stayed alone in Ivy Lodge
during her stay in the hospital, I came across a photograph of a
trip to Florida we took back in the mid-1950s. Once again, the
rest of the world had been temporarily lifted away from us for a
few special moments; I had my father all to myself. I sat on his
lap in our motel room in Clearwater Beach while he taught me
the words to the French song "Frère Jacques." My brothers had
started a game of chess on their double bed; my mother was occupied with unpacking our suitcases while my sister looked on. I
can still see it, can almost trace my love of languages back to
those few moments when he decided to teach me the song,
sounding out the syllables of the lyrics. I didn't know what the
French words meant.

"Say it, Linda: *Frère Jacques, Frère Jacques, Dormez-vous?*
Dormez-vous? Can you say it? It's French! A different language
than English. Maybe you'll learn it someday." I promised I would.

It constituted such a brief moment between a father and
daughter, but while it lasted, I floated in a bubble, a private
world where no one existed but my father and me. He soon tired
of having me on his lap, grew tired of explaining the French song
to me. For a few minutes, though, it was magical. I can trace my
future love of languages back to those few minutes, can look at
what happened when a foreign language was introduced into my
life; a connection had been made.

PLAY IT AGAIN, SAM

Someone downstairs—probably Janet—is sitting at the Steinway grand in the formal living room, playing a few notes; it sounds like the right hand of the classic child's duet, "Heart and Soul." Maybe it's Steve, though, since he's taking the piano. The playing stops after a brief burst of laughter between two people. Definitely Janet. But the laughter and the music from the piano remind me of another happy memory with my father.

One afternoon he sat down at this same Steinway grand piano in the formal living room to play the opening measures to "The Toreador Song" from Bizet's *Carmen*. He did this with great flourish, singing in a faux-operatic voice, dramatically bending over the piano and swaying from side to side to replicate the appropriate theatrics. "*Tor-e-ador, en garde, Tor-e-ador, Tor-e-ador!*" he sang, his voice booming, much to my delight, repeating the opening stanza, all he knew by heart. As he played, he glanced over at me occasionally to gauge my reaction, his eyes twinkling. I sat on the small blue loveseat across from the piano, thrilled at the conspiratorial grin I saw on his face, his theatrics in turn fueled by my enthusiasm, my laughter.

I felt pure glee sitting across from him, watching this warmer, more approachable version of my father, even though I knew it would be short-lived. The spell was broken when my mother walked into the room, dishtowel in hand, to witness this fun-loving display, a scene she wasn't part of. Waiting a minute to take it all in, she winced, whispered under her breath, "Oh, Sam!" as though she'd caught him dancing naked on top of the piano. She failed to see a father—her husband—sharing a special moment with his eldest daughter. Then again, maybe she did.

My parents constituted the perfect storm. They rarely relinquished their roles simultaneously, let their true selves peek through at the same time. One parent had to remain unapproachable, stern, judgmental with their kids, that same parent censoring the other for briefly lapsing into a gentler, warmer stance with us. When my father did his funny piano skit, my mother reminded him of his place in the family. When she occasionally acted fun-loving or silly, he might become impatient, canceling out her goodwill. They behaved like they had an unspoken agreement to display a united front in their parenting. When one let down their guard, the other had to be reminded of this agreement. Every once in a while, though, the heavens would align; they acted playful and affectionate in tandem, but that usually happened during private moments with each other. I'd stand in the doorway of whatever room they occupied, yearning to be part of that special moment, like the times my mother serenaded my father with the "ABCD Goldfish" song, eliciting a warm smile from him.

CHOOSE YOUR WEAPON

At the rear of my father's second dresser, a beautiful mahogany piece I will eventually inherit, its shiny brass knobs and rings clanking when you open or close a drawer, I come across two items my brother Sam will pass on to his only son. I'm intrigued by them, though probably not for the same reasons as Sam. My father kept several weapons in our home during my childhood, not all of them conventional ones, but instruments inflicting harm in the mind of a highly sensitive child. I was easily affected by anything having the potential to be violent or frightening, whether words or physical objects. These weapons ran the gamut from the rudimentary variety, barely capable of inflicting pain, to those with the power to kill you.

We had two German shepherds during most of my childhood years, one a frequent victim of my father's impatience. Heidi was older, a well-behaved dog, friendly, docile. Gretchen, on the other hand, although friendly, didn't behave quite as well, and was frequently the brunt of my father's displeasure.

The weapon—a weapon at least in the eyes of a child—he used to discipline Gretchen was a tightly rolled up magazine. He used it to smack her on her nose, on her hindquarters, or wherever he could get traction. Gretchen always acted predictably as she tried to become invisible, slinking away from my father, flattening her ears against her body, the occasional whimper released when my father's blows reached a vulnerable part of her body.

I don't know what she did to misbehave in my father's eyes, but a noteworthy transgression, paradoxically, involved being "shy," as my father termed it. I'm sure being chased, then walloped, did nothing to break her of that trait, no doubt made it worse.

Guns were more lethal than folded up magazines but were part of the Ivy Lodge arsenal. My father, who had been a special agent in the FBI during World War II, had specialized skills with guns. An early adult photograph I have of him—in his mid-twenties—shows him standing on a firing range, next to a target—in the shape of a man—riddled with bullet holes near the bull's-eye. He looks like an adolescent hunter with his one-dimensional quarry, holding the target for unseen bystanders to admire, a wide grin on his young face. It's logical, then, that he owned guns, knew how to use them. But I hated them, have always hated them.

My aversion toward guns, toward violence, might have had

its origins in foggy snippets I heard as a young child about my father's World War II work for the FBI when he'd been stationed first in San Francisco, then in Seattle, these fragments elusive and fraught with gaps, fitting into a cohesive, cognitive space in my memory. Or it could stem from the incident with the drunken neighbor appearing at our back porch that summer evening, threatening to shoot our wandering dog, followed by my father's threat of retaliatory action. Or maybe its origin lies in an incident just before I turned five when my young aunt—married to one of my father's brothers and living near our home in Kirkwood—used my uncle's gun to shoot herself in the head while he was at work one afternoon, instantly killing herself. Or several years later, the story about my father's only sister who, in the midst of a heated argument with her husband, fired a loaded gun in the air, quickly poured ketchup on herself, and lay on the floor playing dead as her spouse raced back into the room thinking his wife had shot herself. Or it could have been a direct result of the actions of that same aunt's son a decade later. My year-younger cousin took his mother's gun with him to nearby Kirkwood Park when we were both in our early twenties, killing himself, the life of a brilliant young man snuffed out in a flash. Or maybe my feelings stemmed from the death of a cousin, the eldest son of another of my father's brothers, my age, twenty, when his helicopter was shot down in the Vietnam War in 1970, three years after my brother was wounded.

Hard to tell, difficult to pinpoint the source of my strong feelings in this mix of incidents, many of them happening when I was still a young child, traumatized by the images I conjured up of each one, images embellished by my parents' private conversations when they didn't realize I'd been eavesdropping. I was thirteen when President Kennedy was assassinated by a gunman. Three years later my own brother was shot in Vietnam. By then, though, my feelings about guns had become deeply entrenched; an army of NRA zealots couldn't have budged me.

Scholars refer to 1968—the year I graduated from high school—as "the year that shattered America" because of the assassination of both Martin Luther King and Robert Kennedy within a two-month period, and because of the My Lai Massacre of more than five hundred civilians by US servicemen, including young girls, women, small children, and unarmed villagers. Guns and war overshadowed my immediate world and the world I saw around me on TV, beginning in early childhood.

My father kept two guns in our home: a .22 rifle he kept in a long, light-brown, faux-leather gun case, and a BB pellet gun. Since he used the BB gun more frequently, it produced greater anxiety in me. My father's answer to ridding our yard of unwanted creatures, he aimed it at squirrels that dared to leave acorns on his outdoor O-gauge model railroad tracks, sometimes derailing the trains. Given considerations of gauge, the squirrels' acorns represented boulders on the tracks.

When the train cars hit the acorns, the cars came to an abrupt stop, piling up, each car doglegging, one after the other, several falling to the grass below, sometimes damaged in the fall. My father thought that if he could just hit one squirrel with a BB pellet, it would serve two purposes: ridding the yard of that particular squirrel and sending a subliminal warning to other squirrels to leave their acorns elsewhere, as though the squirrels possessed deductive reasoning.

Thankfully, I never saw him actually hit a squirrel, but watching him angrily retrieve the gun made my heart race. I loved animals, couldn't bear the prospect of the squirrels being riddled with BBs, all because they'd left their acorns in the wrong place.

The most frightening of all the weapons in our home

weren't the guns, however, at least from my vantage point as a child. Two smallish items lay in the top drawer of my father's tall bedroom dresser, their meaning shrouded in mystery for me as a child. In isolation, they looked innocuous enough, but when given to a motivated person with skill, I knew they could kill a man or woman.

Rummaging around in my father's tall dresser, tucked behind belt buckles and cufflinks, underneath a wooden tray of loose change, stray buttons, handkerchiefs, miscellaneous papers, and business cards is what I'm looking for: a set of brass knuckles and a leather billy club.

Taking them out of the drawer, I slip four fingers through the rings of the brass knuckles, fitting them against my knuckles to make a fist. I did this as a child when I first discovered them, though my fingers were too small. The large, hard, metallic rings, meant to fit the fingers of a grown man, swallowed them up.

Even as a child, I knew you used brass knuckles when standing close to your victim, to make your punch deadlier. I subsequently learned from friends more worldly than me that American soldiers had used them in World War II. But what frightened me most about my father's brass knuckles wasn't just their presence in his top drawer; what scared me was their used, worn appearance.

These weren't brand-new brass knuckles, souvenirs, or gag gifts passed on to my father by male friends. Beat-up in places, they showed signs of wear and tear. The metal had lost some of its patina, showed scuff marks, discoloration. Specifically, where the fingers brush against the metal, the knuckles had become shiny, polished like silver. Perhaps the friction of fingers caused this. The metal had become slightly tarnished in places where oxidation had taken place. Why? Had my father used them? With whom? What had been the outcome?

Even though a gun could inflict far more damage in most circumstances, the brass knuckles looked more intimate. In order to use them, you had to be in close proximity to the person receiving your punches, maybe even know him. You had to want to inflict great harm. If you were going to be in a fight, why not just use your fists? Why the need to cover them with deadly metal? To me, the brass knuckles had a more intentional aspect about them. No one could use the excuse of friendly fire with them; impossible to accidentally inflict that kind of harm at close range.

He kept the leather billy club in the same top drawer, a small but potent weapon that looked like a miniature punching bag, a leather-covered oval, weighted inside with lead, equipped with a strap used to secure it in your hand. *Why does it show signs of use?* I wondered, turning it over in my hands, slightly indented with the leather, discolored in places, its threads fraying in places.

I eventually learned that the police used this weapon to disperse crowds. Street gangs also made use of it in skirmishes. It could knock you out, or worse. The billy club reminded me of a shortened, miniaturized version of the bolas Argentine gauchos used, twirling them over their heads before launching them at an intended target.

Why did my father keep these weapons in his top dresser drawer? When did he use them? Why? If he no longer needed either, his role in World War II long past, his days in the FBI a distant memory, why had he kept both weapons? Ivy Lodge is in the safe suburbs with a modern alarm system. Did he think he might need to use them again? With whom? Did seeing them bring back fond memories? Of what? Did he take them out of the drawer to elicit these memories? I had no idea.

These are all questions running through my mind, rediscovering these items in Ivy Lodge, unanswered questions I never asked. Back then I told myself he kept the billy club and the brass knuckles as security, in case he ever needed them again, to protect all of us, although I couldn't imagine circumstances warranting it. What good would they have been against drunken Mr. Allen the night he threatened to kill Heidi, for instance?

But I have a different idea. I think maybe each scuff, each dent, each discoloration, each frayed thread on the billy club symbolized a moment when he felt he had control over his environment, when he was in charge, no longer the runt, the bullied kid in school with no power, shoved in a trash can, hoisted up on a classroom shelf. They reminded him of his dominion over certain people, in certain circumstances, at certain times.

Regardless of my questions, it never occurred to me to ask him directly about the brass knuckles or the billy club, to get answers to my concerns. Maybe I feared I wouldn't like the answers he gave me, or that he'd fly into a rage, knowing I'd been rooting through objects in his dresser uninvited. No. Better to keep my fears to myself, even if my mind did wander off to dark places, spin off to uncontrollable musings, a downside of having an overactive imagination. Regardless of how innocuous they look, though, however absent from the daily routine of our family's lives they might have been, their mere presence in his top drawer left me with a sense of foreboding. Once again, the two weapons represent untranslatable parts of my past, their meaning floating above me, unattainable, undecipherable.

CHILDHOOD CLUES

One evening after dinner, my father was in an expansive mood. Instead of rushing off to read the newspaper or tinker with his trains, he shared another story with us from his high school days. Stories like this were rare, ones only he could tell in his engaging style. But, unbeknownst to him, his telling this story elevated my fears about the billy club and the brass knuckles in my mind.

"I probably shouldn't tell you kids this, but the principal at my high school called me into his office one afternoon after I'd been in one too many fights. I didn't take guff from anyone; you know? Anyway, the principal sat me down, stared at me for a moment and then, pointing his finger at me, said, 'Murphy, I'm not a betting man, but I would bet you a year's salary that you will end up down the river in the state pen someday. Mark my words, boy. You are trouble with a capital "T" and you're going to be trouble the rest of your life, or my name isn't John Wilson.'"

The principal paused a moment for effect and then sent my father back to class. My father smirked at the principal, unrepentant as he left his office.

From the way my father told the story, leaning forward in his chair, his elbows resting on his knees, gesturing, laughing, and drawing out all the details of the long-ago conversation as only my father could, I could tell that he thought he'd had the last word regarding this memorable episode. This constituted a laughable anecdote. The principal's words lay in stark contrast to the life my father had been leading all these years. No penitentiary for him. He had shown that principal, by God. A former FBI special agent, a former member of the Missouri Legislature as well as its minority floor leader, a well-known businessman, a prominent attorney; people in St. Louis held him in high regard. A leader at church, a husband, a father. A man people emulated.

But the story stuck with me. Tucked in the back of my mind lay disturbing evidence that the high school principal's words about my father's behavior might still be true, in part: the way he'd fly into a rage, the well-worn brass knuckles and billy club in the back of his drawer, not to mention his use of the BB gun, even the brandishing of the rolled-up magazine at our dog. I wonder if it hasn't been there all along, this side of my father the high school principal referred to, lying in wait for the right catalyst, that red line of rage my father spoke of ready to reappear at a moment's notice.

Thinking about my father, his complex nature, I'm starting to believe that the very traits that upset me the most about him, made me feel unsafe sometimes as a child, probably made him feel the safest, made him feel at least partially in control of his life.

PICTURE PERFECT

There are hundreds of loose pictures, dozens of albums buried in my mother's lower dresser drawer, some dating back to my great-grandparents. Many are still unlabeled, frustrating since I'm not sure who all these great aunts and uncles are, the great-grandparents. While my mother remained in the hospital a few months ago, I stayed alone in their home and, after hospital hours, I'd sit on their bedroom floor, going through boxes of these loose photographs and picture albums, trying to make sense of them. I sorted them into four piles: one for myself, one for each of my siblings.

I noticed there were very few pictures of my father and me, few of him with any of my siblings. In one, a black-and-white snapshot, I'm an infant, casually slung in the crook of his arm while he smokes a cigarette with his free hand. It looks like he's wearing a Hawaiian shirt. The local professional photographer took another one, eighteen years later, at my high school graduation.

My father wears a business suit in the graduation photograph; he's only a few inches taller than me, at five feet four inches. He smiles for the photographer, Francis Scheidegger, a local celebrity of sorts, hired to cover the Kirkwood High School graduation and other Kirkwood events. If I look closely, coupled with the beginnings of a five o'clock shadow, my father's smile looks somewhat menacing. The smile has a tentative hold on him, suggests a darker reality lying just below the surface.

The picture reminds me of a scene from a 1980 movie, *Ordinary People*, based on a book of the same name by Judith Guest. Conrad, the troubled teenage protagonist, is urged by his grandfather to stand by his aloof mother during a holiday celebration. The grandfather wants to take a picture of mother and son. Both initially protest but then assume an appropriate pose, their arms moving this way and that in an awkward attempt at a hug. They can't bridge the emotional gap, though. Ultimately, the picture-taking is aborted, to their mutual relief. When I look back on my high school graduation photograph, I realize that's how I felt when a teacher or friend or parent insisted on taking our picture. It was unnatural; I sensed my father disliked the forced intimacy, adding to our mutual discomfort.

$\backsim\!\!\Upsilon\!\!\backsim$

eighteen

SECOND-FLOOR BEDROOM

*O*f all the rooms in Ivy Lodge, the one holding the most childhood memories for me is next door to my parents' bedroom: the bedroom I shared with my sister when we first moved here, the only other room on the second floor. As I enter it, I know it will look nothing like it did in 1960. My mother took it over after Janet got married in 1977, converting it into her study, leaving one twin bed in place, filling the rest with her coin magazines and metal detecting equipment, along with miscellaneous paraphernalia from various projects, charity work, hobbies. At last she had her own space after almost twenty years in this house, personal space unlike the dingy, ever-shrinking ten-by-ten work space below ground, unlike the kitchen where she had to prepare meals for all of us. Hers alone to use as she saw fit. In theory, at least, my father never needed to set foot in it. The rest of the house is where his physical presence could be keenly felt, but now the bedroom my sister and I used to share had become our mother's small sanctuary.

When this second-story bedroom was Janet's and mine for five years, we had two side-by-side twin beds covered in white chenille bedspreads. I picked at the little balls—a nervous outlet for me—the little round tufts of material dotting the material. Girl Scout curtains hung from our double windows, depicting small groups of Scouts earning badges. I imagined the camaraderie, the friendship of these diminutive, make-believe girls covering our windows. Another feature of the bedroom was a doorbell-like buzzer that produced a piercing, cacophonous noise within the bedroom whenever the button in the kitchen next to the refrigerator was pushed. Family members used it as an unpleasant last resort to summon or, more often the case, to annoy Janet or me. Sometimes, though, I played the role of culprit, pressed the kitchen button to startle Janet up in our bedroom. I could push it and quickly leave the kitchen so no one knew who had done it.

In the early years, just after bedtime, all the lights out except for a small nightlight plugged into a wall socket, I taught Janet little lessons. How to spell simple three- and four-letter words: cat, dog, girl, boy. Using the nightlight as a prop, I made shadow puppets with my hands to create alligators and rabbits on the wall, enacting scenes in which they alternately snapped at or kissed each other. I could easily amuse Janet at four or five; she laughed at my amateur shows. As I poke around the room, I wonder if she still remembers those days. Maybe I'll seek her out when I head downstairs and ask her.

One downside of that second-story bedroom occurred as I drifted off to sleep. Unwanted visitors sometimes appeared. Those same cockroaches—or offspring—I already knew from the downstairs bathtub. They would scurry across my pillow, or my arm, even over my face on one occasion. I'd be almost asleep when I'd glimpse the dark body of one running across my white pillowcase, black on white, or I'd feel tiny legs on my forearm, or —worst case scenario—feel feet scamper across my face. This unnerved me, made me want to stay up as late as possible to avoid any reenactments.

I played with my Lennon Sister paper dolls in this Ivy Lodge bedroom. A popular singing group in the mid-1950s and 1960s, the Lennon Sisters first appeared on the popular *The Lawrence Welk Show*. Janet, the youngest, was my favorite. I also entertained myself with my various Barbie dolls, Barbie a newcomer to the world of dolls when I was eight years old. I had two walking dolls, twelve and twenty-four inches tall, with luxuriant hair: Mary and Barbara, my mother's name. Another was my beloved Raggedy Ann doll, which my maternal grandparents gave me when I was one, a doll that followed me through childhood into adulthood. My kisses had stained her cloth face brown, and I had inadvertently pulled out all her yarn hair by loving her too much. One evening, my Aunt Joan sat in my grandfather's living room when my doll needed repairs, sewing new yarn hair onto her head, bright orange the second time around.

I owned several baby dolls and two life-sized cloth dolls with plastic faces. They had black elastic straps on their feet, and I strapped them onto my shoes, allowing us to dance around the room. The large cloth dolls were like good friends, propped up against Janet's and my bedroom wall, ready to be called into being, dance with me, huggable friends who loved me unconditionally. The face of one had become dented when I accidentally dropped her after one dance.

I enjoyed sitting in the short interior hallway leading from our second-story bedroom to one of the two doors of the tiny bathroom Janet and I shared with our parents. The hallway measured no more than three or four feet across, so if Janet needed to go into the bathroom, she had to climb over my legs —my back on one wall, my stocking feet resting on the opposite wall—or enter the bathroom via the door from our parents' bedroom. Otherwise, I claimed it as my quiet little spot.

I played 45 RPM records on my portable record player in my nook, leaned on either side of the narrow walls, my socked feet on the wall opposite. I'd created my own private little alley, cave-like, where I listened to Elvis Presley singing "Blue Hawaii" with its flip side, "Can't Help Falling in Love." I loved Bobby Rydell and the Everly Brothers, Doris Day singing "Que Será Será." I knew all the verses, sang along with her, though years later I wondered about the wisdom of those words. The lyrics reflected such a defeatist, passive message, namely that young women couldn't determine their own fate. *Why not*, I wondered. *Why wasn't the future "ours to see."* I still loved the song back then, though, and didn't ponder such feminist matters. My favorite, though, remained Mitch Miller's "The Yellow Rose of Texas" with its march-like beat, its rousing opening with drums. A babysitter, Dorothea, had once told me I had "eyes as bright as diamonds," that "sparkled like the dew," like the words in the song. I fell in love with it, without really understanding why. To this day, whenever I hear it, it makes me happy.

BOOKWORM

The bedroom I shared with Janet has two closets: one the size of a small coat closet, the other a larger walk-in closet. Janet and I kept most of our hanging clothes in the larger closet, with a large bookshelf against one wall containing several of our books: Janet's *Blueberries for Sal, The Wind in the Willows*, along with my copies of *A Little Princess, The Borrowers, Mrs. Piggle Wiggle*, a handful of Nancy Drew books, *Charlotte's Web*, to name a few. I read all the Mrs. Piggle Wiggle books, drawn to Mrs. Piggle

Wiggle's warmth, her seeming indifference to being chubby. I loved her.

Books—ones read for pleasure—made me happy. The Kirkwood Public Library was only four short blocks from our home; I went as often as I could, lugging books back home with me after each visit. The smell of the library drew me in, as well as the variety of books, all the choices I had at my disposal.

Five years after the death of my grandmother in 1963, my paternal grandfather remarried, his new wife a never-married, younger woman, Elizabeth, who owned Kirkwood's only bookstore. She played more the role of friend than that of surrogate grandmother and gave me my first dictionary when I left for college. We had a close relationship till her death decades later, long after I'd moved to the East Coast with my own children.

The mere sight, feel, weight of books comforted me. As a child, I wanted to be like Nancy Drew: go on adventures with my friends, spend time with my father the way she did. Or be Sara in *A Little Princess*, live in an attic where magic happened, where fascinating visitors came to call, where my long-lost father searched high and low till he found me. I wanted to be Caddie Woodlawn with her exciting life, or Eloise living an adventurous life in New York City's Plaza Hotel, or Scout Finch in *To Kill a Mockingbird*, with Gregory Peck as my good-natured, attentive father, or be friends with Madeline in Paris, living in a boarding school. Or one of the Boxcar Children, traveling with my kind grandfather who took me to thrilling places. Or Jo in *Little Women*, living life on my own terms, independent, a writer. Like many other children, I did it all when I read these books.

By now Janet and I have both retrieved our books from the walk-in closet we shared. She's even more of a reader than I am, working part-time at a local bookstore. Once, disguising my voice, I called her at her bookstore to drill her about the ambiguous ending of a popular book, asking plot-spoiling questions; she recognized my voice but let the joke play out.

I walk inside the large closet, taking a last look around at a space about the size of the bathroom the four of us shared, probably a quarter the size of the breakfast nook. The dimensions of the house are out of proportion, as though the architect didn't grasp the use for each space or had never thought about what it meant for a family to live in a home. It occurs to me that Ivy Lodge is a home at war with itself, the vast unfinished second-floor "attic" joining forces with the enormous basement and rathskeller to wage war against the formal living room, dining room, and foyer, my father acting as the commander of the former, my mother in charge of the latter. Abraham Lincoln's comment that a house divided against itself cannot stand rang true in our home. In much the same way, our family ultimately couldn't withstand people at the helm with such diverse philosophies, temperaments, and, at the end of the day, goals.

Several books remain on the closet shelf, books my mother owned as a child, ones I never noticed before, although maybe she moved them here when she took over this room. I pull them out of the bookshelf to share with Janet when I go downstairs. She'll think they're treasures. Looking at the titles I notice they're all fiction: Hans Christian Andersen stories, *Happy House*, *A Little Girl of Nineteen Hundred*, *Seventeen Little Bears*, *The Sunny-Sulky Book*, to name a few. They all have decorative bookplates with "Barbara Chivvis" written in various stages of printing or cursive script, gifts from her parents or grandparents when she was a young girl. But I never saw the woman who raised me open a work of fiction. She loved to pore over nonfiction books serving a specific purpose: books about arrowheads, Egyptology, rare coins, gold coins, for example. But maybe she was too practical to lose herself in a make-believe world. Seeing these children's books lifts my spirits; she started out reading fiction, even filled in the black-and-white sketches with her childlike crayon markings in a few, the color spilling out past the lines, onto the page.

I wonder about that little girl, how she became intensely practical, businesslike, adept at hiding her emotions. Did it happen after she married my father, or did it precede their marriage? I can't ask my siblings; when I ask them questions involving either parent's past, they brush me off or become impatient or tell me I analyze life too much, which I guess is true. Regardless, I'm thankful, contemplating all the books the four of us had access to, grateful for the importance my parents placed on reading, on school. Whenever I'm in the home of a friend who has no books in sight, I think how sad that is. Our parents encouraged us to get library cards as children, giving us books for Christmas and birthdays, a tradition our grandparents continued. I have numerous books in my home in Maryland inscribed by one or the other set of grandparents.

During the summer, both when we lived on Gill and after we moved to Ivy Lodge, my mother expected us to spend at least an hour a day reading, a habit that cemented our love of books. Local summer day camps weren't that common. The reading rule became a good way to keep us quiet, at home, occupied at least for a while, especially when we spent the rest of the day running all over the neighborhood or going to the local swimming club.

During one such afternoon session of summer reading, I picked up a book my maternal grandmother Chivvis had given me the previous Christmas, Robert Louis Stevenson's *A Children's Garden of Verses*. I'd never heard of Stevenson or the book, but one poem stood out from the rest. I would read it once in a while through the years: "The Land of Counterpane."

When I was sick and lay a-bed,
I had two pillows at my head,
And all my toys beside me lay
To keep me happy all the day.

Reading Stevenson's poem made me feel safe, content. How wonderful, I thought, to lie in bed reading, playing with your toys spread out all around you. What a pleasant morning—or evening—to be taken care of by a mother, a father, bringing me my toys, fluffing my pillow, kissing me gently on the forehead, bringing me a cup of tea; close, but not hovering. None of these last actions are explicit in the poem, but that's how I interpreted it, the image the poem evoked sounding cozy, safe. As I look at my mother's childhood books in the closet, it occurs to me that I came closest to living that life the year I turned six, when I had hepatitis. This, despite my mother's comments after my convalescence when she accused me of causing my own illness, and later, when she warned me I might have to repeat first grade if I couldn't catch up with my classmates. Aside from those two remarks, I felt like I was living Stevenson's poem, experiencing this Land of Counterpane, if only for a while. Afterward, I longed to return to those seemingly carefree (for me, not for my mother), pampered days, when I didn't have to share my mother with my father or my siblings, when she paid special attention to me.

When the hospital released me, I had to rest at home for several months. Unless occupied with homework to catch up with my classmates, I rested and read all day. My mother gave me a little brass bell to ring whenever I wanted a piece of fruit or Life Savers (both believed to have curative powers for liver ailments back then, or so my mother told me). I would ring the bell, prompting her to stop her chores to bring me whatever I needed, usually applesauce or cherry lifesavers. She worked with me on the homework sheets sent home by my teachers.

During that same period when I convalesced at home, my mother's good friend Pat—my godmother—dropped by each day to bring me small gifts: a tub of silly putty, jacks and a ball, a pencil or pen, a Slinky, a Big Chief lined pad, a tin of Play-Doh, a tiny accessory for my doll house, soap bubbles, plastic toys in tiny plastic tubs sold in vending machines at our local grocery store, Bubble Plastic with a thin straw you used to blow bubbles from a pea-sized ball. Pat and her husband had four boys, no girls, perhaps explaining her desire to spend time with me. I enjoyed her company and thoughtful gifts, slotted her more in the role of aunt than my mother's friend.

Dream Girl

Finished with the upstairs, with looking through my parents' bedroom as well as Janet's and my former bedroom, along with the unfinished wing—the "attic"—I walk downstairs, sliding my hand down the wrought iron banister on the way down to the foyer, checking to see if my siblings are nearby. As a teenager, I used to imagine getting married in Ivy Lodge, making a grand entrance walking down this ornate stairway to meet my awaiting fiancé, my fingers lightly balanced on the railing. I even practiced my walk, how I'd float, elegant, slim—always slim. I visualized the wedding dress I'd be wearing, how beautiful I'd look.

I had an active fantasy life. In college, I played friends' record albums on weekend nights when they all attended parties or went out on dates. Barbra Streisand, Carole King, Johnny Mathis, Andy Williams. I'd think up various scenarios in which boys sought me out, where I remained safe in the arms of some

Prince Charming I'd yet to meet, or maybe a boy I had met, whom I elevated to princely status. Meanwhile, my friends went out, dated flesh-and-blood young men, trying college on for size, learning who they were, whom they wanted to be with. It must have been safer for me to daydream; not that I didn't go out on dates, but they always produced such anxiety for me. What would I wear? What would I say? Did I look fat? Ugly? What if he acted aggressively on our date? College boys scared me, as did alcohol and drugs, relinquishing control of my life. My daydreams never let me down.

---

nineteen

DINING ROOM: DIORAMA OF SILVER, CHINA, AND CRYSTAL

I head to the dining room after my imaginary grand entrance down the sweeping staircase, over to Ivy Lodge's ceremonial room where most major announcements were made, where Sunday dinners took place once our numbers expanded beyond the original six. Walking into it, the room reminds me of a beautiful prom queen whom everyone stares at admiringly, but always from afar, afraid to make a misstep and sully her beauty.

Standing in the wide alcove between the foyer and dining room, I can see that the dining room epitomized everything the lithograph conveyed: window dressing to make a statement about the family who lived in Ivy Lodge. But it was a room where we spent little time. The only activities occurring here were formal holiday dinners, entertaining the occasional guest. Family members walked through it as a shortcut from the family room to the foyer, but only as a thoroughfare; there was no reason to tarry. In hindsight, it all seems like such a waste. It's why, when I moved out, had my own family, and could afford a home, the dining room table took on a different role. It became the place I put homemade decorations for upcoming holidays, where I displayed artwork my children brought home from school, where I put photographs of them. I referred to my dining room table as the celebration table.

Once or twice a year I'd temporarily remove the photographs, the school artwork, the greeting cards, to make room for holiday meals, but only until Christmas or Thanksgiving dinner was over. The dining room played an integral role in my home, not just as a sterile showcase off to the side, not as a diorama to peer at from the outside. No longer would it be a place reserved for outsiders, people valued more highly but with less right to spend time in my home than family members. No longer would it be dead space much of the year, waiting, waiting, to be called into being.

Ivy Lodge's dining room looks bare following my brother and sister-in-law's removal of all the sterling silver monogrammed flatware, sterling silver tea and coffee services, crystal, good china, small treasures as a security precaution following the announcement of our mother's death in the local paper. The chandelier hanging over the mahogany dining room table looks out of place, a misfit. If it could talk, it might express embarrassment at being left behind, nude, its former glory absent. It's nothing without its surrounding finery.

The room is devoid of everything shiny and sparkly. Only furniture remains: the empty mahogany table, expanded to its full length; the buffet table; the large breakfront cabinet. The barren breakfront's glass shelves with mirrored back walls look like thieves entered the house, stripping it of all the treasures it once held: delicate ceramic animals with tiny opal patches, silver chalices, a collection of silver spoons from all over the world, miniature inch-tall Toby mugs my mother collected. Nothing remains except the dusty silhouettes of each object looking like those crime scene silhouettes you see on TV. They're reminders of the room's glory days, expensive items whisked out of the house for their own protection.

One-of-a-kind hobo nickels were displayed in the dining room breakfront cabinet before my brother transported them to his home, part of our mother's extensive coin collection. Homeless or transient men—known back then as "hobos"—carved these original hobo nickels in the 1930s or 1940s using only pocketknives, nails, hammers, or other coins as tools to transform newly minted (1913) Indian-head nickels. The original large Indian faces on the coins—filling almost the entire circumference of the coin—were suitable for carving into different faces.

Back at his home, my brother spread the nickels out on his dining room table. We took turns picking hobo nickels from our mother's collection. I chose ones carved by famous artisans, "hobos" from the 1940s: George Washington "Bo" Hughes and Bertram "Bert" Wiegand. They're an example of my mother's skill at purchasing coins, at being at the cutting edge of trends. She had a knack for purchasing one-of-a-kind treasures no one else had heard of. Proof of her skill in following trends in the coin world—and elsewhere—lies in the story she liked to tell, how she paid for the Steinway grand piano in our living room using a single roll of rare nickels.

Remembering her love of coins, when we were children she gave us each our own little blue cent-holder books with slots for pennies, each slot for the year it went into circulation. We looked through all the pennies we received in change, our mother teaching us to be on the lookout for the rare ones: the wheat pennies in circulation between 1909 and 1959, the rare 1909 S VDB Lincoln penny, the double-struck 1955. Each week when we went to Ruby's after church, the corner shop in the neighborhood where we bought the weekend paper, I'd pore through the pennies we got in change. We all did. We enjoyed trying to collect as many pennies for our coin books as we could. Since our mother also liked this hobby, it became even more enjoyable for us, a hobby we shared. Unfortunately, however, and in keeping with my tendency to try too hard, like the time I overfed my father's fish, I once carried a pile of pennies to my next-door neighbor Donna's house where we sat on her bedroom floor polishing them all to a high sheen with copper polish, thinking what a nice surprise it would be for my mother, her coins all sparkly. We didn't realize that scrubbing them meant lowering their value.

My sister and I shared another hobby with our mother: collecting dollhouse miniatures. She occasionally drove us to Jefferson Memorial in Forest Park—the site of the 1904 St. Louis World's Fair—to visit the museum gift shop; it became a tradition the three of us looked forward to. The shop featured an extensive array of tiny furniture, lamps, wall hangings, appliances, newspapers, food items, dishes, all easily fitting into the cupped palm of your hand. There were also little people: mothers, fathers, children, grandparents, even dogs and cats. Back in the early 1960s, this type of perfectly crafted miniatures wasn't that prevalent; no internet existed, and few specialty stores carried them. Beautiful dollhouses in the gift shop displayed some of the dainty pieces—the dollhouses were not for sale—but others had been wrapped in tiny pieces of plastic for purchase. Our mother always bought us at least one or two of the miniature items for our own dollhouses. When I left Kirkwood to move to the East Coast, I brought my dollhouse with me, partially because of the memories of those Saturday afternoons the three of us spent together.

Conversations during family dinners in the formal dining room were slotted by gender, even after we'd grown up and moved out. The men discussed business, real estate, professional sports, whereas the women talked about children, domestic matters like recipes, home maintenance, shopping, female-oriented groups like bridge club or the altar guild at church. We were like separate teams; attempts to cross gender lines were discouraged.

The summer of 1997, I returned to Kirkwood for a family visit. My father was speaking with Steve about a business matter when I happened to be standing nearby. Although I didn't have much interest in the topic, I half-listened, trying to educate myself about their business dealings, particularly since I'd been part of the family deals since the late 1970s, at least officially. Noticing me standing off to the side, my father stopped his conversation long enough to comment. "You have no idea the kinds of financial transactions your brother and I deal with every day, Lin. You think you deal with big numbers in your life? You'd be amazed at what we face. There's no comparison," then he turned his back to me to resume his conversation with Steve.

I'd wanted to make a sarcastic comment about not caring for business, real estate, or high finance, but decided against it; after all, he was right. I shrugged my shoulders, walked out of the room. Message received, that I couldn't really be part of their world. He spoke to me as though I were a child, not a college-educated woman with an interesting career. But it would have been fruitless to argue with him. Despite our relationship, though, his comment caught me off guard. Well into a successful career as a multi-linguist with the government in the Washington, DC, area, I thought I'd proven myself, earned my stripes, no longer just another female vassal in his kingdom of powerful men. But I hadn't; here lay the evidence.

Queen of the May

Subplots unfolded in the dining room in surprising ways; the concentration of six family members could lead to a surfeit of emotions occasionally bubbling over. One night in 1980 I did something still puzzling to me. I was turning thirty, still lived in Kirkwood with my first husband. After a family dinner I noticed my mother standing apart from the group in the dining room, lost in thought, gazing out at the front yard from the dining room's large bay window, her hand on her hip. Normally she acted like a study in perpetual motion, personifying the dictum of idle hands being the devil's workshop. Washing, scrubbing, polishing, mending, wiping, vacuuming, cooking, chauffeuring (when we were young), serving, ironing, doing our father's—and our—bidding as we grew up. When time permitted, though, at night after all her chores had been completed, she read her books on Egyptology and arrowheads, read numismatic newspapers to research one of her coins. Even when she could free herself to go metal detecting or dig for arrowheads or pan for gold, she was rarely idle. But not tonight. Pensive, introspective, maybe even approachable, I thought.

Meanwhile, my father stood next to the French doors in the dining room holding court about a business matter with my brothers, my brother-in-law, and my husband, while my sister shared an anecdote with my brothers' wives. Without thinking it through, I approached my mother, seeing an opportunity.

I'd been depressed about turning thirty, or maybe the source lay deeper, a problem I wasn't able to articulate. Maybe because I didn't yet have children, or because being married hadn't been the fairy tale I dreamed it would be, the pot of gold at the end of the rainbow. Then again, maybe it stemmed from my disappointment at the prospect of spending the rest of my life in Kirkwood, Missouri. I didn't know. But many times I fought sadness, had little energy; my self-esteem flagged. I needed my mother, or I needed *a* mother, even though I was well past an age to justify that need. Unfortunately, though, I occasionally forgot the history my mother and I shared, forgot our problematic relationship, forgot the play in which we participated, my role in that play.

Walking over to her, I made a few preliminary, lighthearted, innocuous comments. Then, lowering my voice, tears welling up in my eyes, my defenses down, I confided in her that I'd been down in the dumps of late (not daring to use the more clinically accurate term, *depressed*), that turning thirty might have precipitated it. "I don't know what's the matter, Mom. I know I should be grateful for everything I have, count my blessings like you always taught us, but sometimes I'm sad. I don't understand it." Family members had already mocked me at a weekly Sunday dinner after I'd mentioned being depressed about my upcoming thirtieth birthday, their laughter still fresh in my memory. I should have omitted that part, but didn't, blindly continuing.

Before I finished my rambling sentence, I noticed her looking at me with suspicion, as though looking at a new life form, an unpleasant, unwanted specimen she'd just spotted, squinting her eyes as she tried to focus. What did she see when she looked at me? She pivoted, facing me, her reverie broken, her face contorted—the change in her behavior whiplash fast—announcing loud enough that everyone could hear, my confidential tone lost, her voice dripping with disgust: "What are *you* complaining about? You're Queen of the May! You have absolutely no right to say a word. I won't listen to it. Do you hear me? Get off your high horse! Pull yourself together. Just look at the charmed life you've led. You should be ashamed of yourself. Snap out of it right now, do you hear me?"

Not waiting for my response, she gave me one last look of contempt, turned her back on me, marching over to my brother's wife, her smile snapping back into place at lightning speed as though she had flipped a switch. It reminded me of the song I used to sing in Brownies about having something in my pocket that belonged upon my face, the one in which the singer wears a neutral expression until suddenly pulling a hidden smile out of her pocket. The song reminded me of my mother, always at the ready, pulling a smile out of her pocket, out of thin air, whenever she needed it to play a role.

I didn't know anything about a Queen of the May, but I had a general idea based on her tone and her words, words that felt as physical as a slap. Mired in embarrassment, humiliation, sadness, furious with myself for confiding in her, I glanced up long enough to see the disapproving looks of my father, my siblings, their spouses, all of whom had witnessed the rare phenomenon of her raised voice, no doubt wondering what I'd done to provoke her antagonism.

My mother remained untouchable in their eyes. If you confronted her, even using the politest of terms, you'd be met with swift retaliation from other family members; only my father was granted *carte blanche* to say whatever he wanted. And, while none of us shared a close relationship, I was more of an outsider. At pivotal moments in our family's history, they would all band together, leaving me on the fringes. Gaslighting was a term I kept returning to; I became the designated troublemaker to be ostracized.

Even though I'd been asking for emotional support, not criticizing my mother, I had upended a delicate equilibrium. An unwritten rule in my family dictated that you had to stay in your own lane, particularly as a woman. This meant not being assertive ("Get off your high horse! Who do you think you are?")

225

but also not moping around ("Count your blessings!" "Let me know when you're finished crying!" "For crying in a bucket of beer, what's wrong with you?!" or, "What's the *matter*, Linda?!"). A thin balance beam of permissible emotions existed which largely placed you in an invisible no man's land, the only way to avoid conflict.

CONVERSATION OVER

When I stopped by my parents' home to tell them I'd started therapy, shortly after the "Queen of the May" incident, before I'd even finished my thoughts my mother abruptly left the room, rushing off to get ready for a party. Conversation over. When I called her in tears as a recent bride after vandals burglarized the home my new husband and I had rented, everything of value stolen, she reprimanded me, telling me to get a hold of myself, to think of others who had experienced far worse setbacks. Conversation over. When I called her with the good news that I was pregnant with my first child, giving her my due date, she made a point of telling me she and my father would likely be out of town, at their country place that day, seven months in the future. Years before, when I received a devastating, anonymous hate letter in the mail as a teenager, the message cut out of words from magazines like a scene from a mystery novel, she walked out of the room when I tearfully showed her the letter, distraught I'd elicited such angry feelings from an unknown detractor. Conversation over.

In fairness, maybe she hadn't bargained on having a daughter like me, her first daughter. A daughter who cried at the slightest provocation, whose sensitivity was renown, who analyzed, parsed, dissected everyone's every thought, word, and deed. A daughter who could be alternately clingy or impatient while simultaneously maddeningly, fiercely independent. Maybe that wasn't what she'd envisioned about mothering a daughter. Maybe we were just too different, or maybe she'd just gotten in over her head with three other unique children, each with his or her own needs, and having little support in raising them. Her generation had few choices in the matter. Have kids—as many as biologically possible—or risk public disapproval, at least in the Midwest in the late 1940s and 1950s. Maybe she had no choice.

But this was my mother's pattern with me, although she acted like this with other family members, too, when they put themselves in vulnerable positions. The key word: vulnerability. After my father suffered a series of strokes, his mental and physical health gradually, heartbreakingly deteriorating, she continued to visit him at the hospital each day, but would make surprising remarks when no witnesses were within earshot: "Sam looks won-der-ful but, of course, I would, too, if all I did all day consisted of eating nice meals prepared by someone else, sit in a chair, and sleep, without a thing on my mind, no worries. It must be nice to sit around with no obligations. People feed you, bathe you; you don't have to do anything for yourself here, not a care in the world. It's like a resort. Meanwhile, I now have to carry the entire load at home alone." Pausing a moment, then pointing at the diaper he was forced to wear in the hospital, she added in a conspiratorial tone, stifling a giggle, her hand cupped over her mouth, "Wouldn't he just *die* of embarrassment if he could *see* himself, Linda?" The way she spoke about my father reminded me of a young grade-school child mocking a classmate with a disability, not a wife talking about her husband of over fifty years who'd been stricken with repeated health crises.

A few months before his death in 1998, I joined her in my father's hospital room. She greeted me with a harsh criticism of my father, reporting on his behavior: "They gave him a choice between working with Play Doh with the other patients or going to physical therapy to practice balancing, yet he refused to choose. That's *all* he has to do all day, but he can't choose. I wish those were the only choices I had to make in a day," she scoffed. She might as well have been referring to a belligerent three-year-old, not my once-brilliant father.

She wouldn't have dared make these comments if my father had been himself, still the successful commercial real estate owner who read the *Wall Street Journal* each day and performed intricate work on his model trains. Or if anyone but me had been listening. But she must have felt free to express herself now, ever since my father had become incapacitated. What's more, she knew no one would believe me, even if I'd revealed what she said. Maybe, though, her harsh words were also payback for all the years he'd acted unkindly to her.

I still had the tendency to get the last word in. After her negative comments about my father's deteriorating condition had become commonplace, I felt compelled to defend him. We'd just come back from a day at the hospital, finishing up dinner at Ivy Lodge.

"Mom, don't you think Dad would give anything in the world, anything, not to be in this horrible condition, completely dependent on nurses and doctors? He didn't choose this. Why do you talk like that? Don't you think he'd much rather be with you at the country place, or working with his trains, or reading the newspaper?"

She shot me a disapproving look and walked out of the room without a word. Conversation over. Not for the first time, as I cleaned up the dishes, I wondered about her reaction, about her state of mind. These didn't strike me as the words of a self-proclaimed "softie." I'd been given a foreign text to decipher, but I couldn't even identify the language, much less the meaning behind the words; she was speaking in some code.

These episodes about my father opened new vistas for me. My whole life I'd held up their marriage as an ideal the rest of us could only aspire to. But maybe I believed that because I took her comments at face value. When she bragged about the success of her marriage, I believed her, despite evidence to the contrary. When she proclaimed herself to be a "softie," I believed the word, even though she acted nothing like a "softie." Words had a purpose. Language had a purpose; I wrongly assumed that my mother wouldn't misuse it.

In my parents' eyes I'd already proven myself to be a failure after my divorce. Conversely, they had the ideal marriage, didn't they? I certainly wouldn't have—and didn't—put myself in the subservient position she had for over fifty years, but it wasn't my marriage, it was hers. Maybe it was all part of the role she played. Once he'd lost his health, his voice, his power, she turned the tables while keeping up the public image of their marriage. What if she was never happily married? I wondered, recalling the "Queen of the May" incident in the dining room. What if, deeply unhappy, she had rejected any attempt to have her remove her mask? What if this is what had produced the swift blowback?

Even though the "Queen of the May" outburst happened almost twenty years ago, the memory remains. Looking around the barebones dining room now, I know exactly where I stood when she accused me of being "Queen of the May." The incident jolted me as though I'd been a witness at the scene of a crime. The memory still hurts, not just because of what she said that day, but because I exemplified the adage, "Insanity is doing the same thing over and over but expecting different results." That description fit me. I kept thinking the next time or the time after that would have a different outcome. I'd get it right. "If at first you don't succeed..."

LET'S MAKE A DEAL

The most noteworthy scene to take place here, one I'm remembering as I stand alone in the stripped-down dining room, would turn out to be a watershed in my life. Forty years after an announcement my father made in the 1970s, long after we'd begun this process of decluttering Ivy Lodge to put it on the market, I will look back, pull the string of events leading me down a dark, unending rabbit hole. This is the day I will be able to point back to and declare, "This is when and where it began. This is when and where I could have stopped it, changed the course of my personal history, but I didn't." More than forty years later, I will still be paying for not speaking up, for not stepping out of my assigned "lane," for not having the courage to say, "No. Not me. Count me out."

This is my recollection: it was the summer of 1978. After a weekly Sunday dinner in the dining room—filet mignon barbecued to perfection by my father—he said he had an announcement to make. Getting everyone's attention (no grandchildren yet) he informed his four grown children, along with their spouses, that he had bought a building, bought it for us, he said. A medical building in St. Louis. Eventually he would form a company composed of members of the immediate family, calling it "SSLJ," the first initials of his four children: Sam, Steve, Linda, Janet. But in the meantime, he called it the SBM Partnership; SBM were his initials. At this point, he had been in the commercial real estate business for about ten years, finding it more interesting and more lucrative than practicing law. I had watched from the sidelines till now, content to remain an uninvolved observer to his work.

As he made his announcement that day, his face beamed when he looked around the table to gauge our reactions.

What!? I thought to myself the minute the words left his mouth, but didn't say it out loud. A building? I didn't want a building. And a medical building? Looking around the room, my mother clearly knew about this in advance, maybe both my attorney-brothers, too, because they didn't look surprised. Maybe even my then-husband knew. That left my sister and both sisters-in-law, who looked strangely neutral.

I already owned a "building." I had a home, a small, one-story ranch house on a quiet cul-de-sac in Kirkwood. My first home ever, one my husband and I had saved for and purchased the year before with a thirty-year, ten percent fixed mortgage. The first three years after getting married, we'd lived in a rental home, a modest one-story house in a still-undeveloped part of the suburbs, a house that flooded after major rainstorms, had the occasional mouse and cheap linoleum-tiled floors. We'd finally become homeowners, planning for the future: children, a bigger home, college funds for these future children. Owning part interest in a medical building hadn't been part of the plan, in my mind, at least.

Commercial real estate was my father's passion, my father's area of expertise, not mine. He once compared it to playing Monopoly; he loved it all, was good at it. Finding properties, buying them, managing them, building up his portfolio by buying additional buildings. Conversely, I didn't play Monopoly well, hoarding all my cash till the last possible moment, never using it to buy property unless it was Boardwalk or Park Place, fearful of losing control of my stash of money, even in a game.

My then-husband and I had only been married a few years. He worked as an assistant vice president at a small local bank during a period when banks handed out titles instead of high salaries. I'd just finished graduate school and had an average-paying government job. I didn't want a medical building to complicate my life, something else to worry about. My father did things like this, not me.

My principal problem with his announcement stemmed from the fact he had never sat down with me in advance to tell me his plan, to ask whether I wanted to be part of his investment strategy, to ask if I had questions. Never explained the pros and cons. I still would have delivered a resounding *no*, but I wouldn't have been caught by surprise. Commercial real estate is what he loved. Not me. In fairness, though, I didn't ask any questions the night of his announcement, and I should have.

Buildings had cash-sucking vacancies. They had tenants who didn't pay their rent. They had people who fell down in parking lots and sued building owners. They had expensive capital improvements needing the owners' attention, to name just a few minuses. I'd actually been listening to my dad's stories once he'd become involved in commercial real estate. I didn't like the sound of any of it, at least not for me, not my risk-averse, uncertainty-averse personality. I could feel my sense of control leaking out of the room like air out of a balloon as my father made his announcement.

But this was a done deal. I'd like to think that if I'd stood up after my father's announcement, cried out, "No!" it would have made a difference, that financial disaster along with the destruction of our threadbare family ties would have been averted, my future path altered. Or at least that my husband and I would have been excluded from the deals. If only I'd had the courage to say no to everyone in my family, to tell them it wasn't right for me. But I'll never know. I do know, though, that this initial deal marked our eventual transformation from a loosely linked group of six (plus four spouses, so ten) to a group of estranged family members who virtually lost whatever sense of family we'd had back in 1978. Overnight we became a monolingual family, our primary lexicon one containing financial terms, commercial real estate terminology, references to rent, loans, debt, correspondence from banks.

Thinking back on this important day when my father announced the gift of that first building to my siblings and me, I know I also worried that I knew nothing about commercial real estate; this was a language I'd never master, a world I'd never feel at home in. Had I protested, family members might have assured me everything would be fine. "Don't muck it up for everyone," they would have said. "What's wrong with you, refusing a generous gift? How often are you given a building?" they would have said, glaring at me in disbelief. "Don't you trust your family?" they would have scoffed. They did say this later, when the investments started to unravel. But sadly, it was too late by then. I'd already signed on all the dotted lines, on the hundreds of dotted lines in my future, despite my misgivings.

My father rolled over profits from the first building to purchase more buildings, for tax purposes, and to borrow against equity for subsequent deals, specifically, three more buildings in a place called Earth City, Missouri. This meant more papers to sign, more zeros marching across the page, more risk, more terror on my part. The medical building morphed into two, then five and ultimately sixteen buildings my husband and I owned a share of with my parents and siblings. To me, these buildings resembled swamp creatures from a science fiction story, genetically mutating into more buildings, more risk, more debt, more papers to sign, documents systematically destroying any sense of security I'd had previously. They cast a pall over my life, added a level of complexity, of uncertainty I hadn't anticipated.

I like what's solid, certain, unambiguous. I hate surprises. This would be one surprise after another, a decision that would continue to affect me for forty years. I like control, yet I had no control over this. I prefer open lines of communication, but through the years I remained in the dark, trying to piece cryptic bits of information together to form a whole, asking questions no one wanted—or deigned—to answer. "Ask your husband," "Ask your brother," "Ask your father," they'd scold me. Shunted from husband to brother to father and back again, I felt like a piece of baggage with no answers, none I could understand, anyway. It was a business conducted like family. But family was all business. It was like being asked to translate a document in a language I didn't know. With my eyes closed, without a dictionary. Nightmarish.

On one occasion, after I was firmly entrenched in these deals, I went to yet another real estate closing with my family members for the sale of a commercial building. A stack of papers had been placed in front of me to sign, a stack I'd never seen before, rising at least four inches high from the table. Determined to assess what I'd been asked to sign, I began slogging through the pile, trying to make sense of the wherefores and the therebys, the pursuant tos, the numbers, but it all looked like a foreign language I didn't understand. Would never understand. A quiet panic began to set in. Meanwhile, everyone else busied themselves, signing page after page, flipping the sheets over like one of those cartoons where pages are flipped at breakneck speed. No one bothered to read the large or small print, although maybe they understood it all, unlike me. *But what did it mean*? I wondered. Why wouldn't anyone explain it to me in terms I could understand, without becoming impatient or passing me off to the next family member?

Walking in front of the table with all the papers I needed to sign, my mother paused a moment, letting out an audible sigh when she saw me trying to make sense of the documents. "What on *earth* are you doing, Linda? Are you *reading* the documents? Don't you trust your father or your brother? You don't see the rest of us doing that; do you? Look around! How sad you don't trust them, after all they've done for you." Scoffing at me, shaking her head in disbelief, she walked off after broadcasting my behavior to the others. I felt like a traitor. I didn't realize it, but the antagonism I evoked from my family members by questioning their activities, including my role in them, would only intensify over the next few decades.

In 1985 I separated from my husband, moving with my two young children to Maryland where I'd accepted a job working for the government as a translator. As a single parent, being in these deals made me doubly nervous, doubly vulnerable. If something unexpected happened—vacancies, late payments, injuries on the properties, bank foreclosures—I could lose everything: custody of my children, my job, my home. If major improvements needed to be made, I wouldn't have a cushion to cover the losses as a government employee living on one income; I barely had enough to support the three of us. The deals only increased the stress in my life, adding little income, coupled by tremendous risk. I told people that, if I could, I'd keep all my money under my mattress; these deals were the antithesis of my neanderthal philosophy.

Moving out of St. Louis had caused my relationship with family members to further deteriorate. Ending my marriage, leaving St. Louis to embark on a career, they frowned on all of this. Shortly after moving to Maryland, I'd written in my journal, "I feel like I'm just in the wrong family. Not that they're bad, just a bad fit." I felt trapped with nowhere to go.

DINNER DATE

In June of 1998, I flew to St. Louis to visit my mother, to say good-bye to my father, who'd lapsed into a coma following a year of strokes, of repeated stays at the hospital. The accountant who'd worked for my father for many years invited my mother and me out to dinner at his exclusive country club. He reserved a private dining room for us. After exchanging pleasantries, he launched into his speech, reminding me how much money I owed the family business due to cash calls made over the years when there were shortfalls. My father had been paying my share for the time being, but he could no longer help me because of his health.

My mother remained silent while the accountant told me how much I owed. The only words she spoke all evening, aside from nodding in response to the accountant's remarks, were urging me to try a macaroon cookie they served at the end of the fancy meal. "They're simply divine, Linda; you *must* try one. Go on; one won't do much damage to your waistline!"

She sat at the head of the country club table on an elevated chair like an Egyptian queen on her plush throne, decked out in her finest jewelry, a Cheshire cat smile omnipresent on her lips as the accountant read me his tally of depressing numbers. I felt like I'd been the victim of an elaborate trap, particularly since my mother had phoned me in advance of the trip to inform me of the accountant's invitation. "Such a nice offer, isn't it, Linda?

All I do every day is visit Sam in the hospital. This will be such a pleasant change from our routine, don't you think? I'm looking forward to it!"

I drove us home from the country club in my mother's red Cadillac, meeting her remarks with silence as she raved about how wonderful the evening had been. Walking through the back door of Ivy Lodge, she again reviewed events of the evening as though it had been fabulous, asking me repeatedly if it hadn't been the best evening out I'd ever had. "What a lovely dinner, right, Linda? Delightful being in his beautiful country club, having such a delicious meal with both of you. Such a nice break from the hospital. Absolutely wonderful. Don't you think?" The singsong tone of her voice sounded fake to me, though, particularly in light of the nightmarish experience it had been for me.

How could she not have witnessed my distress, noticed that I'd been on the verge of tears. How could she not realize this man, her accountant—who worked for her—had set me up for the kill, perhaps at her direction? How could I possibly have enjoyed myself? What was wrong with her? But I'd said nothing in response to my mother, still shaking, wondering how to "fix" this mess my father had dragged me into decades before, a mess I had tried many times to extricate myself from over the years, without success.

I told her I was going to bed. Still visibly happy, she scurried after me. "Oh, I need a hug! Can I have a hug?" She never spoke like this, never asked for hugs. After lightly hugging me, she then inexplicably removed the portable phone from the guest bedroom on the first floor, my brothers' former room—now the guest room—taking it upstairs to her room, even though she had her own landline phone in her bedroom. No one had cell phones yet; this was the only phone in the guest room. Did she do it to ensure I couldn't call anyone? Once again, I didn't understand why she needed two phones, leaving me with none. She knew I'd want to check in with my husband back in Maryland.

After she went upstairs, I went to my father's first-floor study—my former room—calling my second husband of nearly ten years to report what had happened, to tell him about her strange behavior. I needed to speak to my husband, get a reality check.

Fifteen minutes into our conversation, at about eleven fifteen, I heard a click on the line. "Hello? Hello? Hello?" I said repeatedly. Eventually the phone clicked off. Defeated, I decided to go to bed, signing off with my husband after just a few more minutes. Lying in bed, I was not able to sleep, wondering how I'd ever pay back so much money.

The next morning at breakfast my mother made the comment that she thought she needed to have her hearing tested. I mumbled a few benign words in response.

Then she continued, "Because last night I picked up the phone the way I always do to check the clocks, dialing time and temperature. I dialed three-four-five-six-six, and I heard all this whispering. Linda, I think it was an obscene phone call! I listened and listened to see what I could pick up, but the whispering stopped. I think it was an obscene phone call, and it scared me to death, but here it is morning and I'm still standing, so I guess that's good!"

She spoke the last words with the same childlike glee I'd heard the night before. My head pounding, my eyes puffy, I didn't want to point out the flaws in her reasoning. Again I mumbled an appropriate sentence, but she persisted. "Do you have *any* idea what it could have been, Linda? Do you think the phone lines got crossed somehow?"

No longer able to restrain myself, unwilling to remain silent, I replied that I didn't know, but did wonder why she felt the need to call time and temperature in the middle of the night.

"Oh, I frequently do that," she said. "I want to make sure all the clocks are right."

"So, why do you think you got an obscene phone call since *you* picked up the phone at midnight; *you're* the one who initiated the call?" I asked, adding, "The phone never rang; how did this happen?"

"Well, I don't pretend to know, Linda. I just know I heard whispering, terrible words. It scared me to death. Why are you interrogating me?"

I no longer had any desire to be part of this charade, with her pretending not to know I'd been the one on the phone, the one swearing, crying, that the evening at her accountant's country club had been among the worst in my life. I dropped out of the conversation.

Back in Maryland, I wrote the following in my journal:

"How do I get them out of my life? Just tell me that . . . I would lay down my life for my parents. I would do absolutely anything for them. Why is their mission (mom's now) to hunt me down like a dog? . . . She wants to destroy me and when I try to reason with her, like a lion or tiger or other animal of prey, she has no capacity to stop the hunt because it's instinctual."

Part of the dilemma for me was, once again, that no one ever witnessed her behavior, what she said to me, a phenomenon I wrote about in this same journal: "There are no witnesses, no one ever sees her actions/hears her words. She's like Jekyll and Hyde, but no one ever sees Hyde. No one could believe one's own mother could be that cruel, while still calling herself a 'softie.'"

Reflecting on the debacle in St. Louis and the last time I saw my comatose father, I'm recalling that fateful day in the late 1970s, the day my father gave my siblings and me the building, the first building, the domino that started the chain reaction. I marvel at how his decision took a family with the slimmest of emotional links to connect them, and all but destroyed those links. It transformed a family, barely a family, shoving its members into a business, square pegs in round holes, stripping them of their humanity to each other, of any love or respect they might have previously felt toward each other. What a price we all paid for becoming part of my father's real estate deals.

Now, with all the "loot," all the "wealth" being systematically removed from Ivy Lodge, especially from this once-palatial dining room, I realize that all of it—the silver, the jewelry, the gold coins, the expensive knickknacks, the fancy-looking exterior of the home, the "deals"—all of it just overwhelmed us. It destroyed any family togetherness that had existed before, prior to moving to Ivy Lodge. Realizing this, I sink into a dining room chair, staring up at the chandelier, its light providing the only remaining "sparkle" in the house.

I'm saddened by my thoughts, but maybe it's not too late, I think, sitting up straight, feeling briefly encouraged. Maybe with the sale of Ivy Lodge, with all that it stood for, we can start fresh, four siblings and our spouses, forge a new way of relating to each other, one not linking us solely through buildings, money, debt, legal documents, one in which we don't have to look or act a certain way, can be ourselves. One where we aren't intentionally being driven apart by at least one parent. That gives me a sliver of hope. Most of all, though, I realize it has taken the death of both my parents for me to finally begin to see who I am, but not through their eyes. I'll never forget them; my parents and I have been in lockstep ever since I was a young child, but their words drowned out my own voice. I'm starting to come into my own.

twenty

LIVING ROOM:
THE BEGINNING OF THE END

*E*xhausted from all my memories, the compression of my life into one day, I get up from the chair where I've been sitting. I feel as old as this home. Leaving the dining room, I walk back through the foyer into the living room, the last room I'll look at for the day.

Despite its formal appearance, its oversized stone fireplace flanked by floor-to-ceiling bookshelves, its ornate crown molding running around the perimeter of the room's high ceilings, the majestic Steinway grand, plush beige carpet, it's much more than a showcase. It's packed with images, emotions, conversations, memories. I expect it to look different, though, since both my parents are gone. They filled it with their strong presence. Something is missing. They are missing.

Where is everyone? I wonder. I'm ready to leave. I need to head to my hotel, even though I just stepped into the living room. There's too much here. Too much in the house. Too many memories. I feel like the Ivy Lodge lithograph my parents gave us is undergoing spontaneous combustion before my eyes, consumed by decades of repressed feelings, silence. Everything I held to be true—all the family myths—is gone, replaced by ashes. It's as though I'm trying to escape from the burning building before it's too late, grabbing objects on my way out, ones underpinning the illusion of Ivy Lodge, among them my mother's chipped angel candle holders, dented metal-detecting finds, my father's toy soldiers, cheap basement sign, the train kit cars. I must believe that if I take enough treasures, I can rebuild my own mythology using these pieces. But of course, I can't, regardless of how many mementos I shove into my overflowing bag, talismans I've imbued with magical restorative powers. Besides, there aren't enough of them to cobble together a new family history, a happier one.

Standing on the threshold, anxious to end my day, memories roll over me unbidden about the watershed moment between my father and me that occurred in this room in 1984. If it hadn't happened, I'd still be living in Missouri, not Maryland. I might still be married to my former husband, not my current husband of almost eleven years. I'd still be a housewife. I'd still be miserable. I should have thanked my father for delivering a nightmarish evening, while also the most life changing.

I called on my father one evening a few years after finishing my PhD, made an appointment to see him. I wanted to ask if I could use his name as a reference with local CEOs or CFOs to start my own translating business in St. Louis. An entrée into his corporate world was what I needed, a foot in the door, a short letter of introduction to get my business off the ground. Not money. I wanted the opportunity to prove myself. I'd been doing freelance translating work for five years. Although I had steady work, I thought the next logical step would be to start my own business, bring in more income. Freelancing didn't pay much, only ten cents a word, even if the word in question happened to be a lengthy technical German term for a dental prosthetic technique; a word was a word, worth ten cents in the marketplace back then.

I arrived at the back door, knocking on the kitchen door. My mother greeted me, visibly curious about my mission. I wasn't dressed up because I would be talking to my father, after all. I had dressed in casual, stretchy pants with a loose shirt, my shapeless, baggy uniform, forever trying to camouflage what I thought of as my enormous, unattractive body, all my glaring flaws and unsightliness.

Like a secretary leading a client to an appointment, my mother led me to the living room after giving my outfit a brief once-over and before casting a knowing look at my father. She appeared to return to the kitchen, although not out of earshot, as it would turn out. My father initially acted friendly but somewhat formal since, as usual, he seemed uncomfortable being left alone with me. He inquired about my husband and two small children, at home a few miles away. My siblings, parents, and I all lived within about a ten-mile radius of each other.

We made small talk. Harmless, innocuous topics. But then I got to the point—why I'd come, why I wanted to talk to him. I didn't want to waste his time, forever thinking he—anyone—had far better ways to spend their time than with me. When I broached the subject of the letter, though, experience having taught me to tiptoe up to the topic, his anger suddenly surfaced like hot lava from a volcano when he realized what I wanted. No gradual building of emotions occurred, no follow-up clarifications or questions. He went from zero to two hundred in a matter of seconds. Using every ounce of his vocal cords, he began to shout at me repeatedly, "You are *out* of the nest! Do you *hear* me? You are *out* of the nest!" giving special emphasis to the word *out*. The only interruption from his rant occurred when, running out of steam, his voice laced with sarcasm, he bellowed that he would be *happy* to loan me twenty-five dollars to place an ad in the *St. Louis Business Journal* to drum up business. As though this constituted a generous gesture on his part. As though money were the issue. I somehow managed to interject that I didn't want his money, that it had never been about money, I just needed access to the business world, to the connections he had. But he had stopped listening.

I was dumbfounded. What had set him off? It had taken only a few seconds for him to realize what I wanted, followed by the explosion into inexplicable fury, inexplicable even though I thought I knew my father. He leapt out of his chair, and I witnessed a fury I didn't—still don't—understand. Steve had been a protégé of my father's for years, largely working with and for him since graduating from law school ten years before. He was also deeply involved in the commercial real estate deals, many times acting as our father's proxy. Sam had been assisted by our father. How was this different? This was nothing, just a boiler-plate letter for me, his daughter. Nothing more. A letter I would gladly have written on his behalf, careful not to heap too much praise on myself. I could have done so easily. All he had to do was sign it. Vouch for me, for my credentials, for my eagerness to start my own business, be an entrepreneur.

In the midst of his shouting, I grew even more shocked when my mother appeared out of nowhere to join the fracas, apparently emboldened by my father's words ricocheting throughout the walls of Ivy Lodge. Whenever he became angry, it fueled her tendency to join forces with him. My father had expended the effort; she just had to coast behind him, align herself to his negative energy.

She rushed into the room from the kitchen, reminding me (as if I needed reminding at this point) that, yes, "You are *out* of the nest, Linda. You are on your own; don't you forget it." I looked at their contorted, reddened faces as though looking through the prism of craziness, speechless in my shock. In that moment all I saw was the specter of their anger; their voices were blotted out. I knew I'd never forget the sight of their distorted faces and their shaking fingers, or forget the hurtful words they hurled at me.

Looking back, I'm certain that, had I anticipated the fury my request would unleash in them, I would sooner have walked on hot coals, slit my wrists, stretched out in the middle of traffic than subjected myself to this backlash. It had been a complete surprise. I wasn't certain beforehand that my father would agree to help me, had prepared for that outcome, but I had envisioned him shaking his head no, explaining that he wouldn't feel comfortable writing such a letter. Not this. Never this.

I slowly backed out of the room. Sobbing ugly, breath-snatching gasps, wiping my runny nose on the shirt sleeve of my turtleneck rather than delaying my hasty departure by looking for a tissue, I left the way I'd come in, through the kitchen door, then the back porch, outside to my beat-up red Vega station wagon parked in their driveway, two empty child car seats in the back. I somehow drove the few miles home, blinded by my tears.

This proved to be a catalyst for me, where and when I knew —snap!—I had to save my life . . . get out of this world, their world.

The evening after I asked for my father's help, he drove to my home, made a special visit without my mother, highly unusual for him. When he arrived, I was still back in the bedroom. Looking at my image in the mirror to check my appearance, I could hear the click of the front door when my husband let him into our small ranch home. I was intrigued when I heard their pleasant-sounding voices, wondering what they were talking about without me, given the circumstances the night before. I stood closer to the bedroom door, opening it to listen for a minute before joining them. Incredulous, I listened as my father laughed nervously and then apologized for his behavior—apologized to my husband, who hadn't been there, hadn't been insulted, didn't have a complete picture of what had happened. I'd never heard my father apologize to anyone before. Ever.

"I don't know what got over me. I just lost it, pure and simple. Barbara is always telling me I need to control my temper; last night was a classic example of *not* doing that. I'm sorry."

My husband accepted my father's apology, making light of what had happened, attempting to lessen my father's discomfort. I entered the family room where they stood, now talking about another topic, business-related. Apology over. My husband had acted as my proxy. Business as usual with my father, nothing to sort out between us. My father greeted me, looking somewhat sheepish, but regarded me as though dealing with a business associate he vaguely knew. I sensed no closeness, no remorse. Nor did he ever apologize to me or mention the incident again. The subject of writing a letter of introduction for me never came up again. I never brought it up. The incident was swallowed up into the fabric of our lives, as though it had never happened. But it had. It would signal a major shift within me, be the catalyst to set the wheels in motion for me to leave Kirkwood, to leave my family of origin, to leave my husband.

Thinking back on that moment in my life, I sink into the living room's small blue loveseat, the same loveseat I'd sat in years before when my father had briefly shed his stern countenance to entertain me with his piano-playing antics, his playfulness as he butchered snippets from *Carmen*. It reminded me that my father usually gave his best to others, although occasionally to my siblings or me or our mother. But normally he played to a crowd, loved telling a good story to a circle of friends or business associates, even strangers, entertaining people with his wit, sharing interesting anecdotes that captivated audiences of all ages. Again, though, he didn't like dealing with the tough or messy parts of life, with the rough edges that children—regardless of their ages—sometimes bring to the table. But on those occasions when he behaved like his most charming self, it was like watching TV, seeing this handsome, brilliant, funny man as he hypnotized his audience.

I stand alone in my parents' foyer at the end of that same long day, a day that seems to have lasted weeks. I'm ready to leave a stripped-down Ivy Lodge with the treasures I've claimed, the memories I've unearthed. Turning off the foyer lights, I walk outside into the frigid night air, locking the front door behind me. I will fly back to Maryland the next day. My home. My sanctuary. Where my real family is.

Before driving away from Ivy Lodge, I time-travel back to that first time I came here. I briefly imagine a different scenario, a fantasy in which we all pile into our family station wagon, our father at the wheel, our mother by his side in front, adolescents Steve and Sam in the way back, with little Janet and me right behind our parents, all of us leaning forward to get a better look at where we're going. In this fantasy our father pulls the car into the main driveway of Ivy Lodge, its "FOR SALE" sign hammered into the frozen front yard, slightly off-kilter as though fatigued from having to stand upright so many months.

The house is especially gloomy on this imaginary winter day, uninviting in its uninhabited solitude. Sitting in the car with the heater on full blast, our father leans against the steering wheel and peers up through the windshield at the house, remembering the amazing "deal" he's tentatively struck with Ivy Lodge's nervous owners, a "steal" to buy the large home for far less than it's worth. But then he shifts his focus, looks up at the solitary home again, looks at each of his children's frowning, questioning faces as we register the gloomy façade of the home in front of us. Finally, as though jolted from his reverie by unfamiliar thoughts, perhaps an epiphany of sorts, he shakes his head, commenting almost to himself, "No. I can't do it. I don't need to go inside again. It's just not right for us, for our family, deal or no deal." Hearing his words, my siblings and I sink back into the seats of the car, sighing with relief as our father continues down the driveway, past the house, forking out Ivy Lodge's side driveway, the house receding, becoming ever smaller as we drive away, back to our cozy home on Gill, three blocks from Ivy Lodge, but a world away, where we will continue our life as a family, six souls perfect in our imperfections.

twenty-one

A FINAL TRANSLATION

*T*ranslation involves more than the deciphering of words, words strung together in sentences, in paragraphs, in dialogue, in the years of a life. After all, a machine can do that if you feed all the data into it. Translation also involves making sense of what's left unspoken, those ellipses, blank spaces, the dot-dot-dots when you have to guess what's happening in the person's mind, what the silent messages mean. It calls for the translation of surrounding events, the cultural context, as well as the translation of nonverbal communication. What was being said through that certain look, that ever-so-tiny smile, that flash of a grimace? That spark of anger? Those sarcastic comments? Those prolonged silences? What did it all mean?

During the course of my career, I've translated more than a dozen languages into English. Some of these languages proved more challenging than others; the farther away you go from your language of origin, the harder it is to understand a language, to master it. The greater the distance from what you know, the greater the difficulty. For me, this proved to be true beginning with German, with the way it often tacks the verb onto the end of a sentence. The African languages Xhosa and Sotho proved difficult with their various clicks, unusual sounds, their atypical grammar.

The noun classification system used in Bantu languages required work to master. In this group of languages, which includes Xhosa, Sotho, and Swahili, among others, an entire sentence can be altered depending on the noun class involved. For example, in Swahili *"Kitabu kidogo cha kijani kiko hapa"* means "The small green book is here," whereas *"Vitabu vidogo vya kijani viko hapa,"* means "The small green books are here." Just changing the sentence from singular to plural alters nearly every word in the sentence.

The most difficult thing for me to translate to date, though, has been my own life. To return to Ivy Lodge: trying to make sense of what my parents and siblings said and did, how I fit into that picture of that family in that home. I never found it easy, although I think I began observing them when still very young, long before I became a professional translator. I learned to look for signs, for clues, for subtexts in their behavior. Signs in what they didn't say, didn't do. In what was hiding between the lines, in what went on when a disconnect between their behavior and words could be observed, in their language, their attitude toward me.

For example, when my parents were visiting my husband, children, and me at our home in the East, my father came down to breakfast one Sunday morning to announce that my mother would be missing church, that she didn't feel well. That's all he said. Without talking to her, I knew she was seriously ill. She never admitted to being sick, never missed church, never slept in; three major clues. I rushed her to the hospital where doctors discovered scar tissue from previous heart attacks for which she'd never sought medical treatment. I somehow knew. If that had happened with anyone else, I would have accepted the explanation I'd been given, but I had observed my mother my whole life; I knew what these clues meant.

Those years of being criticized, ostracized, or mocked, when what I wanted most was to connect with them, made me hypersensitive to what my parents communicated in spite of themselves. It made me a detective of sorts, using clues at my disposal to piece together a picture, to translate what I saw/heard/sensed happening and give it meaning.

Studying a language is like that. I learned to put the pieces of the puzzle together, look at the patterns, make sense of it. I did it initially with Romance languages, with Spanish, Portuguese, and French, then with German, and later with Russian. With African languages, most of the ones I studied belonged to the Bantu language family, making use of a similar noun classification system. If I mastered that system, I had a head start in each language. I had the same advantage with my parents when I put that methodology to use, but only decades later, much of it after both of their deaths, after my trip back to Ivy Lodge in 2000.

When my mother told me I was a "big" girl while slapping her thighs in response to my question of how I looked, I now know she didn't mean the dictionary definition, since I was not overweight at the time. She might have meant in comparison to her tiny stature, or she might have wanted to discourage me from asking such questions. Or it might have made her feel good about herself to put me down. Multiple choice translations.

It reminds me of when I questioned a local outside Dar Es Salaam in Tanzania, asking him if the market was far from my hotel. "No. It's close," he'd replied, but to him "close" had a different meaning. It meant at least an hour's walk. Maybe the same applied to my parents. I had to try to be flexible looking back at their behavior, at their words. I had to make allowances for their predisposition to stretch or even destroy a word's meanings, to superimpose their own issues onto their words, even to invent their own languages. Easier said than done during my childhood.

I learned—too late—that my mother telling me, "You won't have a friend in the world," really might have meant that I, in fact, had many friends, but that she was unhappy, isolated in her own life, without as many friends as she would perhaps have liked. My innocent, upturned face, eager for validation, became the exact place to put her verbal fist in order to make herself feel better. The translation of her words had nothing to do with objective reality. When she chastised me for being "too sensitive," that might have meant I needed to learn to tolerate the barrage of words she used as a battering ram against my fledgling self-confidence, like it or not.

When she accused me of being "Queen of the May" following my plea for emotional support, or announced she'd be out of town when my first child was due, maybe the translation was that I'd already had many more opportunities than she, fewer obstacles by far to deal with than she'd had. What right did I have to come to her for help? Maybe from where she stood, my life had been worry-free, ideal. She wanted to level the playing field.

When my father sometimes told me, "You're not too smart, are you?" or instructed me not to be "so thick," he didn't want my opinion. The translation wasn't that I was dumb, as I'd thought growing up. Maybe it meant he'd had a bad day, that being around an adolescent female who didn't understand her place in his patriarchal world, and who talked more than he liked, annoyed him, wasn't how he wanted to spend his free time.

When I cried about a slight or insult—real or imagined—

sometimes eliciting laughter from both parents, it didn't mean my tears weren't valid, that my pain wasn't real. It might have meant they had no interest or time or ability to deal with such matters in their grown-up world, or even that they thought I deserved my tears for something else I'd done or not done. Or that their parenting skills were limited.

When my mother raved about what a "cute little figure" my elementary school friend Patty had, the correct translation probably didn't even include the word "Patty." It might have meant I was becoming a potential rival, someone she would need to devalue in order to feel good about herself. Or it might have meant I wasn't good enough as I was: flat-chested, with poker-straight hair and a mouthful of braces. Or that I needed to *be* different, *look* different, *act* differently, or risk displeasing her.

More often than not, my stabs at translating my parents' words and behavior didn't contain any of the original words used in their statements, didn't bear a resemblance to any of it, to the source language they used. I had to make leaps into the unknown, frequently when no words or clues could help me in my translation. It was like hearing someone tell you, "The apples are rotten today," and having to discern that the speaker actually meant, "I can't stand to be around you right now." So when she asked me, "Are you wearing *that*?" the translation had nothing to do with her wanting factual information from me about my choice of clothes. The message had to do with my appearance. Then I had to dig even deeper for the meaning. Maybe she didn't like the way I looked. My clothes choices just brought that to the surface for her. Or, always a possibility, my father had said or done something hurtful, putting her in a foul mood. So many potential meanings, translations.

Another possibility I don't like thinking about, though, another foreign element in the translation puzzle of my parents, lies with the German term *Schadenfreude*, from *Schaden* (harm or damage) and *Freude* (joy). This occurs when one person experiences joy at witnessing another's humiliation or pain. Many examples of this exist in my relationship with both parents: the out-of-the-nest incident when she piled onto my father's ranting; the evening we went out to dinner with the accountant and she felt pure joy at the sight of my distress. But other, less dramatic examples could explain their behavior. For instance, a year before my father's death, before his strokes, she phoned to regale me about a phone call between my father and my best friend. The friend had wanted to surprise me on my birthday during our upcoming cruise on the Mediterranean and had phoned my father to run the idea by him, since, coincidentally, she was scheduled to be in France when we were there. This inexplicably angered my father. He lost his temper with my friend, who aborted the conversation (and her plan) as quickly as possible. But my mother felt compelled to call me soon after. Chuckling all the while, as happy as a child holding an ice cream cone, she told me in great detail about this incident, how my father had given my friend a piece of his mind, a friend who had always been respectful of my parents. I was dumbfounded on both counts: my father's behavior to my friend and my mother's gleeful reaction. Schadenfreude.

After I began to work with African languages, I studied a new linguistic concept: reduplication. It reminded me of my life in Ivy Lodge. In reduplication, all or part of a word is repeated to intensify the meaning or to make it plural. It exists in English, as well as in other languages: "yum-yum," "goody-goody," "blah-blah," much of it baby talk in English. In Swahili, the word *piga* means "to hit," and the word *pigapiga* means to strike repeatedly. It can also be used with colors. If what you're describing is extremely blue, you repeat the word for blue to make your point.

Taking a linguistic leap, maybe my parents unwittingly did that to make their various points with me. Instead of just calling me lazy or unpopular or fat or stupid, how much better to repeat the word, to intensify the meaning, ensure that I got the message?

My mother's long sighs, her loud shutting of the kitchen cabinet doors, the vigorous wiping of the counters as though she wanted to remove the top layer of Formica. Whipping the dishtowel around, the overzealous straightening of the bed covers, jamming dirty clothes into the hamper. All these nonverbal cues translated into her being unhappy, but that wasn't specific enough. With whom? Me? My father? My siblings? Sometimes I'd have to ask for more information, which you're not supposed to do in the field of translation; you work with what's at hand, like it or not. You're supposed to be an observer, an impartial party. But I had to get to the meaning with both parents. "Are you mad at me? Why are you mad? What did I do? What's wrong? What did I do?" That usually had the opposite of the desired effect, unleashing more anger, the meaning increasingly undecipherable.

I found my father a little easier to read. When his lips pursed into a thin line, or he peered at me over his black reading glasses, or he slammed his newspaper down, I knew it signaled the calm before the storm, that the fuse had been lit and would explode within seconds. Then the translation would be clearer, what had disturbed him as his words spilled out onto me. But I didn't like to stick around for the explosion, even if clarity would follow. If I managed to leave the room quickly, I might avoid his wrath. At least it wouldn't be a direct hit.

When my mother repeatedly referred to herself as a "Pollyanna" or as a "softie," even though this description had no basis in any reality I witnessed, the translation might have been that that's how she *wanted* to be seen. She desperately wanted to be seen as a kinder, gentler person. She reasoned that, if she said it often enough, maybe people would believe her. In psychological terms this is known as the "illusory truth effect" or "the reiteration effect." If you repeat something enough times and convincingly enough, even if it's not true, people may start to believe it. Politicians do this. My mother did this when she called herself a "Pollyanna," a "softie," when she claimed our family was "close." Lies repeated over and over became the truth in many people's eyes.

Admittedly, a number of the translations of my life, of what went on in Ivy Lodge, are loose at best, warranting multiple-choice answers, never ideal in the scientifically based world of translation. You're supposed to go from the source language (the language being translated) to the target language (the language being translated into). A translation is only good when the translator knows—or can surmise—the intention of the person being translated, understands with a fair amount of confidence the exact meaning of that source language. Maybe that's one problem with my attempts to translate my family. Maybe my parents remained unclear in their own minds what they wanted to say, what their words and behavior meant, what their underlying motivation was. In that case, it makes translation doubly difficult if the source of the words and events to be translated is lost in a sea of linguistic confusion. Translators need patterns to make sense out of foreign words, or it all becomes a hodgepodge of meaningless sounds and symbols. Chaos.

A *lingua franca* is a language that is used as a common language between speakers whose first languages are different. English is one in many parts of the world, Swahili is another in Africa, and French still another. It makes it easier for people who do not share the same native language to still be able to communicate with each other, to avoid miscommunications, to have a neutral ground where they can bridge the gap and connect. Looking back at my family, at our years in Ivy Lodge, I think that was a major problem. We no longer had a lingua franca after we moved there. We consisted of six people, our own little Tower of Babel, the single common language we'd shared on Gill Avenue forever destroyed. Six people speaking many different languages, none of them mutually intelligible. Six people bumping into each other in the dark, no longer able to understand each other, wounding one other in the process.

epilogue

*M*y translation of my parents' lives must remain incomplete. Their original language—story—was written in many different languages, many of them indecipherable, some of them now extinct. It reminds me of Walt Whitman's words in "Song of Myself" in which he writes, "I too am untranslatable. . . . You will hardly know who I am, or what I mean." This encapsulates my parents. Even after their deaths, I hardly know who they were or how I fit into their lives. But I know who I am. Maybe that's enough, separating myself from their reality, at long last not seeing myself exclusively through their eyes.

I freed myself from a myth that no longer fit. I moved a thousand miles away with my two small children, built a new life for the three of us with a new career, new friends, new languages, exotic trips to far-reaching locales. I was given another chance at love. I made many mistakes along the way but never doubted my decision to leave. I will always have the same yearnings for that elusive closeness with my family of birth, but I know I can never return to that world.

Back home in Maryland, I still have all the mementos I salvaged from the house in 2000, as well as all the other gifts my parents gave me through the years. The giant Barbarossa key I found in the fruit cellar of the unfinished basement is hanging on a wall in my bedroom. My dad's "ADULTS AT PLAY" sign is in my loft study, tacked to the sloping cathedral ceiling over my desk. I framed the tiny, beaded bookmark I found when we first moved to Ivy Lodge and hung it on the wall of an open stairway just outside my bedroom. The card I made for my mother as a young child and then retrieved from the attic is also in my bedroom, hanging in a short passageway that leads into the room. The gold magnifying loupe my mother used to examine and appraise coins is in my safe along with her intricate beaded necklace with all the charms, the "knight's mail," as I refer to it. I like to take it out and look at the necklace, fingering each of the charms, comparing them to the master list my mother made.

The papier-mâché and ceramic bowls I made in grade school are on a shelf in my study loft. The papier-mâché bowl holds the chipped wooden angel candle holders my mother used for our cakes. I have the sterling silver hairbrush I took from my parents' room to brush my mother's hair during the last weeks of her life in a place of honor on my dresser. It serves double duty, reminding me of my mother, but also of my father since it belonged to him. I keep the plastic Hallmark card I gave my mother on her last birthday in my wallet. The tiny laundry and license plate notebooks with her handwritten tallies are close at hand in my bedroom dresser drawer. My grandfather's jury-rigged coffee-pot-with-clothes-iron-handle hangs in an alcove just outside my basement door, where I see it when I do laundry or other activities down there. I put my father's toy soldiers in two plexiglass cases over the mantelpiece in my family room, a reminder of his too-short childhood.

I sometimes wonder why I placed—still place—so much importance in these objects I brought home to Maryland back in 2000. At the time, I only knew I couldn't abandon them to obscurity, to being thrown out, or even ending up in another person's hands. I think the meaning of all these objects lies in this: I rescued them from Ivy Lodge in part because they represent stand-ins for emotions my parents didn't—or couldn't—express: for love, for affection, for respect, for paying attention to their four children. I try to imagine all those feelings being directed at me.

I translated these gold, silver, metal, wood, and paper things —because that's all they are, things—into tangible proof of their love. I pick them up one by one, convincing myself that these inanimate objects hold all the love I craved. It's right there, stored inside these treasures. What I took from Ivy Lodge that lonely, wintry day in 2000—most of it worthless to anyone but me—was never intended for me, yet I rescued it because at some point it had all been important to my parents, hadn't it? Since they had once loved these objects, paid attention to them, taken pride in them, maybe those emotions would rub off on me, I reasoned. Maybe a connection existed between us: passing through my parents, to the mementos, finally to me. An indirect connection, but still . . . Like Peter Pan trying to stitch his shadow back on, I applied the positive feelings evoked by my parents' treasures, felt the slightest bit of encouragement, of love. Looking at his World War I toy soldiers, the train kits he made with my uncle, along with his "CAUTION: ADULTS AT PLAY" sign, I'm reminded that, like my mother, my father was a complex man with mixed feelings about me, about fatherhood, feelings that can't be reduced to pat phrases or pronouncements.

I kept many of their treasures for another reason: trying to solve the puzzle of who they both were. A mystery to me in many ways, both were complicated, complex people. Keeping these odds and ends, these remnants of their lives, helped me cobble together a more complete picture. The mismatched items I saved have made me ask myself a number of questions: was that really my father who had a hair-trigger temper, or was he the young man who hauled a coil of wire weighing 365 pounds across railroad tracks for his summer job, who, at only ten years old, was put in charge of purchasing food for his entire family of seven each week during the Depression? Was he the teenager who suffered the humiliation of being put in a trash can, high up on the shelf of his high school chemistry lab, or the sometimes-aggressive wheeler-dealer, successful in commercial real estate? Was he the little boy who, seventy years later, still reminisced about playing with his toy soldiers, or the one who rejected open displays of affection? Which one was he? Or was he everything combined? It's a hodgepodge of words, of blurry images that defy analysis or translation.

Was my mother the woman who saved chipped angel candle holders she put on homemade birthday cakes faithfully baked for her children decades before? Or the woman stuck in the dungeon-like basement of a fancy-looking home, sentenced to fifty-five years of waiting on an often-demanding husband? Or was she the woman who enlisted her accountant to order her daughter to pay back a debt from the ill-fated family real estate deals, giddy about her daughter's anguish? Or was she the woman who referred to herself as a "softie," "Pollyanna"? Or the woman who demeaned her daughter about her weight, her looks, her academic record, her eating habits? Or the one who made a special Halloween costume for this same daughter? Maybe she, too, held all that inside. She was like her extensive collection of Russian nesting dolls—*matryoshka*— each doll hiding a different doll, a hidden trait, until you reached the tiniest one, the core of the doll, which none of us ever had access to.

I framed the lithograph of Ivy Lodge several years after my parents' deaths, displaying it in my home, maybe as a reminder of the danger of judging something by its outward appearance. Or as a reminder to myself to hold tight to the good times the six of us enjoyed within those walls. Or as a tribute to my parents, honoring their gift of art to their four children many years ago.

I bristle when I hear anyone toss out the clichéd, facile pronouncement, "Well, they did the best they could," when referring to someone's parenting skills, but I think that, at long last, more than twenty years after their deaths, I might actually believe that sentiment. My parents probably did the absolute best they could. That's the only conclusion in a hodgepodge of contradictory words and messages, of images, physical mementos, experiences that rise up from my memories of both parents, of my siblings, of the home in which we all lived, Ivy Lodge. And, really, what is translation but one person's search for meaning from *other* people's words, opinions, experiences? It's the attempt by a second party to make sense of what seems foreign. Maybe some of it has to remain foreign, though, a cipher. Like Walt Whitman, my parents are forever untranslatable, but I'm not. At long last I know who I am.

The lithograph of Ivy Lodge hangs over a large buffet table in my dining room in Maryland. Visitors sometimes pause to look at it, commenting about the grand-looking home. It always throws me off balance when they gush about the image, but I did choose to frame it and display it, after all. I usually just smile, thank them, sometimes even responding, "Yes, it's a beautiful home."

acknowledgments

This memoir originated as a prompt by Jeremy B. Jones at his weekend workshop at the 2014 Iowa Summer Writing Festival: "Writing about Nowhere," ten pages that eventually grew into this memoir. Thank you!

Without the support, encouragement, and love of my husband, Bill Marshall, there would be no book. I'm so thankful for his patience, wisdom, and love. I'm also grateful for Alex, Mia, Amanda, Tom, Aubrey, Joey, and Jack, who bring so much joy to my life each and every day.

Thanks to the faculty, staff, and students at Vermont College of Fine Arts/VCFA, whose writing, guidance, and example propelled me onward. Special thanks to Harrison Candelaria Fletcher, who joined me on my writing journey back when I had just started to formulate this book, patiently working with me as I struggled to find my voice. Thanks, also, to the inimitable Sue William Silverman, who knows so very much about so many things, and generously shares her vast store of information and inspiration.

My work benefited greatly from the wisdom of numerous talented writers: Dawn Raffel, whose final edits proved invaluable; my friends and fellow writers, Donna Koros Stramella, Rae Rozman, Allison Hong Merrill, Claudia Velez, and Chivvis Moore.

Special thanks to the Missouri Historical Society for allowing me to use portions of their 1996 interview with my father.

Last, but certainly not least, thanks to the amazing team at She Writes Press and SparkPoint Studio: Brooke Warner,

Samantha Strom, Julie Metz, Maggie Ruf, and Crystal Patriarche, Hanna Lindsley, and Tabitha Bailey, who supported my writing and made this book possible. Thank you so much.

about the author

Credit: Larry Bowers

LINDA MURPHY MARSHALL is a multi-linguist and writer with a PhD in Hispanic languages and literature, a master's in Spanish, and an MFA in creative writing from Vermont College of Fine Arts. Her work has been published or is forthcoming in *The Los Angeles Review*, *Maryland Literary Review*, the *Ocotillo Review*, *Chestnut Review*, *Adelaide Literary Magazine*, *Flash Fiction Magazine*, *Bacopa Literary Review*, *PopMatters*, *Storgy* [UK], *The Bark Magazine*, *Catamaran Literary Reader*, and *Critical Read*. She was featured in *American Writers Review*, where she was an Honorable Mention for the 2019 Fiction Contest. She was long-listed in *Strands Publishers's* 2021 International Flash Fiction Contest, and was a finalist in the 2020 *Annual Adelaide Literary Contest* for one of her essays. In addition, she is currently a reader for *Fourth Genre* and a translation editor for the *Los Angeles Review*. Her sketches and paintings have been featured in art shows and galleries.

SELECTED TITLES FROM SHE WRITES PRESS

She Writes Press is an independent publishing company
founded to serve women writers everywhere.
Visit us at www.shewritespress.com.

The Coconut Latitudes: Secrets, Storms, and Survival in the Caribbean by Rita Gardner. $16.95, 978-1-63152-901-6. A haunting, lyrical memoir about a dysfunctional family's experiences in a reality far from the envisioned Eden—and the terrible cost of keeping secrets.

The S Word by Paolina Milana. $16.95, 978-1-63152-927-6. An insider's account of growing up with a schizophrenic mother, and the disastrous toll the illness—and her Sicilian Catholic family's code of secrecy—takes upon her young life.

Don't Call Me Mother: A Daughter's Journey from Abandonment to Forgiveness by Linda Joy Myers. $16.95, 978-1-938314-02 -5. Linda Joy Myers's story of how she transcended the prisons of her childhood by seeking—and offering—forgiveness for her family's sins.

Scattering Ashes: A Memoir of Letting Go by Joan Rough. $16.95, 978-1-63152-095-2. A daughter's chronicle of what happens when she invites her alcoholic and emotionally abusive mother to move in with her in hopes of helping her through the final stages of life—and her dream of mending their tattered relationship fails miserably.

The Space Between: A Memoir of Mother-Daughter Love at the End of Life by Virginia A. Simpson. $16.95, 978-1-63152-049-5. When a life-threatening illness makes it necessary for Virginia Simpson's mother, Ruth, to come live with her, Simpson struggles to heal their relationship before Ruth dies.

Uncovered: How I Left Hassidic Life and Finally Came Home by Leah Lax. $16.95, 978-1-63152-995-5. Drawn in their offers of refuge from her troubled family and promises of eternal love, Leah Lax becomes a Hassidic Jew—but ultimately, as a forty-something woman, comes to reject everything she has lived for three decades in order to be who she truly is.

CPSIA information can be obtained
at www.ICGtesting.com
Printed in the USA
JSHW031220010822
28726JS00005B/8